PORTRAIT OF A NATION

PORTRAIT OF A NATION

Culture and Progress in Ecuador

OSVALDO HURTADO

Translated by Barbara Sipe

MADISON BOOKS

Lanham • New York • Boulder • Toronto • Plymouth, UK

Published by Madison Books
An imprint of The Rowman & Littlefield Publishing Group, Inc.
4501 Forbes Boulevard, Suite 200, Lanham, Maryland 20706
http://www.rlpgtrade.com

Estover Road, Plymouth PL6 7PY, United Kingdom

Distributed by National Book Network

British Library Cataloguing in Publication Information Available

Library of Congress Cataloging-in-Publication Data
Hurtado, Osvaldo.
    [Los costumbres de los ecuatorianos. English.]
    Portrait of a nation: culture and progress in Ecuador / Osvaldo Hurtado,
translated by Barbara Sipe.
        p.   cm.
    Includes bibliographical references.
    ISBN 978-1-56833-262-8 (hardcover : alk. paper) — ISBN 978-1-56833-
263-5 (electronic)
        1. Ecuador—Civilization. 2. Ecuador—Social life and customs. 3. Social
change—Ecuador—History. 4. Quito (Audiencia)—History. I. Sipe, Barbara. II.
Title.
    F3710.H873 2010
    306.09866—dc22

                                                                    2009029680

Printed in the United States of America

CONTENTS

FOREWORD TO THE ENGLISH-
LANGUAGE EDITION

Anyone who has visited Ecuador for more than a few days, and whose travels admit comparisons, has to agree that Ecuador is one of the most beautiful countries in the world. One is tempted to resort to clichés and hyperbole when one speaks of Ecuador, and visitors often do. The word "majestic," one imagines, was created just to describe the soaring, snow-crested Andes that split the country north to south and contain some of the highest mountains and active volcanoes in the world. The beaches, which are extensive, are, of course, "pristine" and "inviting," and the jungles and rainforests, "mysterious" and "prodigious." And the friendliness and hospitality of the Ecuadorian people, the country's most valuable resource and an attraction worthy in its own right, are nothing if not "legendary."

But if Ecuador is one of the most beautiful countries of the world, it is also one of the most enigmatic. With an important oil production and a strong and diversified agricultural economy based on the traditional tropical exports of bananas and cacao and on emerging nontraditional exports of shrimp and flowers, Ecuador nevertheless remains one of the most undeveloped countries of Latin America. With a Human Development Index of 0.772 (89th of 177), Ecuador is below the Latin American average of 0.82. Out of 177 countries tracked by the United Nations, Ecuador ranks 110th in per-capita GDP, 90th in the human poverty index, 101st in people without access to an improved water source, and 74th in children underweight for age. Though the country has shown noteworthy improvement in several indicators (literacy and life expectancy, for example), its progress relative to other countries with similar populations and resource base has been slow. In other words, the rate of economic and social development in Ecuador is slower than in other countries outside of sub-Saharan Africa. How to explain this curious paradox? Even allowing for the vagaries of world markets, the constraints of a primary export economy, and natural disasters, why isn't Ecuador farther along on the development continuum? Why, indeed.

The socioeconomic conundrum is compounded by a geodemographic one. The very feature that embellishes and makes Ecuador so unique—the Andean mountain range—is also a barrier to national unity and a source of bitter divisions of epic proportions. Geographers divide the national territory into four regions: the coast, with its port of Guayaquil; the highlands, containing the capital, Quito; the Amazon or Oriente; and the Galápagos Islands. They might as well be separate countries for all they have in common. The coast is tropical, a traditional center of wealth and riches, and ultimately, power in the country, populated by a happy, outgoing, and fun-loving people whose collective name in Spanish comes from their regional identity: *costeños*. The Andean Highland region is the traditional heartland of the Inca and then the Spanish empires and is proud of that heritage; is the center of landed wealth and aristocratic values; contains the largest concentration of indigenous population in the country; and boasts a population (termed *serranos*—literally "highlanders") that, in its mountain-bound isolation, is reserved, formal, and dignified. The third region, the Amazon, was isolated, forgotten, and effectively removed from the mainstream of life in the rest of the country until its oil reserves began to be exported in 1972. Since then, its role in national life has increased in a way commensurate with its economic importance, a factor that has been especially evident in the effective organization and increasing political role of the indigenous population of the region.

The sharp contrasts between the regions and the isolation brought about by the accidents of geography have had serious and detrimental consequences for the country. Devastating civil wars and rampant political instability are two of the most egregious manifestations of the chronic rivalry between sierra and coast and the ensuing struggle for domination. But more serious still is the somber fact that even after 178 years as an independent country, Ecuador continues to search for a national identity. Why can't Ecuadorians come together under a single vision of country to seek a common future in which all Ecuadorians share equally in the opportunities for education, well-being, happiness? In other words, why are Ecuadorians so divisive, why can't they stop fighting and hurting each other? Why, after all, can't they understand that united they have more to gain than they do divided? Why are they so stubbornly insistent on pursuing courses that are contrary not only to their national interest but also to their individual and class interests? Why?

The enigmas continue into the political realm. The fathers of Ecuador's independence in 1830 declared boldly and righteously that, henceforth, the long night of oppressive monarchy was over and the bright light of democracy would shine over the new nation forever more. But as events would prove, the political soil was not very fertile and the seeds of democracy would founder. What ensued were 178 years of turmoil, instability, dictatorship, civil war . . . in sum, chronic and rampant political strife. As if the formal logic of a political constitution could magically convert an anarchic mass into a democratic order, like some secular kabbalah, Ecuador's leaders produced nineteen of these documents and they are currently working on a twentieth. If they could just get the formula right, they reasoned, reality would follow suit. Yet as Osvaldo Hurtado points out in his introduction to this book, over the entire Republican period of Ecuador's history, dictatorial regimes have outnumbered democratically elected ones, and on average national governments last less than two years! Obviously, democracy doesn't happen by fiat nor is it a product of the good intentions of constituent assemblies. But in Ecuador, the democratic dream has been especially elusive. Why don't democratic institutions work in Ecuador? What is it in the national psyche that on the one hand thirsts for democracy and on the other tramples it? Reasonable Ecuadorians know that without political stability there will be no advancement on other fronts; yet they consistently and stubbornly snatch defeat from the jaws of victory . . . time and time again. Why?

These are some of the enigmas and conundrums and paradoxes and ironies that Osvaldo Hurtado seeks to answer in *Portrait of a Nation: Culture and Progress in Ecuador*. His approach is unique, daring, bold. Simply put, he hypothesizes that culture is behind Ecuador's backwardness. That Ecuadorians' way of being, their view of the world, their way of thinking and behaving—these deep-seated traits, at work over nearly two centuries—have obstructed and undermined and ultimately thwarted development processes in the country. He takes a historical approach to proving his hypothesis, combining description and analysis of economic and social developments with copious citations of foreign and national observers who left records of their travels through the country and their impressions of its institutions, people, and customs. Typically of Hurtado, his field of vision is vast, his idiom, complex, and his style, compact: in under 300 pages he covers with remarkable detail 288 years of colonial rule and 178 years of republican rule, and while the speed and scope are breathtaking, the panorama he portrays is equally so.

In effect, Hurtado has attempted what no other writer, Ecuadorian or foreign, has attempted: to draw a comprehensive, multidimensional portrait of Ecuadorian culture. That he has produced a work of art—a work of fine strokes, sharp contrasts of tone and light, and subtle meanings—is beyond doubt. But the picture he paints is not an unequivocally attractive one. The reader who expects to find platitude, hyperbole, and cliché will be disappointed. Bad habits in the past, says Hurtado, impeded the early citizens of the Audiencia of Quito and the Republic of Ecuador from appreciating the value of work, developing an interest in commerce, establishing relationships based on mutual confidence, seeking improvement through innovation, honoring commitments, and so forth. And in the modern era, though the constraints of tradition and convention have been somewhat relaxed, Hurtado nevertheless concludes that, in the habits and customs that count, that is, that contribute to "development," his countrymen have changed very little:

> Regardless of their economic status and professional level, [Ecuadorians] are not hardworking, efficient, and persevering. Rather, they are indolent, inconsistent, routine-oriented, and given to unproductive spending and not to saving. For this reason, companies and the broader economy are not innovative and competitive, nor do they have enough resources to grow and achieve an international projection. (180)

In his critical view of his country's culture and of his countrymen, however, Hurtado is being consistent with his nature. He has never been bashful about stating his beliefs and opinions, and he has always spoken out when he has something to say. When he speaks, regardless of the medium, he speaks unequivocally and he speaks from principle, and what his countrymen hear is unabashed and informed. For Hurtado, speaking honestly about his country is not betrayal, rather it is the essence of patriotism, because by discovering sincerely and understanding objectively the problems that confront Ecuador, he and his fellow Ecuadorians can better seek and implement solutions that are meaningful and sustainable.

It is not banal to say that throughout the forty years of his professional career as university professor, political party organizer, vice president and president of the country, president of the 1998 constituent assembly, founder/president of the prestigious think tank CORDES, and writer and scholar, Osvaldo Hurtado has been motivated by an unswerving and profound commitment to understanding on the one hand the unique nature of his country, and on the other, to finding, recommending, and implementing solutions to the profound problems that confront it socially, economically, and politically. As vice president of the country he sought to develop and implement a practical economic development plan in Ecuador. As president he desperately and under extremely adverse conditions worked to preserve Ecuador's fledgling and vulnerable democracy. As a member of constitutional and political reform bodies in 1977 and 1998, he endeavored to put into practice his beliefs—based on readings, study, and writings—in the salutary effects of strong and legitimate political institutions for the consolidation and sustainability of democracy in Ecuador. The constitutions of 1979 and 1998, which reform the electoral process, regulate political party formation and operations, and redefine the role and responsibilities of the legislative branch of government, bear a strong and unmistakable Hurtado imprint. Hurtado is the epitome of the activist scholar; his activism is coldly rational and is based on principle and informed judgment garnered over years of study. And his study has been profound and copious, reflecting a wide range of interests and concerns within the framework of national reality: the origins of political power; democracy and its institutionality; governability; politics, economy, and development; populism, citizenship, and values; and the role of culture in national development.

A consummate teacher, Hurtado studies and writes to understand, but also to instruct. Scholarship: yes; academic precision: of course; but always with a view to motivating change in society, to improving the conditions and ultimately the lives of all Ecuadorians, especially future generations. With remarkable coherence, his writings, particularly from the nineties on, all contain the same message regardless of the point of departure: who we are and how we behave, he exhorts, determines our development as a nation. If once he pointed to institutional reform and stability as being the keys to national development, now it is clearly the individual, the very basic constituent element of society, that is the secret to progress. If the individual does not change—change his view of the world; his attitude toward family, work, and nation; his commitment to making Ecuador a better place—then nothing will change and Ecuador will be destined to chronic underdevelopment. There is a clear negative undertone here: "Ecuadorian culture is deficient." But there is also a positive side: "Our future is in our hands." This message, a message of hope and of optimism, comes through loud and clear in all of Hurtado's recent writings, including *Portrait of a Nation: Culture and Progress in Ecuador*, where he points out in the concluding chapter that if progress in a country depends on the cultural values and habits of the people, then the responsibility for future development rests squarely on the shoulders of those same people and on no one else. His profound hope is that the evidence uncovered by his research into Ecuadorian culture will inspire citizens to take stock of their responsibilities and adopt "cultural patterns compatible with . . . individual and collective progress." Ultimately, for Hurtado, the "Ecuadorian people [must] assume their responsibility in constructing their own destiny" (184).

Portrait of a Nation: Culture and Progress in Ecuador is in many ways a culmination. It is a culmination of Hurtado's own intellectual quest for truth in the Ecuadorian context; it is a culmination of his lifelong attempt to capture the soul of his nation. It is a culmination of a thought process that, having explored all the recesses of national reality in the search for keys to the enigma that is Ecuador, has arrived finally at the realization that culture is the ultimate key to understanding and unlocking Ecuador's development dilemma; it explains chronic underdevelopment, but also, ironically, it is that same singular force that can lift Ecuador out of its underdevelopment. Culture, says Hurtado, has both damning and saving faculties. Finally, the book is a culmination of Osvaldo Hurtado's consummate patriotism, of his faith and trust in the power of his fellow Ecuadorians to break the bonds of backwardness, and of his hope and conviction that a better future awaits Ecuador and its people.

Nick D. Mills
Managua, Nicaragua
March 23, 2008

ABOUT NICK MILLS

Nick Mills has lived and worked in Ecuador for many years. From 1973 to 1980 he was director of the University of New Mexico Andean Research Center. He later served as adviser to President Hurtado (1981–1984). He is the author of *Crisis, Conflicto y Consenso: Ecuador, 1979–84*, and the translator of Osvaldo Hurtado's seminal work, *El Poder Político en el Ecuador* (*Political Power in Ecuador*). Currently he is the director of a large community education project implemented by CARE in Afghanistan.

ACKNOWLEDGMENTS

It would not have been possible to write *Portrait of a Nation: Culture and Progress in Ecuador* without the texts left behind by intrepid foreign travelers who, with curious eyes and scrutinizing minds, ventured into the territories of the *Audiencia* of Quito* and the Republic of Ecuador. On returning to their home countries, they published books in which they narrated their adventures and vicissitudes, described the society, and commented on nature and snowcapped mountains in the Andes. In most cases, in their writings they slipped in comments on the cultural habits of the inhabitants of Quito and other Ecuadorians with whom they came into direct contact or simply observed as they carried on their day-to-day activities.

Even though many foreign travelers left behind invaluable testimonials, I would specifically like to mention the Spaniards Jorge Juan and Antonio De Ulloa; the Italians Mario Cicala, Juan Domingo Coleti, and Gaetano Osculati; the British William Bennet Stevenson and Edward Whymper; the Frenchmen Alexandre Holinski, Henri Michaux, and J. Delebecque; the Germans Joseph Kolberg, Hans Meyer, and Ludwig Bemelmans; and the North Americans Friedrich Hassaurek, James Orton, and Albert Franklin. Despite the fact that they were in the country a long while, the most illustrious travelers, Alexander von Humboldt and Charles Marie de La Condamine, left behind few testimonials referring to cultural habits. This was perhaps because their main concern was scientific, or because with discreet

---

Translator's Note: Standard English-language grammar would call for always putting the Spanish word *audiencia* in italics. However, given that some contemporary scholarly articles no longer italicize certain common terms referring to Latin American history and culture (e.g., mestizo, hacienda, and corregidor), in this text such words will appear first in italics and thereafter in regular print. This choice should also create less visual distraction for the reader. For definitions of unfamiliar words, please consult the glossary.

silence they wanted to reciprocate the kind attentions that their generous hosts had bestowed upon them by taking them in as guests.

I rediscovered their books thirty years after I first came across them while conducting the research that resulted in *Political Power in Ecuador*. However, more travel journals are now available thanks to the Spanish translations published by Abya Yala, the Banco Central del Ecuador, and the Corporación Editora Nacional.

Felipe Hurtado, David Molina, and Soledad Álvarez were in charge of the bibliographic research. They also conducted excellent interviews, and Felipe Hurtado researched English-language texts, translated the quotations used herein, and reviewed the endnotes. Lucía Pazmiño researched the French-language texts and translated the quotations. Andrés Dávila created the computer program that made possible the systematization of the information gathered; and CORDES, the research center that I head, made available its abundant research tools.

I would also like to thank John Sanbrailo, Nick Mills, Segundo Moreno, Constanza Di Capua, Juan Malo, Vera de Kohn, Fernando Jurado, Rosmery Terán, Fernando Bustamante, and Carlos Landázuri, who generously agreed to share their knowledge with me. The first two also reviewed the manuscript.

I would finally like to express a special acknowledgment to Barbara Sipe for her smart and thorough work in the translation of *Las costumbres de los ecuatorianos*.

INTRODUCTION

The book that the reader has in hand was originally published in Spanish by Editorial Planeta (Quito, 2007) under the title *Las costumbres de los ecuatorianos* (*The Cultural Habits of Ecuadorians*). Despite its critical vision, it was well received by readers. In fact, it was the year's best-seller in Ecuador in both 2007 and 2008.

Through research in historical documents covering almost five hundred years, this book examines the relationship between culture and development, a topic that heretofore has not aroused interest among Latin American social scientists, even though much research has been done on the causes of backwardness and poverty and much has been written about those topics. As the reader will see, in the colonial period and the era of the republic, first the cultural habits of Quiteños, and later those of Ecuadorians, have constituted a stumbling-block to individual economic success, to the advancement of entrepreneurial activities, and to national development.

Thanks to *obraje* textile production during the sixteenth and seventeenth centuries, the cacao boom of the last decade of the nineteenth century and the first two decades of the twentieth century, and the banana surge in the 1950s and 1960s, the Audiencia of Quito and the Republic of Ecuador enjoyed periods of relative economic prosperity. However, since progress was modest and there were long periods of stagnation and recession, for nearly four hundred years the country remained poor and backward, a circumstance that was somewhat reversed once oil reserves were discovered in the Amazon jungle and oil exports began in 1972. Thanks to this wealth that generously poured out of the ground, without a major effort by the Ecuadorians themselves, the economy grew in the 1970s at a high rate of 9.4 percent annually. This economic growth was curtailed during the "lost" decades of the 1980s and 1990s, when the rate did not exceed 1.9 percent per year, falling below the population growth rate of 2.3 percent. Economic reactivation occurred during the first five years of the twenty-first century, with an annual growth rate of 5.2 percent, due to the stability brought about by dollarization, larger volumes of oil exports, high oil prices on international markets, and the sizeable money transfers made by Ecuadorians living abroad. Just as had occurred previously in the colonial period and was then repeated in the years following the founding of Ecuador (1830), the volatile and insufficient economic growth of the second half of the twentieth century and the early years of the twenty-first century greatly hindered the country's development.

Specialists on Ecuadorian economic development have attributed the backwardness, in which the Audiencia of Quito and the Republic of Ecuador were immersed, to a number of factors: geographical isolation, natural catastrophes, external forces, a difficult geography hemmed in by jungles and mountains, structural weaknesses in the country, and a fragile political system.

In effect, during colonial times and a good deal of the era of the Republic, the country lived in a situation of national and international isolation (between its own regions and from other countries) and underwent economic slumps brought on by earthquakes, floods, droughts, fires, and plagues. Thick jungles and steep mountains made it difficult to build roads, and Ecuador suffered from crises originating abroad that decreased the value of export commodities. To all this must be added the costly armed conflicts that occurred along the border with Peru. However, it must be kept in mind that at the beginning of the twentieth century Ecuador became integrated into the world thanks to the Panama Canal, and in subsequent decades the mountains were conquered and the jungles opened up to roads. Plagues were eliminated or brought under control, fires were contained, territorial problems were resolved, and there were times in which exports enjoyed high prices. However, the country continued to deal with floods, earthquakes, and recurring international crises.

The existence of structures that hindered Ecuador's development led to attempts at economic, social, and administrative reforms in the 1960s and the 1990s. Even though these had different ideological foundations and posited radically different policies and programs, they sought to create conditions that would encourage productive activities and foster national development. The first of these reform programs gave the State a predominant role in the development process, granted it important economic activities, sought the redistribution of wealth through socioeconomic reforms, and established a variety of protectionist measures. On the other hand, the second promoted liberalization of the economy, favored the free operation of market forces, reduced the scope of the state, and encouraged international outreach. In both cases, the programs were only partially implemented and efforts were not made to persevere along the chosen path. For these reasons, the expected economic and social outcomes were not attained.

From the time that the republic was created, inadequate political institutions were blamed for the poor functioning of the democratic system, the recurring dictatorships, and the poor management of public affairs. This reasoning led to repeated constitutional changes, most notably those contained in the nineteen constitutions that have been promulgated, each one conceived with the aim of correcting the political maladies that beset Ecuador. These constitutional reengineering exercises and the institutions that were created to replace the previous ones did not succeed in improving the quality of democracy, guarantee sound government, and promote development. Dictatorial regimes have outnumbered democratic ones; and the governments have lasted on average less than two years. For these reasons, Ecuador has not had a stable democracy capable of guaranteeing national progress, and it has not been able to correct this malady even through the consensual and carefully thought-out constitutional reforms of 1998. Chronic political instability has kept the country from promoting long-term public policies that could guarantee economic stability and growth, which are prerequisites for the creation of opportunities for the poor and of better living conditions for excluded sectors of the population.

This research effort proposes to contribute to the debate on Ecuadorian development by studying a cause that has not merited the attention of those that have analyzed the nation's problems, despite the fact that it has been present throughout the almost five centuries of colonial and republican national existence. Cultural factors, expressed in individuals' ways of being, thinking, and acting, have introduced all kinds of difficulties for the efficient operation of private productive activities, the sound management of the public economy, and the sustained socioeconomic development of the country. Nonetheless, this affirmation in no way implies ignoring the fact that numerous factors come into play in the development of a society.

Among other consequences, a proposal of this nature calls for situating the task of Ecuadorian development within its own borders, under the responsibility of its own citizens; that is, at the opposite extreme of the theories of imperialism and dependency, according to which the country's economic development problems are primarily due to external causes that have to be overcome for progress to be made. These theories have lost force as a result of the collapse of Soviet Marxism and the success attained by the countries that maintain strong ties to the industrialized world. However, even though they have been abandoned by the very ones who once promoted them in their writings, in Ecuador these theories continue to influence the political behavior of an important number of leaders for whom the country's economic and social failures in recent decades were caused by inappropriate policies recommended by international organizations, the opening up of the economy to the outside world, exploitation by industrialized countries, and a lack of interest in participating in Ecuadorian development.

After many years devoted to studying economic, social, and political problems in the country and contributing to their solution through my participation in the national debate and in public office, in the early 1990s I began to reflect on the possibility that cultural factors might explain the country's failure to develop and the democratic system's failure to operate adequately. This reflection led me to write a short essay entitled "Political Culture," published in *Léxico Político Ecuatoriano* (Quito, 1994). I returned to this subject in texts that I wrote in subsequent years, the most widely disseminated being "Culture and Development," published by Siglo XXI Editores in the book *Sociología del desarrollo, políticas sociales y democracia* (Mexico, 2001). This was followed by a report I prepared for UNDP, entitled *Cultura y Democracia, una relación olvidada*, a summarized version of which was published in *La democracia en América Latina, contribuciones para el debate* (Buenos Aires, 2004).

In light of the fact that this research effort is oriented to studying the relationship between culture and development, I am foregoing an analysis of the relationship between culture and democracy, in other words, of the cultural factors relating to the field of politics. However, I believe that a study of citizens' political behavior would help to explain the adversarial political relations, the chronic national instability, the recurring authoritarian governments, and the poor operation of the democratic system. It would also help to explain why the reforms contained in the nineteen versions of the country's constitution (with a twentieth version now on the horizon) have not managed to correct Ecuador's political problems.

For the purposes of this research, "culture" will be understood as the set of customs, attitudes, feelings, ideals, beliefs, values, and behaviors that determine how individuals conduct themselves in their everyday life. Likewise, "development" will be understood as the ongoing improvement of levels of well-being due to sufficient sustained growth of the economy and the equitable distribution of economic rewards.

The mentalities and lifestyles of Spaniards, Creoles, Indians, blacks, mestizos, and mulattos that inhabited the territory of the Audiencia of Quito and later Ecuador are compiled and analyzed in the pages that follow. They are the traits that were habitually shared by broad sectors of society. There were, to be sure, individuals who acted differently and groups localized geographically that, over time, changed certain behaviors. However, since national development is marked by the predominant ways of life and not by the exceptions, the few citizens who behaved differently were not in a position to alter the cultural path laid out by the vast majority.

The novel topic embraced by this inquiry and the lack of previous studies on which to base it made the search for sources complex; and the analysis of the information, laborious. It was necessary to examine numerous books and to exhaust their pages to find some piece of information that could be useful. This called for grueling and meticulous research. It was impossible to forego the task of selecting and analyzing all the material available to make sense of it and fulfill the academic purposes sought. The information gleaned proved to be so evocative and the analysis so engaging that I eventually found that I was working literally around the clock. It was thus that a manuscript conceived of initially as a brief essay ended up becoming a book.

The texts published by foreign travelers from Europe and the United States who visited the Audiencia of Quito and the Republic of Ecuador during four centuries constituted an invaluable resource for the research. They made it possible to learn about aspects of the everyday life of people from Quito and other areas of Ecuador, aspects typically ignored by national authors. Since they came from cultures different from Ecuador's, these travelers were impressed by the beliefs they found and the cultural traits they observed during their travels in the countryside and in the cities. While the Quiteños and Ecuadorians were not surprised by the ways of life of their own countrymen, because they were everyday, common, and shared, regardless of their social condition, these customs were noticed by travelers because they were different from their own and because they seemed prejudicial for individual and collective interests and hindered well-being and progress in the Audiencia of Quito and the Republic of Ecuador. The visitors were so intrigued by what they saw that they recorded their observations and used them in writing books or drafting reports upon returning to their countries, documenting accounts of their experiences and the results of the observations of the behavior of the different social classes.

At a time when there were no roads, inns, means of transportation, or any comforts whatsoever, attracted by the Amazon jungle and the beautiful Andean snowcapped mountains, especially Chimborazo, which was considered the highest mountain in the world, foreign travelers arrived by sea to the river port of Guayaquil and then moved inward through the dense, tangled undergrowth of the coastlands along the Babahoyo River. From Bodegas they traversed the Andes along steep and muddy paths, climbed mountains and crossed immense highland plains, waded through strong river currents or crossed them using lifts or improvised bridges built from logs. They carried with them scientific instruments and all kinds of provisions necessary to sustain them during long journeys and to subsist in isolated stopping-places, such provisions including not only food, beds, and shelters for their nights of rest, but also supplies of ink and paper, which were hard to come by in those days. To transport themselves and their trunks, they were able to rely on help from Indian cargo bearers and teams of mules that they hired in the places where they spent the night, in towns and *tambos* (resting places), all of which were unimaginably rudimentary and dirty. Despite the penuries they suffered, without exception the foreign travelers praised the hospitality and courtesy they received from their hosts, including those who, given their level of poverty, had little to offer.

Unfortunately, there are no travel chronicles written by inhabitants of Quito in the colonial period and Ecuadorians after independence. In addition to the reason noted above, this vacuum is due to the fact that Ecuadorians did not travel for scientific or even sightseeing purposes, or they simply did not have the means to do so because of the high costs. Neither were they willing to abandon the comforts of their homes to venture along unknown paths, expose themselves to all kinds of peril, and suffer deprivations and discomforts. The foreign visitors narrate that they learned of very few natives who would have undertaken the adventure of climbing the appealing snowcapped mountains of the Andes, a challenge that many considered impossible, despite their proximity to the cities and haciendas and the fact that their foothills could be easily reached on mule or horseback. The few who traveled were probably not familiar with writing and even if they were they did not have access to a printing press to publish their books, nor were there people interested in reading them.

The bibliographic review carried out for this research uncovered only three texts referring to Ecuadorian cultural habits and beliefs. These were written not by travelers but rather by scholars, and published in the early nineteenth century: *Psicología y sociología del pueblo ecuatoriano* by Alfredo Espinosa Tamayo; *Ensayos sociológicos, políticos y morales* by Belisario Quevedo;

and *La psicología del pueblo azuayo* by Octavio Díaz. The first of these three was full of useful information.

The first chapter of this book analyzes the customs of the inhabitants of the Audiencia of Quito and the effects that their practices had on different aspects of the economy during the long colonial period. The next three chapters study the same subject, tracing the economic, social, and political changes that occurred in the nineteenth and twentieth centuries, following Independence. The last chapter examines the positive role that cultural values have played in the economic success of certain groups, including the progressive city of Cuenca, the industrious Otavalo Indians, and the successful Arab and Jewish immigrants. The book concludes with a recapitulation of the analysis done in the previous chapters and with a few final reflections.

It should be kept in mind that during the colonial period when one spoke of people from Quito, the term referred to all of the inhabitants of the Audiencia of Quito, except when specified that the reference was only to the people living in the city of Quito or the central–northern region of the Andes.

Readers will undoubtedly take notice of the references made to drunkenness and filth. These cultural habits are examined because of their negative economic consequences. The habit of drinking among all social classes, during both the colonial period and the republic, caused economic harm to individuals and families, curtailed productive activities, and limited the country's progress. Meanwhile, cleanliness is a demonstration of a society's degree of organization, concern, hygiene, responsibility, and modernity. The slight importance granted to cleanliness for almost five centuries explains, for example, why in the twenty-first century it continues to be difficult to eradicate the custom of throwing trash out of car windows, even luxury cars, or of littering by pedestrians, along roadways, streets, plazas, parks, and beaches.

This study is inscribed within the line of thinking initiated by Alexis de Tocqueville (*La democracia en América*) and Max Weber (*La ética protestante y el espíritu del capitalismo*), and continued by Edward C. Banfield (*The Moral Basis of a Backward Society*), Carlos Rangel (*Del buen salvaje al buen revolucionario*), Octavio Paz (*El ogro filantrópico*), Alan Riding (*Vecinos distantes*), Robert D. Putnam (*Making Democracy Work: Civic Traditions in Modern Italy*), Francis Fukuyama (*Confianza*), Alain Peyrefitte (*La sociedad de la confianza*), Lawrence Harrison (*El subdesarrollo está en la mente* and *The Central Liberal Truth*), Gabriel A. Almond and Sidney Verba (*The Civic Culture*), Mariano Grondona (*Las condiciones culturales del desarrollo económico*),

David Landes (*The Wealth and Poverty of Nations*), Lawrence E. Harrison and Samuel P. Huntington, eds. (*Culture Matters*), and Samuel P. Huntington (*¿Quiénes somos?*). This research effort is therefore indebted to these authors for the theoretical instruments they provided and for many of their reflections.

A people's cultural values are not immutable, nor are they inherent to particular races, religious creeds, or social classes. Inconvenient customs, beliefs, and attitudes can be changed through the transformation of socio-economic structures, the organizing role of political and juridical institutions, educational programs designed for that purpose, lessons inculcated by churches, charitable influences from abroad, positive orientations among the mass media, and the example and behavior of enlightened leaders.

The possibility that national culture can be transformed is demonstrated in the study of the changes produced in Ecuador during the second half of the twentieth century. The ones that occurred in Guayaquil during the nineteenth century were particularly significant, and later on those in the indigenous community of Otavalo and in the city of Cuenca. The economic success of Arab and Jewish immigrants was due to their own effort, for they had to deal with more limitations than those that the country imposed on its own citizens.

Reading the following pages could lead one to consider that the description I provide of the national character is too harsh. What a German professor at the first Polytechnic School of Ecuador wrote, more than a century ago, may shed some light on the intention behind what I have written: "A people's best patriots have always been those men that have recognized and assessed (their habits) with sincerity, above all what is wrong, in order to remedy it or improve it in the most suitable way. I beg that what I have said on this point, and what I will say later, be taken in this sense." I agree with Joseph Kolberg on this point and believe that all Ecuadorians need to take a moment to evaluate and reflect, admit their mistakes, and assume their responsibilities, as a necessary step for the country's development.

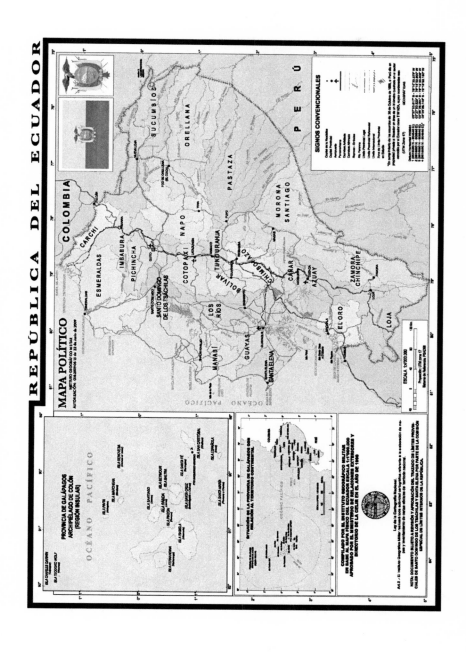

REPÚBLICA DEL ECUADOR

MAPA POLÍTICO

PROVINCIA DE GALÁPAGOS
ARCHIPIÉLAGO DE COLÓN
(REGIÓN INSULAR)

SIGNOS CONVENCIONALES

1

CULTURAL CHARACTERISTICS OF THE AUDIENCIA OF QUITO

John Leddy Phelan, in his study *El reino de Quito en el siglo XVII* (*The Kingdom of Quito in the Seventeenth Century*), examined the meager results attained by the Spaniards, and later the Creoles, in their efforts to extend colonization to the tropical jungles of the coastlands and the Amazon territories of the Audiencia of Quito. These results were due to difficult access and inhospitable conditions. Phelan concluded that colonial life was thus concentrated mainly in the Andean region, a geographical area that years later, in 1830, would be the territorial basis for creating the Republic of Ecuador. The North American historian wrote, "The two Quitos that we have already discussed, the Quito of the coast and the Quito of the Oriente, were marginal to the third and most important Quito—the valleys in the Sierra lying between the two chains of the Andes."[1]

In effect, during the long colonial period the Sierra, or highlands region, was the most advanced and most populated region of the Audiencia of Quito. It accounted for more than 90 percent of the population and carried on farming, livestock-raising (sheep farms), and manual textile-making in mills known as *obrajes*. The subsistence of everyone depended on these activities. In the eighteenth century, the prosperous settlement of Quito in the central and northern Andes declined and became impoverished because of the destruction caused by earthquakes and the ruin of the textile industry. The latter was due to outside competition and lower demand resulting from a decline in the large American mining centers and the contraband introduced by the French, Dutch, and English. Nevertheless, Quito maintained its dominance because of the slight economic and demographic significance that other colonial regions continued to have.

The inter-Andean region offered colonists good land, a healthy climate, and abundant labor. According to Gironaldo Benzoni, Quito was "the most fertile and abundant province of all of Peru."[2] Jesuit priest Mario Cicala was surprised by the "admirable fertility" of the province of Quito, where there was no "kind of fruit, species of grain, variety of flower, type of vegetable, multiplicity of pasturelands, diversity of grasses, that are not seen to take root, grow and germinate in surprising abundance."[3] This observation was shared by the English-Irish chronicler William Stevenson, who served as secretary to Count Ruiz de Castilla in the last years of the Audiencia of Quito, when he noted the different climates that made it possible, in the course of just a few hours, "to experience the cold of the poles, the stifling heat of the equator, and all of the temperatures in between," and also made it possible for its inhabitants to have a large variety of foods at their disposal. The surrounding abundance so caught his attention that he made the prediction that the country would "at a future date become one of the most flourishing countries in the New World."[4] This prophecy was not fulfilled because of the way in which inhabitants of Quito and Ecuador did not make good use or, or take advantage of, the resources that nature had so generously bestowed upon them.

With the exception of Guayaquil, the urban centers of the coast were small, isolated towns that were just beginning to develop at the end of the eighteenth century. One factor that contributed to Guayaquil's progress was its advantage as the only port for the Audiencia of Quito, through which products were imported and exported and contraband entered clandestinely. These activities were stimulated by the reduction of trade restrictions declared by the Bourbon kings. Guayaquil's economy was also nourished by two additional important activities, which were sources of employment for workers migrating from other areas within the Audiencia. The city controlled the production, collection, storage, and exportation of cacao, a crop cultivated on haciendas in the Guayas River basin and taken to the port along the tributaries. And Guayaquil shipbuilders were so important that they came to be considered the largest on the Pacific Coast. Due to its progress, when the colonial period ended, Guayaquil became the second major city of the Audiencia of Quito, even though the population on the coast barely represented 14 percent of the total.[5]

The southern Andean provinces were much less important economically and demographically, but because their economies were not dependent on textiles, they were able to ride out the economic crisis of the eighteenth century and thus attain a larger relative weight at the end of the colonial period. They had also benefited from the profits earned from casacarilla exports, which were used for quinine production. This discovery, which made it possible to cure malaria, generated a significant demand in the Americas and in the European powers desirous of protecting the health of their colonists in the tropical lands of Africa and Asia.

For these reasons, and because it was emigrants from the highlands who populated the coast and the jungle—the latter region having only recently been physically integrated into Ecuador four hundred years later, during the second half of the twentieth century—it becomes germane to center a study of colonial culture on the Andean provinces, and particularly on those of the central and northern regions, which were tied to Quito. These were located between the cities of Ibarra to the north and Riobamba to the south.

A STRATIFIED AND EXCLUSIVISTIC SOCIETY

Unlike other European countries, in which capitalist forms of production were beginning to appear, during most of the colonial period in the Americas, Spain was characterized by feudalism, whose conventions and values marked the behavior of those who conquered and colonized the territories that comprised the Audiencia of Quito. The Spaniards came from a hierarchically organized society dominated by nobility that benefited from land ownership, the economic surpluses that compulsory work generated, and the tribute paid by peasants subject to the status of servitude. It was widely held that land constituted the main source of wealth, as a result of which other economic activities and manual labor were disparaged.

Before the arrival of the Spaniards, during the brief Inca period and the era that preceded it, the Indians had lived in authoritarian societies subject to the absolute power of local political leaders (*caciques*) and sovereigns. They were obliged to provide personal services, pay tribute, and perform all types of work, such as building roads and bearing cargo. Families' needs, including the preservation of life, could only be met through blind obedience and absolute loyalty to those that held power. They did not have land with which they could do as they pleased; rather, land use depended on the will of the person or group to whom they were subordinated. In many social areas, especially the military, which was so important for the conquest of the Andean people, the indigenous society was very backward in comparison with Spanish society. The diseases brought with the conquerors led to a demographic catastrophe, especially in the coastal region, where the indigenous population practically disappeared. However, the Indians continued to be a large majority in the Sierra. In fact, during the colonial period they accounted for between 75 percent and 90 percent of the population of the Audiencia of Quito.

The language of the Incas, which had been adopted by the indigenous people of the Audiencia of Quito, was not prepared to compete with the Castilian language used by the conquerors, colonists, bureaucrats, and clergymen. According to La Condamine, Quechua was lacking in words "that would allow it to express abstract, universal ideas," such as "*time, duration, space, being, substance, matter, body, virtue, justice, liberty, gratitude, ingratitude,*" and many more concepts that could be expressed only quite imperfectly and only after having recourse to long, roundabout phrases.[6] For this reason, the Indians found it difficult to master the language of the conquerors; but had they done so, this knowledge would have enabled them to take advantage of it for their own purposes.

These characteristics of the Spanish world and the indigenous world, and the type of economic structures that were implemented in the colonial period, led to the organization of a highly stratified society in which the top of the social pyramid was occupied by whites and the wide base by people of color. People acquired their status on the day of their birth and kept it throughout their life. Ownership of the obrajes and haciendas, which were the most important commercial activities, was reserved for Spaniards and Creoles, as were political and religious positions of authority and privileged access to education. Furthermore, worldly treasures, economic activities, and representational functions were not accessible to the men and women of color who made up the indigenous, black, mestizo, and mulatto peoples. They, on the other hand, were obliged to pay tribute to and to work for their masters in conditions of servitude or slavery. Naturally, reciprocal cultural influences did not fail to occur, especially among the Spanish with regard to the Indians. In the end, the centuries-long domination of all types, including religious domination, made it possible for the customs of the conquerors to prevail.

The Catholic religion gave ideological support to colonial hierarchical society by justifying as God's will the widespread economic, social, and political inequalities that existed. If society's development was determined by divine will and men were merely an instrument, they could do little to change the social conditions in which they lived. Since poverty was considered a blessing, rather than a burden, men should accept it with resignation and seek consolation in charity, an attitude that would eventually be compensated for in "the other life" through "eternal salvation." Profit-making, moneylenders' collecting of interest on money loaned, and scientific research were morally scorned, or at least looked upon suspiciously, because they went against the natural order determined by God. These values were transmitted by Catholic clergymen through the education that they imparted in schools and universities, and through their preaching of "the word of God" in the churches that, by then, were the social hub of colonial life. To these were added the close ties existing between the Church, the political authorities, and the white society; the direct exploitation that took place through the collection of economic contributions; and the Church's commitment to the system of domination and exploitation by virtue of the religious orders' direct ownership of obrajes and numerous large haciendas.

Scientist Alexander von Humboldt, who visited the Audiencia of Quito for an extended period, wrote: "In America, fair skin is what decides the rank that a man holds within society" since the color of their skin establishes "a sort of equality among men that affirm that they have certain degrees of superiority due to their race and their origin." The German traveler illustrated this racial differentiation with a story about the way in which disputes were settled. He cited a person of high social status who, when he disputed some matter with a common man, would be heard to say "Perhaps you consider yourself whiter than I am?"[7]

The Spaniards, as Phelan noted, "were racist and ethnocentric in their own fashion." Although they collaborated with different races, much more than other people from other nations, they "never for a moment doubted their own superiority over them." So, "the only equality that they were willing to grant to the Indians was the equality of the other world."[8] This segregation was confirmed by a contemporary researcher, who stated that Indians, despite the rights and privileges consecrated under secular law and religious canons, were faced with the cruel paradox that they were treated "like animals or mental retards." He provided evidence of this reality by citing a 1609 source that showed that renting a horse for one day cost four *reales*, whereas hiring an Indian guide only cost his food and "sometimes two or four *reales*."[9]

Jorge Juan and Antonio De Ulloa, Spanish sailors who accompanied the French Geodesic Mission that laid out the equatorial meridian, in their celebrated work entitled *Noticias secretas de América* wrote: "The Indians are truly slaves in those countries and they would be fortunate to have a single master to whom to contribute what they earn with the sweat of their brow." Farther on, they added that in the case of the black slaves, only they and not their families were obliged to work and any financial losses were borne by the master, whereas the Indians had to carry the burden of the losses that they produced and share their chores with their wives and children.[10] Stevenson remarked that in the area of Mount Chimborazo, he saw Indians dispossessed of their lands, obliged to work for meager pay, subjected to "the whip and other corporal punishments," and "reduced to the most abject state of servitude and slavery."[11] Caldas, upon seeing how a peasant family was fascinated by the light of a candle, expressed his amazement at the fact that, "barely thirty leagues" from Quito, Indians lived "in almost the same state as in the time of the Conquest."[12]

The lands initially received from the Spanish Crown by Spaniards and Creoles by virtue of "royal favors" or dispensations, together with the concessions made by the municipal councils (*cabildos*), were expanded over time, especially in the seventeenth and eighteenth centuries, leading to the formation of large haciendas. According to historian José María Vargas, "The origin of the social structure of Ecuador's agrarian property lies in the way lands were distributed by the Cabildo."[13] Some land was purchased by the officials who had gotten rich in the performance of public office or in the unscrupulous administration of the obrajes. However, some of the Indians' properties were usurped; they were forced to abandon their land, obliged to sell at ridiculously low prices, or had land taken away in the courts, thanks to the whites' influences in the legal system. When the colonial period came to an end, the whites had appropriated the best lands and relegated the Indians to ownership of small, not-very-productive plots far away from the fertile inter-Andean valleys. The stratified social structure was built on the basis of a "planned division of the land" that took into account "space and labor available and estimated revenue," whereby some benefited and others were deprived.[14] Some of the largest and most prosperous haciendas belonged to religious communities, but church involvement in hacienda ownership did not entail any change whatsoever in social and economic structures, perhaps with the exception of haciendas belonging to the Jesuits.

Since there was a caste system, with definite social and legal limits, similar forms of discrimination occurred with other individuals of color. For example, in 1690 the Cabildo of Guayaquil established different sanctions for people who set up tables in the plazas and the churches to sell merchandise. Mulattos, quarterbreeds, blacks, and mestizos were flogged with fifty lashes, whereas the "leading people" were only obliged to pay a fine of fifty pesos.[15]

Thus, colonial society did not offer conditions for equal opportunities and thereby the possibility of social and economic mobility as a function of individual merits as opposed to ethnic background.

The most pernicious segregation existed in the field of education, on which a people's economic future so depends. Only the sons of well-to-do white families were admitted to the aristocratic colonial university, since the students who intended to register had to prove "cleanliness of blood." For example, to be admitted to the university, Eugenio Espejo had to employ subterfuges to "prove" an imaginary Spanish ancestor from the nobility. Indians did not even have access to schools because their ethnicity excluded them from any form of education. Special establishments run by the Franciscan monks were reserved for the mestizos, who learned artisan trades that were known back then as "mechanical arts" or "vile trades." The priesthood—which was a source of wealth, prestige, and power—was off-limits to Indians and even mestizos.[16]

A society that consecrated social inequalities from the time of birth—and maintained them for life thanks to a system of domination that ensured their immutability—curbed the incentives for those who occupied the lower strata of the social pyramid to use their work as a means of rising out of poverty and improving their social and economic status. On the other hand, certain that their social situation would not be challenged, those who occupied higher positions did not find it necessary to perform their activities with dedication and determination since there was no threat of competition and their economic position would not be improved through greater effort.

The historical origins of colonial society, with its structural characteristics and rigid hierarchies, added to geographical and demographic factors, eventually gave rise to the paradigms that shaped the beliefs and dictated the behavior of the inhabitants of the Audiencia of Quito.

WIDESPREAD IDLENESS

Despite the centuries of exploitation that the Ecuadorian coastal region has experienced, it continues to be an extraordinarily fertile land. A contemporary study affirms

> It has the richest combination of soils and climates of the Western Hemisphere. In its overall profile, the soil contains approximately twice as much organic matter and is comparable to the soils of some of the richest black plains found in the United States. Add to this abundant sunshine, a lack of wind, daily temperatures of around 80°F (27°C), and an average annual rainfall of over 75 inches. All of this explains why Ecuador's agricultural potential is unequaled.[17]

If the coast is that fertile nowadays, one can only imagine how fertile the lands were four hundred years ago.

Even though the highland soils were of poorer quality and were less readily available because of the extensive plains and the numerous Andean mountains, the region had fertile valleys, frequent rainfall, and abundant irrigation water. The temperature changes were greater, but the region did not suffer summer heat or winter cold as in the countries with four seasons. Its climate fluctuated between cool spring-like weather and moderate autumn.

The coastlands and highlands could be cultivated all year long, and the two regions had a variety of climates. This permitted rich and poor to have a wide range of food year-round. The existence of a mild climate made it unnecessary to stock the provisions that the people who lived in harsh geographical environments were forced to have because they could die of cold or hunger if they did not store up food and firewood for the long winter months. In the case of the highlands, the temperate climate also contributed to the fact that the inhabitants did not endure the plagues that afflicted the coastal settlements.

Juan and De Ulloa contrasted the "abundance of crops" produced in the Sierra with the "idle, lazy life" of the inhabitants.[18] Stevenson, referring to the natives of the Province of Esmeraldas, wrote an observation that was valid for all the coastal inhabitants: "It may with truth be asserted, that industry is certainly not a prominent feature in their habits," he noted and then added, "where a sufficiency is easily procured, where luxury in food or clothing is unknown, where superiority is never contended for, and where nature appears not only to invite but even to tempt her creatures to repose, why should they reject her offer?"[19] This opinion was confirmed by Cicala, who wrote: "If care and solicitude in farming and working the land had been on a par with their disinterest and neglect," the wealth that whites and Indians would have obtained would have exceeded that attained by peasants in Europe.[20] In a report that they sent to the Crown in 1814, two natives of the Audiencia of Quito, José Joaquín de Olmedo and Vicente Rocafuerte, reiterated these concepts when they wrote: "The fertility and abundance of this province are so great that, with another level of development and under other auspices, it would today be the richest in America. But the vigor of nature left to its own devices, without labor, without cultivation, without art, remains almost intact under this climate; and even cultivated continuously, it seems never to weaken."[21]

The existence of a numerous indigenous population and therefore the possibility of cheap, unlimited labor that was available first to the conquerors and colonists, and later to the Creoles, allowed them to avoid performing tiring manual labor in manufacturing textiles, working the lands, extracting precious metals, and keeping house. All of this work was left to the Indians. They were recruited by whites and put at their service through the encomienda system, despite the fact that the estate-holders (*encomenderos*) had no right to do that, since the Indians assigned to them were only obliged to pay tribute in money or in kind, in exchange for receiving protection and religious services.[22] Against express legal prohibitions that they be subjected to forced labor and personal services, and despite the sanctions that the Crown established for those who did not comply, they were obliged to work on haciendas and in textile mills, and to do domestic chores in the country and in the city. In some cases the tribute was transformed into work; in others they received meager remunerations or simply none at all. The "assistance" that the Indians received in food and clothing kept them permanently in debt and subject to mandatory work on haciendas and in textile mills by means of which they tried to work off their endless debt.[23]

The Creole pretensions to nobility constituted another obstacle for them to earn a living through hard work and to take the lead in economic progress through their own initiatives. According to a contemporary researcher, during the late colonial period in the Audiencia de Quito there were eleven families with titles of nobility that had been bought from the Crown, all located in the city of Quito. In his research, Christian Büschges, save one exception, did not find any evidence that they would have been interested in carrying on economic activities and in one case only a "slight" interest in enterprise, risk-taking, and success.[24] In reality, many other whites, merely because they considered themselves as such, attributed to themselves imaginary titles of nobility, which they displayed before all foreign travelers who passed through the Audiencia of Quito—even though their nobility could not be demonstrated since almost all of them had some Indian blood in their veins. This behavior led the visitors to express their amazement at the fact that the natives would lay claim to such distinctions and privileges in total ignorance of their own ethnic condition, their merits, and their lack of effort to make a name for themselves through their own devices and the provision of important services.[25] Such was the banality and the ostentation of the upper classes in Quito that, to rub elbows with European visitors and demonstrate their personal worth, they showered upon them excessive attentions. According to the testimony of the Frenchmen who formed part of the Geodesic Mission, they were "welcomed as kings" with opulence, luxury, and lavishness, and the most influential families fought over "housing them, showing them the city, and inviting them to their table."[26]

The aforementioned German researcher found in these characteristics of the Quito nobility and in the nobility's co-optation of those who prospered economically through their businesses the reason why the Audiencia of Quito did not experience the formation of a bourgeoisie, a social class differentiated from the nobility, with its own values and interests, different from those that made up the inherited colonial hierarchy of the home-land.[27]

Travelers and officials of several nationalities that in different eras vis-ited the Audiencia of Quito coincide in describing its inhabitants as people unwilling to do any type of work requiring sacrifice, regardless of their social or ethnic condition (Spaniards, Creoles, rich, poor, white, or people of color). Some had supervisory responsibilities or did manual labor in farming, livestock-raising, trading, mining, textile-making, handicrafts, and in colonial and ecclesiastical administration. Such activities allowed them to have a means of subsistence, but according to the visitors, those who had jobs did not perform them with the determination and dedication they had seen in workers and supervisors in their countries of origin. Furthermore, there were whites, mainly Creoles, who did not have any occupation what-soever, and did not seem to be concerned about it. A variety of expressions were used to describe the lack of a work ethic among the inhabitants of the Andean region of Quito: idleness, laziness, languor, slothfulness, vagrancy, indolence, apathy, etc.

Alexander von Humboldt remarked that he found a country "where anything requiring an effort is avoided," especially in the case of the whites, whom he characterized as "lazy bums."[28] Romualdo Navarro wrote that in the province of Quito, which God blessed with a mild climate and "rare fertility" of its soils, most of its inhabitants gave in to "a detestable idle-ness and those who did have employment disdained their work in a vile manner, which gave rise to the great wretchedness in which they currently find themselves."[29] Jorge Juan and Antonio De Ulloa considered that most of the inhabitants of the Audiencia of Quito "do not occupy themselves in exercise, nor work to keep themselves busy and their imagination en-gaged," some "because they have nothing on which to spend their time" and others because "laziness keeps them unoccupied." They added that, among the members of the white society, there was an aversion to perform-ing manual labor since the Spaniards "do not feel comfortable with any mechanical exercises," considering them a blemish "beneath them" due to their social condition and viewing them as activities reserved for "blacks, browns and bronzed." About the Creoles they said that there were few that devoted themselves to commerce, since "the only exercise in which people of distinction are employed," except for those who were members of the religious orders, is "to visit the haciendas or chacras during the year" where they spent "the whole harvest season"[30] of July and August. Stevenson confirmed this appreciation when he wrote "the principal employment of persons of rank is to visit their estates, on which they generally reside during part of the year."[31]

Three Ecuadorian historians have coincided with these observations made by foreigners regarding the softness of the Quito inhabitants. According to historian González Suárez, regardless of the social condition and profession of those who came to the Audiencia of Quito (soldiers, noblemen, university graduates, bureaucrats, businessmen, artisans, clergymen, and peasants), "All of those who came to this region looked disdainfully at all industry, all trades and in general all work: the workers, the artisans themselves, when they came here, were ashamed of their trades and they seldom returned to them." Thus, "The field work and even some trades were reserved only for the Indians because the whites thought that they were beneath them."[32] This opinion was shared by historian Luis Robalino Dávila when he indicated that no sooner had they settled in the territories that they populated than they sought to ennoble themselves by acquiring agricultural properties and collecting tributes in the encomiendas, while at the same time refusing to perform "lowly" manual labor, which was "beneath the dignity of a well-born person."[33] Francisco Aguirre Abad affirmed that

> In the tranquil and vice-ridden life of the colonists, in which they had almost no productive activity to perform, living off the abundance of the haciendas so as not to tarnish their nobility with any sort of commerce, the country's youth gave themselves over to sensual pleasures of all kinds. The lower classes followed the bad example, so that, without the work of the Indians, one does not know how the colonists could have lived, nor how commerce and trade would have progressed if it had not been for the arrival from Spain of new immigrants who fortunately devoted themselves to work, taking over economic activities that otherwise were reduced to practically nothing.[34]

Due to the poor economic condition in which they arrived or the need to get ahead by making their fortune, some Spanish immigrants, whether settled or in transit, were more inclined to work. They performed commercial activities, particularly those related to trade between provinces and regions and the business of imports and exports. Some got rich, and this situation allowed them to acquire lands, marry upper-class Creole women, and become incorporated into the dominant white group. They provided manufactured food and goods from Europe and China (wine, liquor, oil, soap, iron, copper, tin, lead, quicksilver, dishware, woolens, fine cloth, and silver and gold threads), and to the viceroyalties of New Granada, Peru, and La Plata they exported the ordinary cloth made in the obrajes. Coleti confirmed this when he indicated that "Those who sustain the traffic and the business are Europeans who travel from city to city, taking merchandise from these areas and bringing back those from other countries," to whom were added the foreigners that "keep the shops open" in Quito.[35]

Cicala found in the Indians who lived in the cities a "singular ingenuity and capacity" similar to that of Europeans. He considered them very adept at "the servile and mechanical arts," especially manufacturing and building. On the other hand, he described the Indians who lived in the country and worked on haciendas or in obrajes or performed other types of work, as inclined to stealing, drinking, and lying.[36] This opinion was shared by other foreign travelers. Benzoni[37] noted that in Quito the goldsmiths made "wonderful things" despite the fact that they did not have suitable implements and that the greatest pleasure among the Indians, just as among the other people, was drinking. Jorge Juan and Antonio De Ulloa found in them "very little fondness for work," which they attributed to the lack of incentives, since they would have the same income "working or not working," since it was the same difference to them "to earn money by sweating for it or not to earn any at all since it passed through their hands so quickly that it practically went unnoticed." This view was supported by the observation that the free Indians "cultivate the lands that belong to them with so much application that they do not leave any scrap wasted"—and when recalling their hard work of old, which in the pre-Columbian era allowed them to build bridges, avenues, and roads, and communication routes that were mostly left to disappear due to "the lack of upkeep by the new inhabitants," that is, the whites that came from Spain and the Creoles born in Quito territories.[38]

That observation was shared by Stevenson when he said that in the "Kingdom of Quito," as a result of the degradation to which they had been subjected by the whites, the Indians evidenced the "vices of indolence, apathy and laziness" more than in other places in the colonial empire where "the curse of the conquest was not as strongly felt."[39] Belisario Quevedo added other observations on the character of the indigenous people. If the Spaniards were characterized "by a lack of discipline," the Indians went overboard "in the opposite direction." They did not know "covetousness and the desire to get rich" because they were "lazy and a friend of the indolent life," in addition to being "poor planners" since they consumed only "as a function of their present desires" and were very given to promising but evasive in complying, since the commitments they made were worth little if they were not "generated by fear."[40]

Indians worked in the few mines that existed in the Audiencia of Quito, in the important textile industry, and on the haciendas, working the land, caring for flocks of sheep, and shearing their wool. In the cities and towns they worked in convents and hacienda houses as domestic servants (*huasicamas*) in charge of the stables; running errands; hauling water supplies, firewood, and grass; carrying litters; and making textiles in small household workshops. The servants were so numerous that they outnumbered the masters that they waited on.[41] With so many servants at the disposal of the Creoles and Spaniards to carry out any task that might occur to them, there was no work whatsoever in which the whites could entertain themselves, not even everyday household chores. The Indians also worked in urban construction and provided a much-appreciated passenger transportation service that scandalized Humboldt. They carried the whites, especially women, on their backs, in chairs made specially for that purpose to help them traverse the nearly impassable Andean paths.

Mestizos were considered to be those whose ancestors were a mixture of indigenous people and whites, and those who through acculturation had managed to pass as such, many of them to avoid paying the tribute that the Indians were obliged to pay.[42] Cicala wrote that the mixing of Spanish and Indian blood led to the mixing of "the worst conditions of the Europeans with the negative part of the Indians." Even though he recognized that there were exceptions and that in general they were intrepid, valiant, smart, clever, and ingenious, he also attributed to them a number of shortcomings: being "shameless, negligent, drunkards, gamblers, lazy, *ladinos*, malicious, liars and friends of fraud."[43] Juan and De Ulloa both affirmed that the mestizos, who were numerous in the highlands, were people "of little or no use" economically because their "lack of application" to work "reduced them to a life of idleness and laziness." The authors attributed this passivity to the fact that they were a social group that lacked incentives, since "they knew very well the little or no esteem in which they were held in their countries" so that, despite any initiatives that they might take, fortune "could not favor them more . . . because of the little luck that befell them at birth." They concluded by saying that "if for failing to work and being given to idleness and laziness, forced work (the *mita*) should be imposed on them as a punishment, no group of people could benefit more than the many mestizos that exist in those countries."[44]

The mestizos, by virtue of being "less presumptuous" than the whites, agreed to carry on arts and trades, especially those "of greater esteem, such as the trades of painters, sculptors and silversmiths, and others of that kind," leaving to the Indians those that they considered "less appealing," such as those of cobblers, masons, weavers, barbers, carpenters, and others. The handicrafts that they made and the services that they provided were negotiated directly with their customers, who were primarily Spaniards and Creoles. Many of these artisans were occupied in the construction and decoration of the rich Quito churches and the splendid nearby convents. Juan and De Ulloa indicated that the artisans were not known for finishing the work entrusted to them in a timely fashion, according to deadlines, especially when they had received their fee in advance. Due to the "slowness and laziness" with which they did the work, it thus became necessary to lock them in until they finished.[45] In the ability to do paintings, sculptures, and other works of art, the Quito artists were better than those of other South American countries, but they were only adept at imitating and copying. They lacked the conditions to create works of their own invention and imagination.[46]

The mestizos were also in charge of small neighborhood stores that dispensed articles for the day-to-day consumption of the city's residents, mainly food and clothes made in the textile mills. This commerce was minimal because, due to the level of poverty, many families supplied their own food and made their own clothes, especially the Indians, above all in the critical eighteenth century, during which, given the crisis of the obrajes, there was a dramatic drop in living standards.

As for the residents of Guayaquil, the Spanish official Francisco de Requena described their character as "similar to that of the rest of the province." They did not take advantage of the possibilities offered them by the fruits of the rich soils because they were lacking in an "inclination to laborious exercises: they desire tranquility more than fortune; and when attained, earnings cause them great worry and fatigue, and thus they love idleness and slothfulness . . ."[47] Cicala diverged from this appreciation when he wrote that he had heard foreign businessmen say that "they had not experienced similar honesty and punctuality in any other part of America, and not even in Spain, as in the agreements and contracts" signed by the people of Guayaquil. He added that they were a people of capacity and ingenuity that were "in continuous activity from morning to afternoon," that they carried on an "extraordinarily large and active" trade, that their artisans were excellent craftsmen, and that the vice of drunkenness was not as deeply rooted as in other cities and regions.[48]

LACK OF ENTREPRENEURIAL SPIRIT

The cultural habits that the Spaniards brought over from the cities of their homeland, the Creoles' adoption of these habits, the hierarchical society that they established, the availability of an unlimited labor supply, the vast extension of farmlands, and the hacienda and textile mill owners' and administrators' negative attitudes toward hard work did not create favorable conditions for entrepreneurial initiatives to flourish. To the contrary, they created all sorts of obstacles for Spaniards and Creoles, the only ones in a position to undertake such initiatives, generate and invest capital, form partnerships, seek profit, become interested in introducing innovations, improve production processes, increase yields, and, in short, promote the progress of the Audiencia of Quito. The Indians, due to their conditions of poverty and subordination, were unable to do this and to a lesser extent so were the mestizos. For these reasons, during the long colonial period there was no public- or private-sector economic advancement, despite the propitious environment for economic activities created by day-to-day peace, which would be lacking during the convulsed era of the republic.

Land ownership was considered a factor of social prestige and an instrument of power, but not a productive resource that had to be cultivated carefully and conscientiously to achieve optimal economic results. In that regard, Phelan wrote that "As soon as anyone acquired either the capital [through obrajes or commerce] or the desire to belong to the cabildo elite, he turned himself into a landowner. If he continued his commercial operations, he did it through intermediaries."[49] The vastness of the lands that the Spaniards and Creoles had at hand made it unnecessary to introduce techniques aimed at increasing crop yields and adding livestock pasturelands. It proved easy to obtain these by expanding the cultivated area and making land-extensive use of the soils. Furthermore, since they did not intervene directly in the production process, hacienda owners did not have a good idea of the deficiencies and of the possibilities for improvement. The control of the farming and livestock-raising work was in the hands of the administrators and overseers or foremen, since the large landowners did not live in the countryside but rather in urban areas and only visited their haciendas during harvest seasons, which coincided with the dry, sunny weather of July and August.

Textile production became an important economic activity toward the end of the sixteenth century and reached its peak in the seventeenth century. "Common or low-cost" cloths such as cotton, wool, and hemp-cord were produced, as well as baize or felt, coverlets and blankets, flannel, linen, ponchos, thread, and hats. The larger mills operated in the rural areas near the large haciendas, and the small ones in the cities, especially in Quito. In the case of the "community or public" obrajes, they were overseen by administrators who were named by the colonial authorities; in the case of "private" ones, administrators were named by their owners, which could be a religious order. In either case, tribute based on income had to be paid to the Crown. Between one hundred and five hundred Indians worked in the obrajes (because it was the "work of Indians"). They performed their work in conditions of subjugation that bordered on slavery. In exchange, they received as pay a minimal part of the production in the case of public obrajes, or a salary in the case of those privately owned. In reality, this was pay for each batch completed, because each worker was obliged to produce a previously determined amount of thread-making, weaving, dyeing, or nap-raising. Despite the fact that he was well remunerated, the administrator illegally appropriated a good part of the benefits obtained.[50] In the "private" textile mills, there was greater abuse by the owners in the exploitation of the indigenous labor force, whose pay was negotiated as a means of increasing profits for the owner.[51] Exceptionally, there were obrajes belonging to the Crown, for example in Otavalo.

Due to the particular characteristics of the production process, the obrajes were not really factories. Robson Brynes Tyrer noted this when he wrote that "it must be kept in mind that the technology and the social context of the economy of Quito's obrajes had nothing to do with the characteristics of modern manufacturing societies. The technology was primitive, so textile-making was a quite an arduous task."[52] This "preindustrial" nature of textile manufacturing remained predominant throughout the colonial period without modifications in production structures or technology, whereas in Europe there was a proliferation of inventions that gave rise to the Industrial Revolution. For three centuries, no obraje owner thought to introduce elements that would make it possible to improve the manufacturing process and make it more technical, even though the prosperity of the most densely populated region of the Audiencia of Quito depended on the success of this economic activity. Furthermore, colonial policy itself created obstacles that thwarted the success of entrepreneurial initiatives. Stevenson noted that the Count of the Casa Jijón brought over mechanics and artisans from Europe to manufacture fine cloths and good designs. However, this activity had to be suspended because of the interference of Audiencia officials and an order from Spain that "obliged him to destroy all of his machinery and ship the artisans back to Europe."[53]

Textile production experienced ups and downs depending on demand, especially the demand originating outside the Audiencia of Quito. Textiles were highly profitable as long as there were buyers for them in the rich mining centers on the continent and as long as their production was protected from foreign competition. These two strengths became weaknesses when the demand fell as a result of the depletion of the mines, the consequent reduction in employment, and the economic crisis of the cities that had flourished around the mines. The decline was also due to the entry of European and Asian textiles by virtue of free trade and contraband, against which a technologically backward type of manufacturing was not in a position to compete. For these reasons, the local obrajes began closing during the eighteenth century and finally almost disappeared, depriving Quito of the activity that had been at the heart of its progress. A deep economic crisis made money scarce, caused concern, increased unemployment, and impoverished not only the rich textile mill owners, but also all of those who were involved in the production of raw materials, industrial transformation, and internal and external commercialization of textiles.

Even though the obrajes were exploitative,* they also constituted a source of wealth because, given that most of the production was exported, they generated significant revenues for the Quito economy. Their wealth explained the prosperity of the seventeenth century and the sumptuous religious architecture built in the capital of the Audiencia. All those involved in the production process got rich: cotton growers, sheep breeders, wool producers, suppliers of raw materials, textile mill owners and administrators, and those that marketed the products internally and externally. One exception was the indigenous workers, but even they had a source of employment and some remuneration.

The owners of the obrajes must have had unusual entrepreneurial skills for their time if we recall that colonial society in general was lacking in hard work and entrepreneurship. They had to oversee enterprises with a certain level of specialized labor, since the workers in the textile mills performed multiple individual functions such as washing, spinning, weaving, napraising, and dyeing. Other responsibilities included obtaining raw material supplies (cotton, wool, dyes), organizing the manufacturing process, keeping the equipment in good operating condition, and distributing the final product to markets, especially foreign ones. This was an extremely complex task due to Quito's isolation, the absence of roads, and the enormous distances that had to be covered by the merchandise—by land on mules and by sea through Guayaquil, to places as far away as the viceroyalties of Lima, New Granada, and La Plata, and the capitancy general of Chile. To appreciate the weight of the entrepreneurial dimension of obrajes and the significance they had for Quito's economy, it is worth pointing out that almost three hundred years would elapse before the Northern Highlands

---

*Phelan described them as the "sweatshops of South America."

once again became an exporting region, which occurred just recently, toward the end of the twentieth century.

Creoles and colonial Spaniards did not work with their hands on the haciendas and in the obrajes; and they were sure they would never have to use them given the abundant work force and the nature of the power structures that had been created to protect their privileges. For these reasons they lacked motivation to reverse hard manual-labor practices through the introduction of innovations, technologies, machinery, and new resources. The lack of technological change and entrepreneurial drive hindered the modernization of agricultural and livestock activities and of the textile mills, and thus curtailed greater productivity, competitiveness, and larger profits. This type of progress would have had impressive economic effects on the economy as a whole.

The meager salaries and the practice of paying in kind hampered the formation of a monetary economy and the development of a domestic market, both of which would have been necessary to increase the demand for the goods produced in the obrajes and on the haciendas. In turn these would have created incentives for their owners and administrators to take measures to increase crop yields and manufacturing outputs. Robson Tyrer noted that "The obraje workers' low salaries and their payment in kind restricted the development of a cash money economy in Quito and completely eliminated any possibility of domestic market expansion . . . generally associated with the growth of manufacturing."[54]

The market was in fact limited to the few wealthy whites and some mestizos. The Indians, who constituted the vast majority, lived in an economy of subsistence and barter supplemented by the food that they grew on the small plots available for their use on the haciendas. Those who lived in the cities lived off leftovers and gifts they received from their masters. Their clothing consisted of a single change of clothes composed of rough materials that the women wove or put together, "not much better than what they wore in the times of their heathenism."[55] In that regard, Cicala indicated that the Indians did not think about "the next day" because they did not have a sense of foresight, so they did not put away money or anything else, not even food, clothes, or provisions.[56]

The whites' usurpation of the lands that belonged to the Indians was not the only manifestation of the lack of respect for their property rights. A Spanish official wrote that "the damage that the powerful, distinguished and privileged classes caused the artisans was notable, because without touching their assets, they 'borrowed' work and artifacts and delayed payments, many of them recurring to military privileges or to other important and titled citizens, a practice that caused the ruin of many of these tradesmen's families and worked to the public detriment because the trades neither flourished nor prospered."[57] This observation was shared by an anonymous English author when he wrote that when the owner of a business had lower social status, "the traveler takes the provisions that he wants and decides how much to pay or does not pay anything," so that "in order to avoid the looting to which they are exposed, they do not collect more grains than those necessary to sustain their family."[58]

In Quito and the surrounding areas, the lack of respect for others' property was so widespread, and the insecurity about the ownership of large pieces of property so great, that the neighbors of the district were forced to establish a sentinel service.[59] The constant robberies that the members of the Geodesic Mission suffered at the slightest inattention, while they were working in the field doing scientific investigations, led them to leave behind the harsh testimony that "Indians and mestizos have one thing in common that adds to their doubtful qualities: all of them are inveterate thieves. They steal absolutely anything."[60] Caldas described the way in which on repeated occasions someone tried to charge him "two or four times" the value of anything he wished to buy or any service that he needed to hire, just because he was a foreigner.[61]

Neither were there feelings of responsibility to assume and fulfill commitments, nor aptitudes for efficiently organizing a task, perseverance to focus on following it through to completion, ability to identify an objective, vision in finding means to make it possible, willingness to follow the chosen path despite difficulties, effective use of time, and a practical sense of living. These attributes are a necessary condition for an enterprise or a community to face day-to-day problems, find solutions, implement entrepreneurial initiatives, carry out projects, and attain overall economic progress.

After having praised the friendly nature of Quito's inhabitants, Stevenson noted that one negative trait was "a kind of inconstancy or volubility" that always had them ready "for any change." He wrote that a Quito resident who was a friend of his told him that "If we have a penitential procession in the morning, all attend in their most penitent attire, and put on their gravest looks; if in the afternoon we have a bull fight, none are absent; they will leave the circus in the evening to attend a missionary's sermon and spend the remainder of the night at a dance or card party."[62] Sociologist Belisario Quevedo noted the same thing when he referred to those known as "Spaniards." He cited "indiscipline, changeability, fickleness, a facility for forgetting the rules, difficulty in sustained and patient obedience, a habit of relying on others' support, always expecting something of others . . . avoiding responsibility but demanding it of their neighbors."[63]

The travelers and officials that described colonial society did not discover among the inhabitants of the Audiencia of Quito the virtue of savings. To the contrary, the chroniclers portrayed the inhabitants as wasteful of the much or little money they had. Jorge Juan and Antonio De Ulloa repeatedly affirmed that in Quito there was a widespread inclination to hold festivities (the improvised bullfights on city and town squares were the most popular), to drink, and to gamble. This was true among whites, mestizos, and Indians; and even "some of the most decorated and respectable people, given their rank and status" were addicted to such activities. Both authors say that these activities led rich men to lose their fortunes and poor ones to be left indigent, because of card and dice games, dances and parties (*fandangos*), and "sumptuous funerals" whose "pomp and vanity" surpassed what had been seen in other places, with extreme and ostentatious spending that "destroyed many people's fortunes and left them in ruin" because no one wanted to seem less than others.[64] One colonial official wrote at the end of the eighteenth century that residents of Quito "were Asian in their grandeur, friends of luxury and decoration."[65] A scholar from the Geodesic Mission noted that La Condamine, "despite having been accustomed to the luxury of Parisian parties" felt "uncomfortable before such ostentation" at a reception to which he was invited by the president of the Audiencia of Quito.[66]

These affirmations were shared by other foreign visitors. The Italian Coleti mentioned the case of "very noble families reduced to extreme necessity" not only because of the economic decadence of Quito during the eighteenth century, but also "because of the great luxury squandered by each one, whether they can afford it or not, in competition with others." They might not have even "a bit of bread until midday," he added, to be able to buy "rich apparel or go in debt up to their ears" because the husband and wife were of one mind in letting "the household go broke and leaving their children in extreme poverty." He warned that the residents of Quito "during the day abandon themselves to their sleep in order to digest their intoxication and at night return to the same occupation, and they do not think of anything else until their money runs out." He adds that "Gambling does not take second place, being another child of the common father of all vices: idleness," a pastime in which "even distinguished people" lost their daily income and their belongings.[67] Cicala said that "noble persons, priests, monks and even nuns" were not exempt from the vice of drunkenness, and that it was not easy to enumerate the "families that had been reduced to misery and need in the city of Quito and its surroundings." He said that "the amount of liquor consumed every day was incredible," and the vice of gambling had led the city to a "deplorable state of poverty and wretchedness."[68] Such observations were repeated when he visited other cities of the inter-Andean region. The affirmation of historian Jouanen was conclusive when he said that it was easier for the Jesuits to divest the Indians of their "superstitions and witchcraft" than their vice of drunkenness, which "could never be completely eradicated."[69]

The use of the capital that was built up despite the aforementioned constraints was not compatible with the economic development needs of the Audiencia of Quito and the progress of its inhabitants. In some cases capital was hidden away; and in others, allocated to the building of churches and convents rather than invested in improving families' well-being or in productive activities and public services. Instead of investing savings in activities that would yield profits for their owners and the community, the rich of those times—and they were not the only ones—were accustomed to stashing away precious metals, jewelry, and gold and silver coins. They would hide them in secret places to ensure their protection and preservation from relatives, friends, and strangers who might try fraudulently to appropriate their wealth, obtaining through trickery loans that would never be repaid or simply stealing the treasures outright. In those days it was a common and sometimes lucrative pastime to search for and discover the buried treasures of affluent people, to whose discovery the sudden wealth of families that had no economic means would be attributed. At the end of the colonial period, Humboldt wrote that the sums collected by the bishop of Cuenca to build the cathedral turned out to be "dead money, kept in strongboxes" just as "were all private funds," which explained why "there was no industry."[70]

Another part of the capital, especially in the case of the rich religious orders, was allotted to building churches and convents. For the people of that era, that effort deserved more attention than building infrastructure, opening up roads, putting up bridges, and improving the cities' sanitation. All of the sumptuous churches and the monumental convents of Quito were erected during the colonial period. Hassaurek said that "if one tenth of the millions that it cost to build these churches and monasteries—not to mention the thousands of Indians that perished from beatings as they carried out the ungrateful task of transporting on their trembling backs each one of the blocks of these buildings—had been used to build roads, this country would have long ago had a place among the civilized nations."[71]

For these reasons the physical condition of houses in Quito and other Andean cities, according to testimonials of the era, were poor, precarious, and ill kept, not only in the case of the people of modest income, which would have been logical, but also of those that had abundant resources. Surely this is why the rich people in colonial Quito did not leave behind any palaces, and why there is a sharp contrast between the modest civil architecture and the opulent religious architecture. The elegant, spacious, and comfortable hacienda houses are the one exception, which is difficult to explain because the large landowners did not live in the countryside. However, it must be kept in mind that only a few such homes had these characteristics.

The lack of public and private savings and investment kept the society from having the public services that would foster progress and attend to the citizens' basic needs. The lack of public investment was a constant throughout the three hundred years of the colonial period in the fields of education, health, and communications. There were few residents of Quito who could access education, none enjoyed even minimal hygiene conditions, and roads were virtually nonexistent in the Audiencia. The isolation was so great that each province supplied itself exclusively with goods produced from within its geographical basin.

When Caldas, who was not European but rather came from the neighboring Santa Fé de Bogotá, visited Quito at the end of the colonial period, the capital's deplorable sanitation caught his attention. He observed that the "houses were very dirty," only three had "permanent water for cleaning and [other] needs," and the streets served as "common sewers."[72] This lack of sanitation must certainly have been the reason that, years before, the city had lost "nearly half of its population to two strong epidemics" that occurred in 1759 and 1785.[73]

The lack of roads made mules, donkeys, and horses the only means of transportation that travelers, merchants, and farmers had available. Given their versatility, the mule teams gave rise to a much-appreciated service and a lucrative business that lasted nearly four hundred years, until the early twentieth century. In their chronicles, the travelers pondered the sagacity and skill of these sure-footed animals, which, guided by instinct, could climb steep paths without putting their riders in peril. The riders simply held onto the animals' backs and left the reins loose with the certainty that they would arrive safe and sound at their destination. In the places where it was not possible to use pack animals due to the perilous narrow trails or the fragile goods being transported, the beasts of burden were replaced by teams of Indians. The lack of paths for coaches and wagons made the wheel, which was unknown to the Indians and introduced by the Spaniards, a useless technology that could not contribute to progress or facilitate communications and commercial exchanges using carts and coaches. According to a traveler who visited Quito at the end of the colonial period, these vehicles were "just barely known."[74]

Despite the fact that the indigenous people were not familiar with the wheel, they had paid more attention than the Spaniards and Creoles to the construction and maintenance of roads, if we recall what Juan and De Ulloa said. The whites' disinterest in road-building was confirmed by Humboldt when he said that during his trip in the area of Cuenca he found vestiges of a "magnificent road" built by the Incas with "carved and well-suited" stones, but that road had been lost due to neglect by the local authorities, so that when traveling along it, he got mired "in mud up to the mule's belly."[75] Cicala coincided with this appreciation when he noted that Spaniards and Creoles had not made the least effort to repair dangerous paths, deep mud holes, steep hills and slopes, and river crossings over which mule drivers, travelers, pack animals, and merchandise passed.[76]

The Jesuit religious order was a notable exception to the indifference to progress that reigned in colonial society. Hence, their expulsion—which was ordered by Charles III in 1767 and lasted eighty-seven years—proved to be detrimental for the education of the youth, the progress of the country, and the modernization of cultural habits. The importance of the Jesuit educational establishments, whose academic level was higher than those of the other religious orders, was noted by Jouanen, when he affirmed, "Undoubtedly great and very lamentable was the damage that the expulsion of the Jesuits caused to public instruction, of which they were mainly in charge, especially outside Quito."[77] The Jesuits also transmitted ethical values, so necessary in permissive colonial society. This contribution was pointed out by an author who noted that the Jesuit school in Ambato contributed to the inhabitants' abandonment of their bad habits.[78]

The forced exile of the Jesuits directly influenced the economic deterioration of the eighteenth century because the Audiencia of Quito lost the last advocate of modernity and progress that remained following the bankruptcy of the textile mills. According to Nicholas Cushner, author of a study on "Jesuit agrarian capitalism," for that religious group, "The land was a business to be run as effectively and profitably as possible." For this purpose, they put a Creole member of the Order in charge of their haciendas and obrajes, someone familiar with the tasks entrusted to him and living in his place of work, with authority to take initiatives and adopt innovations.

The Jesuits placed high priority on saving, building up capital, and investing because they felt that business success was based on sound finances. To improve business management and increase economic returns, they vertically integrated their operations through the specialization of each one of the farms or workshops, to produce food for the workers, cultivate pasturelands for pack animals and cattle, provide mules for transportation, produce cotton, and create wool-bearing sheep for the textile mills. To market their end products, they used the networks created by the convents; and to obtain better prices, they imported capital goods directly from Spain and made centralized wholesale purchases. Each production unit was independently financed and worked with its own budget, accounting, inventories, and records of income and expenses, so that the administrator and his bosses could verify compliance with the tasks assigned and the profits expected. All of this made it possible for the Jesuits' investments to yield high rates of return.[79]

In the last decades of the eighteenth century, the first manifestations of a positive cultural change appeared in Guayaquil thanks to the economic opportunities opened up by the production and exportation of cacao, increased imports, and the successful shipping industry. This mercantile spirit contributed to the port's leaving behind colonial immobility and embarking on sustained progress that lasted until the early decades of the twentieth century.

The shipbuilders prospered due to the privileged geographical location of Guayaquil, which operated as both a river port and a seaport, as well as to the abundance of fine woods that existed in the plentiful surrounding woodlands (the mangroves were used for the ship hulls) and the ease of transporting them along the rivers of the Guayas River basin. On the other hand, they had to purchase abroad other raw materials necessary for shipbuilding, especially iron. According to Spanish, English, French, Dutch, and Flemish sailors, there was "no [other] shipyard that enjoyed the conveniences and facilities and the most apt woods to be assembled, the finest, strongest and most durable, and best suited to build this type of ship."[80] The shipyards came to produce five-hundred- to seven-hundred-ton ships, which at the beginning of the nineteenth century made shipbuilding "Guayaquil's most important activity."

The shipyards promoted arduous, specialized work; employed a great number of mechanics, carpenters, and other artisans; fostered the circulation of money; and facilitated "the economic independence of a large part of the inhabitants" of Guayaquil. Unlike what happened with other activities that were limited to trading goods in the state that they were extracted, the shipyard "managed to give the highest value possible to natural products."[81] In contemporary terminology, this means that the shipyards gave significant value added to the raw materials resulting from the felling of trees.

Shipbuilding promoted the development of entrepreneurial capabilities needed to undertake the complex productive process of raising capital, transporting enormous logs, importing raw materials, substituting for them with local products, organizing work, reducing costs, incorporating technologies, and selling end products. According to a contemporary researcher, the shipyards "produced a surprisingly egalitarian community based on merit and work capacity," so that for the people that worked in them there were no distinctions as to "origin or skin color."[82]

Despite the entrepreneurial progress, the residents of Guayaquil could not distance themselves from the cultural values that for centuries had been shared with other inhabitants of the Audiencia of Quito. Even though the ships produced in the shipyards were highly appreciated "for their architectural merits," their construction did not use techniques that were common in other places, such as bending wood and milling it with machines.[83] Toward the middle of the nineteenth century, the lack of technological innovations and the depletion of the forests that provided the raw material led the shipyards to lose their comparative advantage and to collapse.

One researcher found that in the eighteenth century in most cases the residents of Guayaquil themselves, "through their neglect and negligence," were responsible for the constant fires that plagued the city.[84] They did not take precautions to avoid fires, nor did they fulfill the responsibilities that were entrusted to them to monitor the houses so that they could act in a timely fashion and avoid the propagation of fires. The researcher concluded by saying, "It would be necessary to wait until 1764, when the most terrible fire of Guayaquil's modern history occurred, the celebrated *big fire*, for the authorities to decide to adopt more severe and effective measures for this problem." Stevenson also noted that at the end of the colonial period "Notwithstanding the danger to which the city is exposed, the dreadful examples which it has experienced, and the easy means by which water may be procured in any part of the town, for the prevention of general conflagrations, there is not one engine for the extinction of fire, nor any regular body of firemen."[85]

They reacted with similar indolence to the flooding of the Guayas River, despite the fact that their houses were endangered. This problem could have been prevented if, with the "joint action of the neighborhood" and "a small expenditure," a "medium-sized breakwater had been built" to guarantee "the complete protection of Guayaquil."[86] One official reported that in "this city, the richest in America because of its nature, and the poorest" because of the "indifference of its governors and neighbors," the inhabitants drank water from the river "mixed at the very least with seawater, and they do not have the drive nor the agility to make this water flow readily from the heads of the rivers, a flow that would easily fertilize all in its path and enter the aforementioned city."[87] Stevenson considered that the farmers did not pay "due attention to growing and harvesting" cacao; and if they had, their production "would have increased in quantity and quality" because "there is no better soil and climate for the growth of this plant." He added, "The only thing that is lacking here is an increase in capital, in activity and in inhabitants because the climate and the soil are propitious for producing anything found between the tropics."[88]

Given the wealth generated by cacao, the shipyards, and the import trade, it is surprising that in Guayaquil there did not occur an accumulation of capital, so necessary for the growth of existing activities and the creation of new businesses. Stevenson attributed this situation to the destruction of homes and merchandise by the frequent fires and the ensuing economic losses that could not be recovered because there were no insurance companies; he further attributed it to the fact that the Guayaquil merchants were intermediaries for large buyers in Lima, Panama, and Mexico, with whom they had to share their earnings.[89] To this must be added the looting by English and Dutch pirates that, in 1624 and 1687, "left the city in shambles."[90]

PATERNALISM

Colonial society favored the formation of a paternalistic mentality that became a determining factor in the relations among individuals and between individuals and institutions. Other elements contributing to this phenomenon included the nature of pre-Columbian indigenous society and Spanish feudal society; the existence of rigid social hierarchies; appalling economic, social, and educational inequalities; the lack of equal opportunities; the idea that people could not take care of themselves; and the Catholic belief that social and economic structures were immutable.

The enormous power that hacienda and obraje owners exerted, plus the isolation of the rural areas, created conditions for them to assume functions inherent to political authorities in fields that extended beyond the economic activities of farming and manufacturing. In fact, they became the authorities to which indigenous people and mestizos habitually recurred to address their problems and settle their conflicts. Due to the fact that interpersonal relations were not governed by a legal system that attributed rights and demanded obligations, attention to the needs of individuals became discretionary. Since the peasants were not in a position to have direct access to political and religious institutions—because of their economic limitations, scarce knowledge, unfamiliarity with the Spanish language, and the isolation in which they lived—they needed their masters to represent them and "recommend" them to authorities. In this way, a paternalistic society grew up in which the *patrón* provided those that depended on him with protection, support, guidance, advice, and intermediation in exchange for which the beneficiaries of his favors paid him respect, adherence, and loyalty and provided diverse services. This paternalistic relationship became so important that the peasant who had the aid of a benefactor was privileged, while he who did not was left out in the cold. Stevenson noted these social behaviors when he observed that the mestizos were "surprisingly docile, friendly and attentive and that they saw any sign of attention from a person of higher social status as a true honor."[91]

The remuneration earned by the Indians for the work they did on haciendas, in obrajes, and in the homes of their masters, sometimes with their families, was not seen as pay for the work they did but rather as a gift. The ridiculously low stipend was credited to the sum that as an advance the *patrón* had made to them in money or in kind, so that it could slowly be paid off with the consequent dependence of the indebted peasant. In a paternalistic way, he was somehow compensated by certain favors that the master granted him, such as the use of a small plot of land and a hut to live in, with the possibility of having irrigation water available and a place to pasture animals and gather wood. In the encomiendas the Indians were also obliged to pay a tribute in exchange for protection and for religious instruction.

Personal and family relationships, friendships, and loyalty—led by a patriarchal authority figure that operated through clans and clienteles—were decisive when it came time to distribute favors or designate public officials. Historian Pilar Ponce remarked that an individual's capacity "to support a clientele formed by relatives, friends, protégés or servants that completely depended on him" was a status symbol and a sign of prestige. In other words, this was a household organization that shared home and table and whose members received "all sorts of concessions, favors and support from their protector."[92] Those that were in a better position to head up such networks, the nucleus of which was an extended family made up of *compadres*, close friends and clergymen, were men who, in addition to having wealth, held public offices as presidents of the Audiencia, councilmen, judges, magistrates, and intendants. The position of councilman was particularly important. According to Ponce, between 1593 and 1701, 68.6 percent of the councilmen had some type of family tie to other members of the municipal organization.[93] It was from such positions that favors were distributed to family members and other dependants, incorporating them into the heart of the group and granting them lands, distributing Indians, and giving them licenses for commerce and trades.

To the extent that laws were frequently reduced to the mere formality of an intranscendental written text and institutions only occasionally exerted their authority, they did not count for much in the everyday life of the peasant world, as a result of which they were not useful in regulating the citizens' economic, social, and political relations, which generally took place at the margin of legal formalities. The absence of norms meant that, instead of institutional relations, personal relations prevailed, based on family ties, friendships, relationships with godparents, dependence, and loyalty. The following testimonial of a Spaniard, related by Belisario Quevedo, is pertinent: "When addressing a superior, a subordinate is often heard to say 'I don't pay attention to you as an authority, but I do what you ask me to do as a friend.' We have respect for people, but it is hard for us to respect a law, an authority, an institution, just because of their nature as such. We are better at obeying personal orders than general dispositions."[94]

The interventionist nature of colonial administration and legislation contributed to the strengthening of paternalism. The excessive legal regulations and the interventionism of the authorities limited opportunities for citizens to take initiatives or make decisions and thus resolve their own affairs and problems. The municipal council regulated almost all of the realms of day-to-day life in the urban centers by setting prices for food and fees for artisan services, prohibiting the exportation of goods, regulating people's departure from the cities, and authorizing the sale of weapons. As historian Robalino Dávila has said, all of the manifestations of colonial life were so strictly regulated that there was no activity "in which the Government did not interfere and did not at least try to regulate." This occurred to such an extent that "the Law of the Indies, the Cédulas [Royal Orders], and the decrees of the Audiencias prescribed what should be planted, which branch of industry would be undertaken in this or that district, where purchases could be made and what could be sold, with which ports trade could be done and which ones could be accessed or not, and when imports or exports were authorized."[95]

The paternalism emanating from legal norms and administrative practices led to a slump in economic initiatives and to the absence of a business class. Competent and talented people that could have taken initiatives became dependent on the State and those that represented it: the King, the Viceroy, the Audiencia, and the Cabildo. They resorted to them directly or through intermediaries to respond to their needs and to settle their problems, many of which could have been handled by the individuals themselves through their own efforts. The way in which the State numbed private initiatives was noted by Humboldt when he wrote that the "absolute power" exerted by the municipal government "reduced the independent spirit of the small communities" and hampered their development by not forcing them to "exercise their freedom."[96]

This social and economic paternalism and the Catholic preaching of conformity, analyzed above, worked to create a passive, contemplative mentality that kept individuals from assuming their own responsibilities and shaping their own destiny. Regardless of their social condition, people believed that to obtain a job, a benefit, a solution, an improvement, or advancement—in sum, to achieve economic success—what mattered more than merit, effort, and initiative was access to the person or persons that could dispense favors and make concessions. Also common was the idea that the shortages that affected them, the failures they suffered, and the difficulties that they encountered in trying to get ahead in life were not due to their mistakes, guilt, omissions, and carelessness, but rather to circumstances that were outside their control, the lack of external assistance, and even damages that were deliberately perpetrated by others. At the same time, in the relations between those who occupied higher positions and their subordinates, granting favors and making concessions were worth more than the laws and their fulfillment.

The cultural characteristics of colonial society, analyzed in preceding pages, had a negative impact on progress; the outcome would have been different had the transformational forces of education, ideas, and laws been given free rein. These instruments of progress would have made it possible to replace inconvenient structures and behaviors with others that were compatible with individual and collective economic improvements. However, this could not be achieved due to the nature of the educational system, the restrictions that existed for the free circulation of knowledge, and the inveterate noncompliance with laws.

NONEXISTENT EDUCATION AND KNOWLEDGE

The colonization of the territories that comprised the Audiencia of Quito coincided with the introduction of the Inquisition by the Catholic monarchs. This institution outlawed and persecuted any idea considered contrary to true Christianity, and this position led the Crown to demand that whoever might wish to go to the New World previously demonstrate his status as an "old Christian."[97] For this reason the Crown prohibited outright the immigration of Jews, Moors, and "heretics" to the colonies, precisely the groups of people most capable of disseminating new scientific knowledge and undertaking entrepreneurial activities, as demonstrated in the European countries where they developed banking, trade, and industry. "The doors to the colony were closed to the immigration of 'strange' people, people of books and ideas. The inhabitants did not enjoy freedom to settle and trade; much less did they enjoy freedom of conscience and speech,"[98] historian Robalino Dávila pointed out. Phelan added, "All over the empire there came to prevail the cautious and conservative sprit of the Counter Reformation, with little room for innovation and experiment."[98] So limited was the contact of the residents of Quito with the outside world that "The arrival of mail was a novelty that caused amazement" to such an extent "that the mail chest from Spain was received with the ringing of bells."[99] Thus, as historian Aguirre recognized, "It should not be surprising that, with such a system of complete isolation, the Spanish colonies have not progressed at all in the long period of more than two centuries."[100]

The universities founded in Quito in the early years of the colonial period—the only ones in the Audiencia—were established so that the descendants of Spaniards could be educated according to Spanish culture and Catholic principles, which were transmitted dogmatically and sectarianly. The State's theocratic nature, the Church's monopoly on teaching, and the fact that the clergymen were the best prepared men of the era, allowed Catholicism to determine the content of education and establish what was true and false in every matter in which discrepancies or doubts arose. Due to the fact that the metropolis was never interested in promoting science during its long colonial domination because all ideas had to pass through the filter of the Catholic Church, the residents of Quito could not access the knowledge that would have allowed them to correct the existing scientific deficit, change behaviors contrary to progress, and modernize productive activities.

According to historian González Suárez, long after the founding of the Real Audiencia, "there was nothing more than schools of basic letters in Loja, in Cuenca, in Guayaquil and in Quito, one in each city."[101] A little more than half a century before the end of the colonial period, according to Coleti there were two universities in Quito. San Fernando University imparted classes in philosophy, theology, civil and canon law, and medicine, but this last area was always closed because of the lack of a professor. Theology, philosophy, sacred writing, and civil and canonical legislation were taught at San Gregorio University. With respect to course content, he noted that "the distinguished youth, after two or three years of poorly taught and poorly learned grammar, proceeds to the study of the major sciences such as philosophy, the oldest and stalest in the world, a descendant of the fetid peripatetics, the speculative theology of everything, commonly occupied with useless questions and the study of possibilities." And he added that "Mathematics is totally ignored, mechanics disdained" and if someone "approves of something of the modern philosophers" he is immediately seen "as a common enemy, and persecuted as such."[102]

At the end of the colonial period, the wise Caldas noted that Quito had "a prodigious number of doctors" and that, except for those that had learned something by their own effort, the others were doctors in name only, for there existed "an endless condescendence" on the exams, so that there was no memory of "a single person that had failed." After describing the corrupt practices of the superiors of the religious communities, he added that little could be expected from the education imparted by people of this nature, who considered "Kepler's laws of astronomy a fable," had an "endless addiction to the letters of Saint Thomas, little severity in work and discipline, and much concern about adornment."[103] Around the same time, Humboldt observed that the Jesuit library had been reduced to a third of its size as a consequence of the losses suffered supposedly during their expulsion—that the price of books was four times higher than in Europe because it was so difficult to obtain them and the history, medicine, and exact science texts were "very poor."[104]

These weaknesses in education kept the colonial period from producing changes in ideas and in the cultural values that the Spaniards had brought over and implanted when they arrived in Quito's territories as conquerors, authorities, or colonists.

Foreign travelers that visited the Audiencia of Quito and observed the conduct of its inhabitants coincided in mentioning a widespread lack of scientific knowledge. Juan and De Ulloa, in the language of the whites, said that even though they were "subtly ingenious and proper for study" since with little effort they learned what was taught, they were, on the other hand, "quite lacking in political news and historical facts, and in the other natural sciences that contribute to the greater cultivation of understanding, or those that enlighten them and lead them to a certain degree of perfection."[105] Stevenson shared this opinion when he said that the young people in Quito were not interested in the sciences due to "their misfortune, and not their fault" since the teachers' lack of freedom, the ecclesiastical restrictions, and the unsuitable selection of books and academic instruments kept the university of Quito from being able to compete with those of the "most polished countries of Europe."[106]

Theological education was merely theoretical and speculative and did not provide practical skills. It emphasized religious matters and was not interested in current problems; it trained lawyers, clergymen, and those versed in letters but was not able to exert a positive influence on the cultural habits and beliefs of the inhabitants of the Audiencia of Quito. Instead of promoting cultural changes that would make the values of the new generations consistent with the requirements of individual and collective progress, education instead contributed to reinforcing traditional behavior. The education imparted in schools and universities did not provide the students with technical knowledge and skills either, which would have led them to work to transform the reality around them. The isolation of the colonial society and the restrictions imposed by Spain kept immigrants with more open mentalities and professional capabilities from other European countries from contributing to the progress of colonial society.

One experience of Jorge Juan and Antonio De Ulloa demonstrated how alien scientific knowledge was for the elite of the time. They told how during a visit to Cuenca "well-read people of rank" refused to accept that those who had managed to "verify the figure and magnitude of the Earth" had not "discovered many minerals in the plains." They could not convince them otherwise despite the arguments they used, since the residents of Cuenca thought that the French scholars and the Spanish mariners possessed "some art of magic."[107] A paragraph written by geographer Villavicencio one hundred years later summarized very well the fearful backwardness of colonial ideas. The Audiencia of Quito, "cloistered by its immense cordilleras and the oceans, and dominated by the obscurantism of the monks, knew as much about men and things as we now know about men and occurrences on the Moon."[108]

NONCOMPLIANCE WITH THE LAW

In 1542, eight years after Sebastián de Benalcázar founded Quito, Charles V issued the New Laws of the Indies, which, together with those published later, comprised the Compilation of Laws for the Kingdom of the Indies, enacted by Charles II in 1681.

The Spanish monarchs' concern for protecting the rights of indigenous people was notable, with norms in some cases similar to those contained in twentieth-century labor laws. They prohibited personal services and forced labor, work shifts longer than eight hours per day, payments in kind, employment of minors and pregnant women, Indians' work as bearers, transformation of tributes into work, the authorities' holding of economic interests in the territories under their jurisdiction, the encomienda holders' possession of lands at the site of their encomienda, and lending of money to Indians for its later repayment through work. They provided that all work should be remunerated, that salaries should be set as a function of needs, that domestic work should be voluntary and paid, that those who had accidents in the mines should be indemnified, that the Indians' lands should be protected, that those [lands] that had been taken away should be returned, that "annoyances and abuses" should be impeded, and oppressors punished.[109]

As has been seen in preceding pages, colonial society's structure and operation were radically different from what the Laws of the Indies provided for, as if they did not exist. Throughout the colonial period, the royal orders repeatedly mentioned noncompliance with the dictates of that body of laws. Hence, systematically until the end of the colonial period in the early nineteenth century, complaints reached the Royal Council of the Indies regarding the tributes exacted from, and the abuses suffered by, the natives.[110]

Noncompliance with the Laws of the Indies was due to the fact that the officials in charge of enforcing them in the Audiencia, municipal governments, *corregimientos*, governances, and intendancies were closely tied to the interests that they wanted to control and the abuses they wanted to correct. The members of the municipal council were hacienda, encomienda, or obraje owners, or merchants. This was a status requirement that typically had to be met to gain access to such an institution. Something similar occurred in the case of those that performed other functions in the colonial administration; and those that did not usually had a relative in some public office. Furthermore, the custom of having officials buy their positions was widespread. This investment led them to occupy their positions with a view to using their functions to the greatest advantage. Making fortunes was the objective of those that left Spain, crossed the Atlantic, and climbed the Andes to become part of the colonial bureaucracy. When local authorities considered that the Laws of the Indies and the orders issued by the monarchs were inconvenient—because they were contrary to what they deemed the reality of their territory—they could be exonerated from compliance by recurring to a sacramental formula of kissing them and pronouncing the phrase "I obey but I do not comply."

When some envious official wanted to enforce them, he was obliged to desist because of the resistance of those that based their wealth on the exploitation of the indigenous people. Those who persisted in enforcement became unpopular and ended up losing their positions, as happened with Audiencia presidents Manuel Barros and Francisco López. The so-called revolt of Las Alcabalas, organized by residents of Quito in 1592 for the purpose of keeping new taxes from being collected, had a great deal to do with the pro-Indian policy of President Barros, whom the people that were revolting considered to be contrary to their interests. For these reasons, during the colonial period any regulation that diminished the benefits of the dominant sector was "difficult, if not impossible, to enforce."[111]

The fact that the law had a simply ornamental role led the populations of the Audiencia of Quito to become accustomed to living in illegalities. Violating legal principles, manipulating them, or simply ignoring them became an everyday practice of all sectors of colonial society, particularly among whites, for whom the law was not—as it should have been—a necessary point of reference for their lives but rather a nuisance that it was necessary to get around, with complicity from the authorities, by taking advantage of their negligence or exerting power over them. Few thought that with such behavior they were not recognizing the rights of other members of the community, committing illegal actions, favoring private interests, consecrating privileges, causing economic damage to society, and harming the State represented by the exchequer or royal treasury agent. The lax and permissive morality of the residents of Quito justified the violation or utilitarian use of the law. It is worthwhile to quote an expressive saying of the times: "God is very high up, the king is very far away, and I am the boss here."

Several testimonies confirm how widespread attitudes contrary to the law were, and how legal provisions conflicted with the widespread custom of evading them. A magistrate (corregidor) from Cuenca wrote in 1765:

> In this country there is no one more despicable than a judge: if he gives an order, they do not obey him; if he corrects them, they reprimand him; if he begs, they look down on him [. . .] and if at some point he attempts to punish, there are no people that come to his aid, nor ministers to carry out the order; to the contrary, there is a surplus of backers that support and defend the delinquent.[112]

Jorge Juan and Antonio De Ulloa noted that, as a way of "consenting and even sponsoring" contraband, they called it "eat and let eat" and the judges put up with "men of a good sort, that did no harm to anybody."[113] One researcher referred to the way in which the seventeenth-century shipbuilders in Guayaquil eluded royal dispositions that intended to guarantee the use of suitable wood. Despite demonstrating the violation of legal norms at repeated hearings, the Council of 1689 ended up blaming the "mestizos, zambos, Indians, mulattos and blacks" and overlooked "investigations and trials for the past 40 years" that "unequivocally implicated members of their own class."[114]

The failure to enforce the law meant that there was a lack of what today would be called "legal security," that is, norms of a general nature to which individuals are voluntarily or coactively subject. This absence was aggravated by the fact that doubts about the upright intention of people were common in colonial society when they were discussing an economic agreement or making a deal. As tends to occur in such cases, the seeds of distrust were sown regarding people's disposition to fulfill the economic commitments agreed on with the backing of legal principles, as well as the institutions' capacity to protect the affected person by enforcing the law. The lack of legal protection for agreements and contracts left the parties' compliance up to their good will.

Since relations were not based on reciprocal trust, but rather on suspicion, and they required all kinds of safeguards to cover the consequent risks, people did not tend to form partnerships to implement initiatives, carry out projects, resolve shared problems, and combine their capital and their efforts. In this deficit of partnerships can be found the explanation for the fact that in the chronicles of the travelers and in the reports of officials there were no references to the spirit of unity among residents of Quito. Since innovative projects were always individual, people did not manage to amass funds sufficient to implement them. This was the case of the initiative of building a road to connect Quito and Esmeraldas, so that the capital city could break out of its Andean isolation and have a nearby port that would allow it to boost its commercial exchanges. This was the sole initiative of a wise man, Pedro Vicente Maldonado, who lost a good deal of his fortune on this venture.

The custom of ignoring the law ran so deep in the collective soul that not even the laws, orders, and dictates issued by the authorities at the request of those interested in them were complied with, despite the fact that they did no harm to anyone and everyone agreed on them since they protected assets against the risk of catastrophes. This is what happened in Guayaquil with the dispositions issued at the request of the inhabitants to avoid the repetition of fires that had destroyed entire neighborhoods and endangered the entire city. Despite the fact that they would have helped their neighbors to preserve their homes, sell their belongings, and avoid sizeable economic losses, the dispositions were not respected.[115] Once the scare had passed, the residents of Guayaquil "were found to be indifferent and careless," and the ordinances that obliged them to take precautions to avoid fires "gathered dust in the municipal government files."[116] According to Laviana, because they ignored the dispositions of the authorities, disobeyed safety regulations, and displayed irresponsible behavior, after a short while they ended up causing new and devastating outbreaks.[117]

2

CULTURAL VALUES IN THE NINETEENTH CENTURY

In 1822 the Battle of Pichincha did away with the colonial regime and sealed the independence of the territories of the Audiencia of Quito, which, once liberated from Spanish domination, formed Gran Colombia; and then a few years later, in 1830, the Republic of Ecuador. The new state adopted the democratic system. Even though this term did not appear in any article of the constitution, it was present in defining the government as "popular, representative, alternative, and responsible" and in dividing authority among executive, legislative, and judicial powers. The constitution also recognized the equality of citizens under the law, guaranteed freedom, and consecrated certain rights such as the right to property, the right to petition authorities, and the sanctity of jurisdiction.

The republic was founded when agriculture had become the only source of national wealth, due to the disappearance of the obrajes and the later collapse of the shipyards. Calculations done by Hamerly established that in 1832, in the district of Guayaquil, 75 percent of adult males lived off the land and the sea.[1] The importance of farming and livestock-raising activities must have been greater in the highlands due to the irrelevance of other economic activities. For a foreign visitor in the mid-nineteenth century, Ecuador was an agricultural country, not because of the "painstaking" work of its inhabitants but rather because of the variety of rich soils and the high prices paid for its exports, which were the reasons that it progressed and yet remained "stationary."[2]

The efforts aimed at reactivating poor colonial mining deposits or finding new ones proved fruitless. The country suffered from the aftermath of the economic life of the Audiencia of Quito and the continued influence of the stratified society. To communicate and trade, Ecuadorians still had to use impassable colonial roadways. As in previous centuries, the

37

Catholic Church kept its privileges, controlled education, and dominated knowledge.

In the nineteenth century, even though the highlands continued to account for more than two-thirds of the Ecuadorian population, that region began to lose its hegemony due to the increasing economic and demographic importance of Guayaquil, fostered by the immigration it received and by the progress it made. This city's development was due to the fact that it continued to be the only port, and also to the opening up of commerce decreed by the government of the republic; the growing foreign trade, on which it held a monopoly; and the natural communication routes formed by the Babahoyo, Daule, and Guayas Rivers and their tributaries, which compensated for the absolute lack of roads. In addition to cacao ("the golden seed")—of which the country became the world's largest supplier—tobacco, wood, leather, straw hats, asphalt, hemp, and casacarilla were also exported. Depending on the era, the value of these commodities managed to add up to amounts equivalent to those generated by cacao. According to Hamerly, thanks to these favorable economic conditions, toward the middle of the nineteenth century Guayaquil had "stopped looking like a large village and had become an industrious port."[3] The other coastal populations, none of which held economic importance, could only communicate with each other through maritime trade and through summer paths that became mire during the rainy season. The exceptions were the settlements near the Esmeraldas, Chone, and Jubones Rivers, which could take advantage of their channels.

The Amazon region remained uninhabited and its small population was limited to scattered indigenous tribes, a few missionaries, and occasional rubber traders. The region continued to be isolated from the rest of the country without roadways to connect it to the cities of the highlands. The marginalization that it underwent was so great that its southern areas had greater economic ties to nearby Peru—with which it was connected by the rivers of the Amazon region—than to the distant Ecuador from which it was separated by the giant Andes Mountains.

During the economic stagnation from which the country suffered in the nineteenth century, in addition to the aforementioned reasons, the economic aftermath of the costly wars of independence, devastating earthquakes suffered by provinces in the highlands, and the epidemics and fires that affected Guayaquil were all a burden.

Especially costly were the day-to-day political conflicts that had not existed in the peaceful colonial period. Many times they came about because of military confrontations between government forces and rebellious groups that paralyzed agriculture, trade, and transportation activities and caused economic damages to all social sectors. The groups in contention forcibly recruited urban and rural workers and took supplies from stores, by force, and without paying for food, manufactured goods, horses, mules, donkeys, and any wares that they found along the way on haciendas and in cities. To this looting the triumphant caudillos added all sorts of retaliations against those defeated, some of which lost their assets, died, or were exiled. According to the historian Cevallos, the military chiefs, for their part, appropriated public resources allocated to maintaining and paying the troops because, unlike other federal government officials, they did not render accounts for their expenses.[4]

Several testimonies from travelers confirmed this. Osculati wrote: "Trade is almost nonexistent because of the disputes and civil wars to which that republic was continuously subjected."[5] Orton commented that "The unstable condition of the country does not encourage great undertakings; all business is periodically paralyzed by revolution."[6] The campaign armies were "one of the calamities of Ecuador," according to Holinski, since they expanded "the devastation and famine around them." The French traveler's description of one such "army" was shameful:

> One cannot imagine a stranger and more ragged spectacle than the movement of marching Ecuadorian troops. The men carry all sorts of arms and are dressed in all sorts of clothes. Some carry rifles, others spears, and some absolutely nothing. Half of the band is dressed in gray and the other half wears no uniform at all. Wearing shoes is a privilege for only a few, while the vast majority go barefoot.[7]

MacFarlane provided a similar description of the regiment of a revolutionary general that exhibited "the most shameful variety: one man wore a blue coat with metal buttons whereas another had long sleeves; one soldier had shoes but his comrade did not. All coincided in just one thing: they all wore pants of some kind, whether white, black or a kind of pajamas." He added that the Ecuadorian revolutions took on the role of strikes, but their objective was not to increase salaries but rather to provide government jobs to their supporters.[8]

At the end of the century, the American writer Graff recounted the military victory of General Alfaro near Guaranda. Even though the officials in his army wore uniforms, the regular soldiers were a "ragged crew," half of whom were armed with rifles and the other with different types of implements that hung from their necks and "made them clash like cymbals." The most fortunate ones rode mules, horses, or donkeys, which were sometimes mounted by two or even three men at a time. No one was killed or wounded in the battle because both those who attacked and those who were attacked shot as long as they were not within firing range. According to the author, in those years of the revolutionary tumults, it was "customary that, if the noise and smoke of the defensive troops did not intimidate the enemy before it reached the front line," those who defended the city evacuated or ran home to change clothes in order to go out into the streets—accompanied by a band—and cheer for Alfaro.[9]

In the rest of the budding Ecuador, the poor and backward society of the Audiencia of Quito continued, so that the nineteenth century was in many senses a prolongation of the colonial period. Several elements came together to make the citizens of the new State maintain their ancestors' beliefs, attitudes, and behaviors: the continuation of old economic structures, the survival of rigid social hierarchies, the abundant indigenous labor available, bountiful nature, the ideological sustenance provided by the Catholic Church, the theoretical and elitist nature of education, its nonexistent connection to the needs of the economy, the country's international isolation, and the absence of the rule of law.

CONTINUATION OF SOCIAL HIERARCHIES

The *latifundios*, the name given to large agricultural properties, were consolidated with the advent of the republic, when Creoles appropriated the lands that had belonged to the Spanish king and the Juntas de Temporalidades. These were added to those that were taken away from indigenous communities through legal proceedings brought before officials of the republic. On the coast, the cacao boom made it possible for hacienda owners to incorporate unused lots into their extensive production, plus those of small landowners that, through different kinds of pressure, were obliged to leave them or hand them over.[10] Thus, the haciendas, which had begun to take shape in the previous century, became the institution that organized farming and livestock-raising activities. In the republic, newly added characteristics made them the hub around which Ecuador's economic, social, and political life revolved during the nineteenth century.[11]

In the haciendas of the highlands, through a system of bonded labor (*concertaje*), the large landowners gave social and legal form to servitude, the subordination to which indigenous people were subjected during the colonial period. In his work as a peon, the Indian laborer was forced to work most of the year in agricultural/livestock activities and periodically in domestic chores in the master's home in the city, where he had the role of houseboy (*huasicama*) and his daughters were maids (*servicias*). In exchange for this he received remuneration in money, grains, or animals; a small lot for a house and a garden (*huasipungo*); and authorization to use irrigation water, pasture his livestock, and collect firewood and straw. He remained permanently in debt because the calculation of the wages used to pay off his loan was habitually manipulated by the landowner. The subjection of these "peons of one's own" was so complete that, when a hacienda was sold, the laborers that worked there were transferred as well.[12] The Indians lived in wretched huts made of adobe and straw, some of which seemed like "doghouses" entered by stooping to go through a hole.[13] Debtor prison provided the hacienda owners with a coercive legal instrument to force the permanently bonded laborers to follow orders and fulfill their work obligations. In addition to the hacienda owners, their oppressors were the government and the clergy, the latter being "the worst of all."[14]

The aforementioned North American traveler became the partner of a rich hacienda owner for the industrial extraction of the salt contained in an Andean spring located in what is today the prosperous Indian settlement of Salinas. He later wrote that the day they had offered to pay the salary of the Indians who worked the furnace they had built, no one showed up because they thought it was a trick since they were accustomed to "no Indian ever receiving" pay for his work. When his partner learned what had happened, he scolded the foreigner for the "foolishness" of paying the workers a salary. This error became the motive for the disagreements that led him to abandon his industrial project and the family that he had asked to travel from the United States to "strike it rich" by exploiting Ecuador's wealth of natural resources.[15]*

The debt bondage or bonded labor system was also present on the coastal haciendas, and it had similar characteristics with respect to the granting of the use of a parcel of land in exchange for farm work. The peons, known as *sembradores*, *finqueros*, or *aparceros*, were in charge of the cacao plantations. However, the conditions in which the *montubios* worked for hacienda owners on the coast were less oppressive than those of the highlands.

Whites, by virtue of being whites, maintained ownership of the haciendas. Even though they continued to live in the cities and only occasionally in the country, their influence encompassed rural and urban spaces. They held in their hands all forms of power and excluded other ethnic

---

*One of hacienda owner Domingo Cordovez's children, a son who was Graff's roommate at a U.S. university, hosted him in Ecuador. Cordovez owned several large properties in the highlands and on the coast, one of which, located in the Province of Chimborazo, near Riobamba, included "several Indian populations."

groups from access. They owned the land, which continued to be the principal productive resource, and they had privileged access to education and held political and religious power. Governors, legislators, judges, officials, and clergymen invariably belonged to the ethnic group of whites; and mestizos and Indians were habitually excluded. The segregation was such that in the military corps the whites reserved the rank of officials for members of their race, although others that were seen as whites could, in exceptional cases, also have access. The troops were comprised of blacks and mulattos ("zambos and cholos" as Joaquín De Avendaño described them), who were forcibly recruited because, according to the Spanish consul, those of color "belonged by right to the army" regardless of their "stature, age, status or profession." Curiously, the Indians "never formed part of the militia."[16]

Just as had occurred in the colonial period, land continued to be a symbol of personal excellence, rather than a productive good from which it was convenient to extract the maximum economic profit through work. Since haciendas were a place of rest and social prestige—instead of a farming business—the large landowners lived in the city and only occasionally visited the country for a couple of months during the dry harvest season, accompanied by numerous family members. This perhaps explains why the hacienda houses were spacious, elegant, and comfortable. Thus, a French traveler said "the families of Quito have such lovely country homes that neither those of Peru nor those of Chile can compare with their elegant rooms adorned with beautiful gardens and located amid charming places."[17] Apparently this was not true of the hacienda homes located in provinces far away from Quito.

The Indians, who in general did not know the Spanish language or spoke it with difficulty, comprised the largest ethnic group in the highlands. Nonetheless, they were relegated to the mountains, as the whites continued to amass the best lands and removed the Indians from those that they previously had, to leave them merely what they could reap from small plots of land. They continued to be subject to various forms of exploitation that included forced labor and the payment of tributes to the State and to the Church. These tributes came to account for one-fourth of their meager income.[18] According to Hassaurek, their social and economic status was below that of a black slave in the United States. Frequently, they were whipped and subjected to all sorts of abuse. The contempt with which whites regarded Indians and mestizos reached such a point that the harshest insult that could be used to belittle a person was to call him an "Indian."

Ironically, the members of the Indian community also recurred to that expression to insult others of their own race.[19]*

The rigid social hierarchies, which were somewhat more flexible on the coast, continued to perform a function of discrimination in the nineteenth century, by ensuring the whites their privileged position and keeping mestizos, Indians, and blacks excluded from any possibility of economic and social advancement or anything that could help them out of their marginal positions. They were also deprived of incentives that might have led the mestizos, through sustained efforts, to fight to maintain and better this position and might have made others determined to rise out of poverty. For these reasons the society of the republic did not offer its members options to forge their own destiny and be rewarded for their efforts, just as had happened in the colonial period. It was of little use that, with independence, a political system was established that—at least theoretically—recognized equal rights and that these were expanded in the constitutions that came afterwards.

The Catholic ethics transmitted by the Church's teachings and preachings contributed to the fact that Ecuador remain immersed in backwardness, that social hierarchies were accepted, and that traditional cultural values were maintained. Instead of encouraging progress, innovation, ideological renovation, productive savings, entrepreneurial initiatives, and accumulation of wealth, Catholicism made selective social hierarchies legitimate, praised poverty, numbed initiatives, and disapproved of making profits and collecting interest. In addition, it censured books and the free circulation of ideas, and demeaned the advances of science when it considered they were contrary to the natural order of things.[20] Holinski says that "Throughout the highlands, and one could say throughout Ecuador, the public education in its [the Catholic Church's] hands is nothing more than the maintenance of ignorance," because "the vast majority of people's learning" goes only as far as the Catechism so that if individuals were instructed rationally, "indicating their rights and responsibilities to each one," the existing status quo would soon have ended, which was not possible because "the priests were there to stop it."[21]

The beliefs that the economic and social order was desired by God and that people's destiny was determined by fate made Ecuadorians adopt attitudes of resignation and contemplation. If poverty, instead of constituting

---

*The author says that around 1870, even though Indians did not pay tributes on the coast, the tax burden there was heavier.

an unfair burden, was a beatitude that ensured the salvation of the soul, it did not make sense to change it through forced labor and the pursuit of earthly gains. For their part, those who were wealthy fulfilled their duties to others through charity, not out of respect for their rights and commitment to individual and collective obligations. If what counted for eternal salvation was a priest's pardoning of one's sins—rather than upright everyday behavior and abandonment of bad habits—the kind of conduct that people had had before facing death did not matter. Hassaurek noted a consequence of this view of the earthly world when affirming that "stealing is hardly considered a sin by the common people." To confirm this, he recalled that on a certain occasion he heard a housekeeper "express her abhorrence of Protestantism" because Protestant clergymen had "no power to forgive sins." She considered this "horrible" because it implied that "little insignificant thefts, which, in her opinion, everyone committed, should without absolution in this world, be carried to the other side of the grave."[22]

For the reasons noted above, negative economic habits from the colonial period continued to be alive in the nineteenth century, despite the fact that Spanish domination had ended, the political regime had changed, and a democratic republic had been established. Even though there were exceptions, that is, citizens with cultural habits somewhat different from the common ones, which some travelers noted in their writings,* the visitors repeatedly coincided in characterizing Ecuadorians, particularly highlanders, as people imbued with noble pretensions, indolent, contemplative, lazy, inconstant, unreliable, given to deceit, lacking initiative and entrepreneurial spirit, of little character, not very practical, reluctant to take risks, incapable of setting up enterprises, without conditions for partnerships, drinkers, neglectful of personal hygiene and cleanliness in their homes. These attitudes and behaviors were common to the rich, the poor, whites, Indians, blacks, mestizos and mulattos, and even members of the clergy.

DISINTEREST IN WORK

The person who wrote the most insightful description of the Ecuadorians' ways of life was one that shared four years with them during the

---

*Those who most thoroughly described the cultural habits of the highlanders admit that there were exceptions. Hassaurek himself said that his opinions referred "to the average resident of Quito" since there were "many honorable intellectuals that sincerely deplore the intellectual lethargy of their countrymen, especially those of the new generations" (Hassaurek, *Cuatro años entre los ecuatorianos*, 197).

sixth decade of the nineteenth century, as a diplomatic representative of the United States. He repeated the observations made by foreign travelers in their chronicles when they visited the Audiencia of Quito during the colonial period.

According to Friedrich Hassaurek, the "descendants of the old noble families," known as gentlemen, viewed work as a "disreputable" activity so they preferred to "starve than perform manual labor," which they considered degrading because it "becomes only an Indian or cholo." He added that "no white man will condescend to menial offices" since "poor as the white native may be, he will generally manage to maintain himself without working." These observations were confirmed by an anecdote. An industrial entrepreneur and large landowner planned to install a factory of woolen goods in a settlement near Quito. To implement it, he brought in from Europe "a Scotchman, a very intelligent and well-educated man, and an excellent machinist" who began to work with great determination and did much of the work himself. The Quiteños of noble lineage that heard of this traveled to Chillo to see this unbelievable occurrence with their own eyes. Upon returning, they commented "in a state of amazement" that they had seen "'a white man who worked like an Indian.'" The Indians also found this hard to fathom because there was no one of their race that the hardworking Scotsman could have descended from.[23] De Avendaño confirmed these views when he wrote that "the youth of the early society of Quito study and work very little" and the "softness in which they are immersed leads many to excesses that are degrading."[24] So presumptuous and prejudiced were the upper-class Ecuadorians that men and women alike considered it "disgraceful . . . to be seen carrying any thing through the streets of Quito."[25] They were not even capable of carrying an umbrella, which was so necessary in the rainy Quito of those days. A servant carried it for them and solicitously walked alongside his master or mistress, protecting him or her from the rain.

In keeping with Spanish tradition, commerce was considered "incompatible with nobility" because it was not a "respectable" activity, noted Hassaurek. He added that "sound business practices" were lacking and that the merchants of Quito "lacked any entrepreneurial initiative" because they were victims of "indolence and inactivity." Thus, during the day they closed their shops for several hours to have breakfast or lunch.[26] Orton wrote that in Quito "Of commerce there is scarcely enough to deserve the name," and that it was "nearly supported" by Guayaquil because "without capital, without energy, without business habits, Quitonians never embark in grand commercial schemes and industrial enterprises." He added that the "merchants never trusted their clerks," so these usually did not even exist. Moreover, merchants had "no fixed price, but get what they can . . . The majority know nothing of wholesale, and refuse to sell by the quantity, fearing a cheat." Some even had difficulties in performing simple arithmetic. For example, to sell ten *reales* of oranges, some counted out amounts coin by coin, because they could not calculate the number of units in the total sum.[27] The same thing occurred to Whymper when he wanted to buy bread in a rural town, but he overcame the difficulty by buying the same amount several times.[28]

Those for whom idleness was not a way of life and who had to be engaged in some trade, as in the case of the mestizos, were not diligent either. Referring to the artisans, in almost the same words Hassaurek repeated the observations on behavior that other travelers had made hundreds of years before, regarding not meeting deadlines for delivering what had been ordered. "Mechanics will work for three or four days, and then suddenly stay away, especially when they have succeeded in getting some money in advance," said the author.[29] Orton remarked that in Quito "it is impossible to start a man into prompt compliance" so that he would begin work "when you wish" and not when he wanted to, and said that any "amount of cajolery, bribes or threats" to get him to do anything in the time agreed on was futile.[30] "Unreliable fellows" was the expression that Ecuadorian highlanders coined to describe the artisans who did not fulfill their work commitments: masons, carpenters, stonecutters, ironsmiths, locksmiths, beltmakers, cobblers, carvers, cabinetmakers, etc.

Since the whites' culture of idleness was shared by all social classes and races, the Indians were no different. Spanish consul Joaquín De Avendaño, in his first stroll around the city, found that Indians in Quito remained seated on the ground, surrounded by filth, drinking a fermented drink (*chicha*) and liquor (*aguardiente*), with "very few individuals being occupied at something" such as peddling wares, running errands for their masters, or sweeping streets, a chore that they performed badly since they habitually just stood around on corners.[31] Theodore Wolf found them "phlegmatic, melancholy, negligent, taciturn, humble and very distrusting," in addition to "strong and vigorous" for carrying "enormous loads" on their backs "for great distances," and "light-footed and untiring when making long journeys on foot—but also weak and slow for other work and exercise."[32] According to Hassaurek, Indians were "lazy and dishonest like the common people of the highlands" and "submissive" to the extreme of tolerating all types of insults and abuses, including whipping, "as if nothing had happened." Both authors attributed this passive temperament to the mistreatment the Indians had suffered for centuries.

The U.S. diplomat affirmed that, unless there were some pressing need that "would move them to work a little, they did not go out to look for work nor did they accept any that was offered them." As servants, they did not seem very efficient to the American since "three or four servants together do not work as much" as "just one of the Irish or German servants" in his country. These harsh opinions were attenuated when he admitted that "these poor creatures [the Indians] are the most useful members of Ecuadorian society," since they "work more than all the other races together." Nonetheless, their "position in the social scale is in an inverse proportional to [their] usefulness" since they work the land, build houses and roads, carry heavy loads and perform "all that hard and heavy work which nobody else could be hired to do."[33]

Even nineteenth-century Ecuadorians did not demonstrate any inclination to hard work requiring effort and perseverance, traits on which the possibility of earning higher income and living better depended. Travelers noted with surprise that in the minds of these people there was no desire for profit, in other words the desire to get rich, which has been so important in other nations so that individuals and societies will thrive. "I never saw a people who cared so little for making money," lamented Hassaurek,[34] "though all are in sad need of it," added Orton after confirming his countryman's observation.[35] The first of these authors pointed out that "getting someone to finish something is a difficult task" because "no one hurries," "everything is problematic," and "every step of the way is full of difficulties, delays, postponements and disappointments." He added that even "the simplest transactions of daily life are full of obstacles, impediments and abuses," making it difficult to complete an operation once started because it can be abandoned at any moment. He ended by saying that to reach an agreement with a highlander on a business transaction "is the most difficult task in the world" since slowness "is one of the worst vices of this country" and "there is no occupation so pressing as not to be able to be postponed" with a "come back tomorrow."[36] This criticism was shared by Whymper and Orton. The former said that generally speaking, "Nothing is to be done *to-day*. Everything is *promised* for *to-morrow*, and when the morrow arrives it will be promised for mañana again."[37] The latter remarked that "nobody is in a hurry; nobody is busy save the tailors, who manifest a commendable diligence. Contempt for labor, a Spanish inheritance, and lack of energy, are traits which stand out in alto relieve."[38]

In the whites' unwillingness to work, especially if manual labor was involved or effort was required, there was influence from social prejudices incubated during the colonial period, the presence of a large indigenous population, and nature's bounty.

The social aspirations of the whites continued alive, even among those that were not racially white. Because they were white or considered themselves as such, they believed they should be exempt from any type of work except for the occasional oversight of their haciendas. Whites continued to be a minority, despite the fact that they included those that, while having Indian or black blood and being easy to identify by their skin color, their hair, and their facial features, had managed to "whiten" themselves thanks to their high economic status and family ties forged with the upper classes through marriage—and in other cases, thanks to the fact that during the colonial period families of black descent had obtained decrees that declared them white.[39]

One traveler noted that "since some strain of *mestizo* blood enters into almost the whole 'white' race," it was not unusual to find people of "some slight shade of colour . . . occupying high positions."[40] His observation was confirmed by Orton, who noted in 1868 that of "the white population— a stiff aristocracy of eight thousand souls—that inhabited Quito . . . not more than half a dozen can boast of pure blood. The coarse black hair, prominent cheek-bones, and low foreheads, reveal an Indian alliance."[41] This was made evident when parents of light skin, hair, and eyes had off- spring with a Mongolian blue spot on their lower back.

Despite the fact that the dominant groups had Indian and black mixes, they continued to cling to the Spanish ancestry that supposedly proved they were pureblooded, and in some cases of noble origin, a pretension that led them to segregate their countrymen as Indians, mestizos, blacks, mulattos, and cholos. This attitude was less apparent on the coast, which was a land of immigrants, with a minimal indigenous population and an absence of noble families during the colonial period.

Whites did not feel compelled to work because in the highlands there was still abundant indigenous labor in a situation of dependence. Their *pa- tronos* could make use of them whenever they wanted, to perform all sorts of jobs (working the land, picking fruit, herding cattle, opening up trails, working as household servants), without having to pay them. Otherwise, this would have entailed a considerable expense. The abundance of labor illustrates why homemakers led idle lives, surrounded by servants so nu- merous that there were four or five servants in the home of a "respectable family" and ten or twelve in the home of "large families."[42] This was not the case on the coast, where, despite emigrants from the highlands, it was necessary for whites to work because the indigenous population had been reduced to isolated tribes, the mestizo labor was insufficient, and the abundant fruits produced by the land were being lost. Nonetheless, inhabitants of the coast were not motivated to move to the country to do farm work, due to ancestral colonial prejudices against manual labor.

Since bountiful nature generously continued to provide food every day of the year and to offer a mild climate that encouraged softness, Ecuadorian people did not need to make sacrifices and amass provisions to protect themselves from adverse times. Foreign visitors mentioned this fact repeatedly as an impediment for the progress of Ecuador, and not an advantage, as previously believed and believed still today. In 1832 Terry wrote that "most of the people in the province (of Guayaquil) only cultivated the soil to obtain sustenance" and that "a country that could supply all the South American Pacific Coast barely had enough for its own sustenance."[43] In 1847 Osculati believed that in Ecuador "the cultivation of cereals was generally very careless" and that the lands were "discretely cultivated" but "extremely productive" due to the fertility of the soil more than to "the activity of its inhabitants."[44] In 1851 Holinski thought that the hot temperatures "numbed or killed the taste for work."[45] Years later Hassaurek referred to the little advantage that the inhabitants of Guayaquil obtained from the "great generosity of Nature" which had made the social classes "poor, indolent, lazy and short-sighted."[46]

In 1868 Orton noted that "The soil and climate of Ecuador, so infinitely varied, offer a home to almost every useful plant. The productions of either India could be naturalized on the lowlands, while the highlands would welcome the grains and fruits of Europe. But intertropical people do not subdue nature like the civilized men of the North; they only pick up a livelihood." After pondering the fertility of the region of Guayaquil, he added that they only harvested "a fraction" of the cacao that grew naturally, due to the "scarcity of laborers" and the shortage of Ecuadorians because of those "exiled or killed in senseless revolutions."[47] In 1871 Kolberg praised the extraordinary fertility of the soil around the Guayas River basin, "which, without exaggeration" could sustain "a thousand times more men than it sustains" if it were "worked in earnest." He went on to lament that "the warm and stable climate" made the inhabitants "indolent and soft."[48]

POOR ECONOMIC PRACTICES

The inhabitants of the Quito highlands, and Ecuadorians in general, were not noted for honoring commitments, fulfilling agreements, and acting honestly in day-to-day economic relations. For these reasons, in the incipient republic, relations were not based on reciprocal trust regarding the good faith with which the parties were acting in the activities they undertook, the contracts they signed, and the business transactions they carried out. Scholars of contemporary development identify such trust as an important element in the progress of nations. The lack of constructive relations and sentiments of cooperation hindered establishing enterprises, conducting business, and undertaking economic initiatives. These are necessary steps for exploiting the vast natural resources available to the country.

The lack of trust was so negative for the economic progress of Ecuador that Hassaurek considered it more damaging than the political instability and social convulsions that afflicted the country during the nineteenth century. His affirmation that "There are few people whose word can be fully trusted" was supported by stories about the many instances of noncompliance when he hired someone, organized a trip, or received offers. "It takes forever to reach an agreement with a seller, with a mule driver or with a tradesman." And if an agreement is reached, "the other party wants to change things again and demand more favorable conditions." Hassaurek concluded, "To agree with a serrano on any business transaction is the most difficult task in the world," and when an agreement has been reached after long bargaining, he "makes new demands, or invents additional conditions." He also observed that "after you have paid them their own price, they will commence to bother you for an additional sum."[49] According to Graff, due to the lack of trust, the foreign businessmen in Quito did not set up partnerships, and no storeowner "dares to leave his employees in charge for even five minutes." He therefore considered it to be the only place in the world where the merchant opened his shop in the morning, stayed there the whole day, closed up himself and slept "with the key in his pocket."[50]

There were no guarantees for property rights, as seen previously in the case of Indians' lands. However, that was not the only case. Among the risks that travelers had to face was that of losing their belongings, not only at the bottom of a cliff because of poor roadways, but also at the hands of Ecuadorians accustomed to viewing foreigners as naïve victims. The roadway thieves were not the most dangerous, but rather those who worked for the visitors, especially the mule team drivers. Osculati recounted how, at the recommendation of other "explorers" on a trip from Guayaquil to Quito, he never lost sight of his bags while sailing, riding on horseback, or resting, but the muleteers had still managed to make a hole to extract his belongings.[51] Whymper recalled how Riobamba officials and a Quito banker tried to take advantage of him, and how a Guaranda merchant and a Riobamba hacienda owner actually did. Convinced that the purpose of the English alpinist was not to climb Chimborazo but to look for a treasure hidden under the snow instead, they asked him to share it. However, they withdrew their claim "with a sour gesture" when he told them that he would gladly share the treasure if they covered half of the expedition expenses. When he closed out his temporary bank account before returning to England, the banker that waited on him retained "his advances," which he said was "customary." However, he desisted when Whymper announced that he would mention that custom of Quito bankers in the book that he planned to publish. On another occasion, he discovered that he had been tricked by a merchant who sold him rotten meat when he opened one of the trunks to eat before beginning his ascent of Chimborazo. A hacienda owner who called himself a marquis even locked him in at the Chuquipogui stopping-place until he had paid an exorbitant sum for bad food and worse lodging.[52]

In interpersonal relations, individuals did not know what to believe because of the "tendency to substitute words for facts." Enock said that "truth becomes distorted, exaggeration takes its place, and expediency or opportunism tends to colour social dealings, and chicanery to influence commercial and political matters." He went on to note that "Often an agreement is an instrument which may be broken if circumstances so dictate."[53] Holinski shared this opinion when he said that there is a custom of "double talk" and that through "sophisms, most men conceal an absolute lack of principles, a comfortable theory whose aim is success and . . . personal interest."[54] The opinion of Ecuadorian José Peralta was no different; among "the ugliest passions" he pointed to "the personal interest that takes on all disguises in order to deceive the credulous society and end up with a profit, without reservations as to the means."[55]

Another Ecuadorian author tells how cacao growers were deceived by intermediaries who arbitrarily imposed quality and weight standards for the product they bought and then tricked them when it came time to settle accounts and pay them.[56] This practice was repeated everywhere with other crops, especially when the seller was an Indian or a person of lower social status. None of this scandalized anyone, and it was even viewed favorably by many. According to Graff, whoever deceived others was praised for his cleverness; and on the other hand, whoever fell for the deceit and believed in the commitments made was considered a *"pendejo"* ("poor fool").[57]

Since behaviors such as not being punctual, distorting the truth, and failing to comply after giving one's word were common to all social classes and different ethnic groups, they made economic relations highly uncertain. One traveler who visited Ecuador around 1832 noted that the constant extensions of the periods for matters involving more than one person were "an almost universal disposition" expressed in all the acts of everyday life. He noted that when he made a business appointment he could be "sure that the person he was to meet would not arrive at the place agreed on" or that he would arrive "quite a bit later than the time agreed on." This also occurred when he was planning an excursion or a trip, which often had to be postponed "due to frivolous delays."[58] The lack of a sense of time and its economic value could have been due not only to a cultural reason, but also to the fact that few people had watches. Orton suggested this when he said that in Quito "there are only one or two watch-tinkers . . . and, as may be inferred, very few watches are in running order. As a consequence, the people have very little idea of time."[59]

The "custom of making high-sounding promises, which are not intended to be kept, is universal among Ecuadorians of the Sierra," who at the moment that one requested services or accepted the assistance proffered so insistently, always found an excuse not to fulfill them, said Hassaurek.[60] His fellow countryman, Orton, added that there was a "contrast between big promise and beggarly performance," among other reasons because the speaker did not expect his words to be taken seriously.[61] Such opinions were shared by Theodore Wolf when he said that highlanders were "not very good at keeping their promises and not very scrupulous about telling the truth."[62]

According to Colonel Franciso Hall, one of the precursors of Ecuadorian liberalism, in Quito the terms "lie" and "liar" had lost their harsh etymology because the first was a common practice and the second an everyday occurrence. So, they could be used without offending the speaker, unlike what would have occurred in "a high London circle." He then added that the tendency to change the literal sense of things made the country "a nation of lawyers who easily twisted words and their meanings as they pleased."[63] These concepts were expressed in 1828, two years after the founding of Ecuador and five years before he was assassinated by his distrustful enemies. A foreign traveler also attributed to President García Moreno the phrase that "If my countrymen had to survive by telling the truth, all of them would starve to death."[64]

A society in which individuals believed that those with whom they had connections would act maliciously, by virtue of their awareness of their own bad faith, did not offer conditions for joining efforts and resources in order to undertake initiatives that could not be carried out by individuals. For this reason, they failed to set up enterprises and to carry out projects that would have contributed to the country's progress and to the partners' wealth. Rather, those who discussed a business deal did not spare precautions to protect themselves against possible thievery, and sought to ensure each transaction through all sorts of cautionary measures.

This shortcoming of Ecuadorian society, which proved so costly for the country's progress, was described by Hassaurek in the following terms: "An important trait of serrano character is their great distrust of each other, which precludes all spirit of association. Partnerships are not customary; corporations are unheard of. Great enterprises, therefore, are an impossibility."[65] This was confirmed by Orton, for whom "mutual distrust" made partnerships "almost unknown." Therefore, he did not "remember a single commercial firm, save a few made up of brothers, or father and son."[66] Whymper shared similar reflections when he wrote that there was "universal reservation and distrust" due to a "general disposition not to respect the sanctity of contracts" and to file "later claims." He gallantly explained this strange behavior by saying that Ecuadorians had "a different code of honour" from his.[67] Historian Cevallos, in referring to the Indians, said that "In all of their contracts, in all of the actions of their lives, one can see that, from sunup to sundown, they do not believe anyone, that [they believe] people are trying to trick them, or that offers will not be honored," mainly when dealing with whites.[68]

Distrust ultimately limited the productive use of savings through investment in agriculture, commerce, and industry, and curbed the possibility of capital formation that was necessary to finance the exploitation of the country's natural resources, which visitors coincided in viewing as an "emporium" of abundance and prosperity. Instead of being used for productive investments, the capital that was left after paying tithes and "first fruits" to the Catholic Church was stashed away in secret hiding-places, with the belief that it did not matter if the funds were left idle if they could be kept safe under the watchful eye of their owners, far away from the artifices of relatives, friends, and possible unscrupulous partners interested in appropriating others' money though loans that were never repaid or other fraudulent means. In the nineteenth century, buried "stashes" continued to be found; this was the name for the valuables put away by people who died without leaving indications about their location. "Finding buried treasures is not something rare," said Hassaurek. During his stay in Quito "on many occasions" he witnessed that "the tearing down of old buildings led to the discovery of considerable sums of money buried by their owners," which they had hidden instead of investing them in activities beneficial for them and the community; and before dying they did not have "time to communicate the secret to their children or relatives."[69] Another of his countrymen reflected that there could not be industry in a people "who spend much of their time repeating traditions of treasures buried by the Incas, and stories of gold deposits in the mountains."[70] This deluded belief was shared by many inhabitants of the Andean region.

The fact that the profession of moneylender was looked down upon did not help savings to have a productive use either. Moneylenders were known by the deprecatory name of *chulquero*, meaning "usurer." For this reason there were difficulties for establishing and operating credit institutions that would function openly in the financing of farming, livestock-raising, and manufacturing activities, especially in the highlands. The two banks that were founded in Quito had to close shortly after their establishment. At the end of the century, Graff commented that "the degree of commercial morality was so slim that there was not a single bank in the city" and that he would have found amusing the idea of an Ecuadorian walking up to a teller's window to deposit cash in a bank account.[71]

This way of life of Ecuadorians, and the passive way in which they lived, kept the country from developing and kept the citizens from improving their well-being. Except in Guayaquil and its area of influence, the economy remained stagnant, as it had been during most of the colonial period. It is not possible to obtain figures to confirm this, but the fact that agriculture and commerce did not progress during the nineteenth century, except on the coast, could serve as an indicator. Only a handful of manufacturing centers were installed; and the country maintained, almost unchanged, the deplorable colonial levels of education, health, roads, and urban services. Poverty was so great and so widespread that it affected all social classes, even those that had a certain amount of resources. Except for relatively few exceptions, the latter also had economic constraints and some had a daily and "constant struggle between ostentation and want."[72] Since "well-to-do people," because of their indolence, did not manage to increase their inherited wealth during their lifetimes, when they died they only bequeathed to their children whatever was left of the assets they had inherited.

The major obstacle for the country's development continued to be the absolute lack of roads. According to Wolf, in the mid-nineteenth century, in the area around Guayaquil—but not in other coastal areas that were in need of roads—there were a very few precarious bridle-paths that during the rainy season "were not bad but rather awful, and many times impassable." Along some of them "the untamable vegetation" that invaded them made it necessary to use "hatchets and machetes and a great deal of patience in order to cut open a path."[73] Referring to the roads that left Babahoyo toward the highlands, MacFarlane spoke of places where travelers passed by "hanging or dragging" and had to "lift their feet and put them on the mule's neck" to avoid the mud, trusting that the intelligent animals would also place their hooves in the right places. He added that, in going up the Andes mountains, the mud was so compact that at the mule's every step one heard a sound like "when a very large bottle is uncorked." He concluded by saying that along the trails of Ecuador, the mule did "the work of the cart and the wagon" because, since there were no roads, "wheels were useless."[74] Wolf's appreciation was similar when he said that climbing the Andes to reach the highlands was a great accomplishment, because one had to zigzag up steep slopes where one advanced thanks to the useful ridges, consisting of small transversal ditches full of mud in which the beasts placed their hooves in order to obtain a firm hold, avoid slipping, and continue advancing.[75]

Just as in the colonial period, there was only one "road" between the coast and the highlands. Travelers left Guayaquil upstream along the Babahoyo River in sloops impelled by oarsmen and polesmen until disembarking at the settlement formerly known as Bodegas and currently as Babahoyo. Then they climbed the cordillera on mules led by mule team drivers along muddy trails full of ridges, along the edges of precipices, wading across creeks and making their way across ravines, in order to cross the Andes at an altitude of almost four thousand meters and then traverse valleys, plains, and mountains and finally arrive in the distant city of Quito. A trip between the port and the capital took at least two weeks and sometimes longer depending on the condition of the road, on which traffic was interrupted during the rainy season between December and March.

In the highlands, due to a lack of maintenance (already a national malady) the old trails had become impassable so that, according to a popular saying, "Our roads are roads for birds, but not for men." Due to their precarious nature, it was not possible to use coaches and carriages to transport people, merchandise, and materials. These were carried on pack animals or by Indian bearers who were in high demand in the cities,[76] or pulled by donkeys or oxen when necessary. Osculati wrote that the highland roads could only be transited by mules and horses, which were the only means of transportation "compatible with the nature of the soil and the condition of the roads."

Referring to the road between Latacunga and Quito, he wrote that in Ecuador there were no roads for vehicles and that the paths "were terrible, the bridges mostly broken and in ruins, without the Government thinking about repairing them, not even in the most frequented places."[77] Kolberg made fun of the so-called Royal Road of the highlands, as just an illusion of the Ecuadorians, since travelers had to put up with "an infinite number of anxious moments and deep miry places," finding themselves with "a number of gullies as deep as a man is tall, large blocks of stone scattered everywhere, and ravines so deep that the horse and its rider were entirely concealed," all of which gave the appearance of soil that had been "sunken and destroyed by an awful earthquake."[78]

This shortage of good communication routes between the port and the capital and the other highland provinces kept Quito in the same confinement it had experienced during the colonial period. In mid-century, the French chronicler Holinski wrote that Quito and the provinces of the sierra were "submerged in a labyrinth of mountains that isolated them from the world." This situation made the capital "a Spanish city with the customs, culture, spirit and innocence of the sixteenth century" and put Ecuador at the "tail-end of most of the Spanish republics."[79] North American visitor McKenzie coincided with that view because, for him, Quito at the end of the century was "a retrograde city" that had "remained excluded from the rest of the world and still retained the atmosphere of seventeenth-century Spain."[80]

In the nineteenth century the state did not exist as a public service provider because the country had been immersed in political and military disputes. It was the lack of authority and of government that MacFarlane depicted when he said that in Ecuador the state "seems like a parent that did not have enough authority over his children to keep their face and hands clean."[81] To this incompetence of public power, or simply its absence, must be added the country's difficult topography and technical lags. There were no picks, spades, and shovels to dig and remove earth, nor carts or wheelbarrows to carry it away; and worse yet, machines and other implements needed to build roads. The Indians transported the loosened earth and the necessary materials (wood, stone, bricks) in their ponchos or in sheepskins.[82]

In the second half of the nineteenth century, García Moreno was the first president to confront the problem and begin to provide solutions. All of the foreign travelers who met him or heard about his work expressed admiration for the modernizing spirit and enterprising nature of the authoritarian president, so different from the listless Ecuadorians of the times. Thanks to his integrity, as of 1861 the inveterate deficit of roads began to be remedied with the construction of a railroad from Guayaquil to the highlands, and a road from Quito to the south. His notable road-building efforts, along with those of other presidents without the same determination in subsequent decades, made it possible to connect Quito and Rio-bamba with a bimonthly service of mule-drawn stagecoaches by the end of the century.[83] Guayaquil, Milagro, and Yaguachi were also connected by railroad; the Vía Flores passed through Guaranda to the western edges of the Andes; and the horse and mule trails were improved.

Political instability, fiscal shortages, and the absence of priorities, along with everyday conflicts of different sorts, kept the state from completing the few works it started (roads, bridges, buildings, and other constructions), as well as from performing maintenance. Many initiatives and investments were wasted. The citizens did not cooperate either to improve urban and rural spaces or at least take care of public goods. Travelers noted that in the barren Andean landscapes there were few trees and the Ecuadorians had no interest in planting more. One traveler wrote that Quito's main plaza (now Independence Square) was filled with dust in the dry season and with mud in the rainy season and was used for the popular bullfights. There, Garcia Moreno built "a beautiful park full of evergreen trees and healthy flowers with lovely walkways and lined by immaculate streets." However, this progress, an important innovation for the times, was not valued by the neighborhood, which at night "destroyed the saplings or tore the leaves off plants and trampled the flowers," thus obliging the president gardener to protect them with soldiers until the plants grew and "the people left behind their bad habits."[84] He was also concerned about introducing eucalyptus trees and planting them all over the country, but nobody thought of recovering and propagating the lovely native trees by establishing nurseries.

The problems and delays that poor roads caused, even for traveling short distances, made transportation a dangerous and costly venture that had negative impacts on production and commerce since agricultural surpluses could not be sent to provinces that had not had good crops. Osculati wrote that in the province of Quito "a large part of the products spoiled" or they were sold at low prices because they could not be sent to other places.[85] MacFarlane also noted that it was a pity that farmers had to travel four days across the Andes "to sell their products at prices that barely compensated them for the time and the animals used."[86]

One researcher said that at the end of the century, due to the lack of roads in the highland provinces, the cost of transportation was prohibitive, so that whereas in some inter-Andean valleys there were abundant farm products, in others there were shortages. She added that it proved so oner-ous to take products from the highlands to the coast that for the residents of Guayaquil it was cheaper to import wheat and barley from Chile or California than to bring them down from the highlands.[87] At the end of the century the transportation of the component parts for the first cotton factory installed in Quito cost more than the amount paid by a highland businessman to buy cotton in the United States.[88]

In Quito there were shortages of coffee, an article that the country could produce in abundance, and the paradox was that it exported casacarilla and wheat while it imported quinine and flour, in the latter case because there were few and deficient mills.[89] Thus, Holinski rightly said that "the difficult communications kept commerce from prospering, and without commerce there was no work, and without work there was no progress."[90]

The limitations that isolation placed on the growth of demand hindered investments to improve farming and manufacturing, which for the aforementioned reasons had to be limited to production for the surrounding market. Traditional wooden plows pulled by oxen continued in use, and pigs were sometimes used to move earth with their snouts. Grains were threshed by horses and Indians, the first of which flailed them with their hooves and the second with their shoes. Hoes were made of wood, and there were no shovels, "and no one even dreamed of having modern machinery for farming activities."[91]

Even when the century had ended, the United States consul reported in 1902 that agriculture in Ecuador was performed in a "very primitive way" since they "seldom" used fertilizers and "modern plows and other new farm implements were unknown."[92] Livestock production [the "pastoral industry"] was just as behind as agriculture. According to Enock, the economic yields that it generated were due more to the "favourable natural conditions rather than to improved methods."[93] For this reason, in the late nineteenth century Quito had shortages of milk, and even more of butter and cheese, to which only "the very wealthy" had access, and both were of poor quality.[94]

Even though goldsmiths, woodcarvers, and those that worked on stairway railings were very skilled, the other tradesmen were centuries behind them. They did not produce good crafts due to the fact that they used "the crudest tools and implements" so that "what, in other countries, would be accomplished in a few days" in Ecuador "took weeks and months."[95] There were few and very elementary manufacturers that produced thread and cotton and wool cloth (baize and coarse material) for the local market. Some of these were used to make ponchos and shawls, and were located in the industrious towns of Cotacachi, Otavalo, Atuntaqui, Chullo, and Guano, as well as in the city of Ambato, where a foreign traveler found "numerous indications" that it could become "the center of the country's manufacturing."[96] At the end of the twentieth century, this prediction seemed to be coming true.

One author commented that Ecuador's industrial and commercial life was "but little developed in comparison with that of the larger Latin American communities."[97] Banks, which are so necessary in the financing of productive activities, were recently founded in Ecuador in the mid-nineteenth century. They failed initially and only became relevant at the end of the century.[98] In 1890, an Ecuadorian described the Sierra as an "unproductive [sector] submerged in poverty, with no credit abroad; a dead point, in sum, where work has no stimulus and existence is similar to lethargy."[99]

About 1860, with the exception of the churches and convents that occupied one-fourth of the city, and some public buildings, there were only two or three houses in Quito with a third floor.[100] This reflected the poverty of civil construction, which contrasted sharply with the richness of the religious edifications. Nineteenth-century visitors remarked that the capital was one of the dirtiest cities they had found during their journeys. The homes of the rich were no exception, for in their parlors dust covered the furniture and furnishings, and in their kitchens and dining rooms poorly cleaned dishes were used.[101]*

Holinski, alluding to the city's topography, said that "going up and down, up and down is the luck of the inhabitants of Quito," the streets "cannot bear any type of vehicle because they require jumping between one ditch and another," the "canals that wind through them are obstructed by filth," and "as soon as you turn a corner, you are in the country."[102] In the same era, about 1868, the North American Orton said that Quito seemed to be "a useless feudal town sitting on a mountain" in which "not a chimney rises above the red-tiled roofs, telling of homely hearths beneath. No busy hum greets the ear." One heard "jingling church bells in place of rattling carriages . . . [and] the wandering eye does not look for a railroad or a telegraph, for even the highways, such as they are, seem deserted." He described the outlying Indian houses as dirty, disorderly "low mud hovels." He concluded by saying that Quito was "more than a century behind this age of steam and lighting."[103] However, at the end of the century, Festa found the city relatively clean, with paved roads—but not the outlying areas, which were dirty "beyond all description."[104] Around the same time, Graff wrote that there was still the custom of throwing garbage out of

---

*Hassaurek said that Quito was "one of the filthiest capitals in Christendom" (Hassaurek, *Cuatro años entre los ecuatorianos*, 54).

windows, while yelling "Careful below." This waste was later trampled by animals, dried by the sun, and scattered by the wind.[105]

All of the foreign travelers noted the highlanders' lack of sanitation and hygiene. De Avendaño remarked that "The lack of cleanliness was very common in Quito," due to "the false idea of hygiene" that "washing one's face and hands daily, like the Europeans did," damaged the skin and was harmful to one's health. So, they only washed when they took a bath, which was "once or twice a month"[106] for the cleanest ones. Hassaurek had a similar opinion about the hacienda owners in the province, who only occasionally cleansed their faces because in their modest country homes there was a scarcity of wash basins.[107] At the end of the century, Graff was surprised that in Quito there was only "one place to take a bath," and the hacienda house where he stayed, which belonged to a rich provincial landowner, was "rustic and scantily furnished," did not have a bathroom, and had "numerous and mortifying fleas," while chickens "strutted around the rooms looking for crumbs," firewood was used to cook, and the hacienda owner's children "were not familiar with the use of soap and seldom changed clothes."[108] If these were the hygiene habits of the most well-to-do people, one can imagine what occurred among members of the other social classes, especially in the countryside.

The lack of hygiene, just as in the colonial period, led to periodical epidemics and meant that a sizeable part of the population continued to have fleas, lice, and jiggers. One pastime of two people who were together was to remove fleas from each other, and in the case of the lower social sectors, especially Indians, to catch the insects, crush them between their teeth, and then eat them, according to stories told by several travelers. To protect themselves from bug bites at night, Whymper and his traveling companions thoroughly cleaned the rooms of the inns where they stayed. This hygiene caught the attention of the neighbors, who "open-mouthed from ear to ear" congregated to watch what the "extravagant gringos" were doing.[109]

No different were the cultural habits of the people living on the coast. Foreign travelers described the residents of Guayquil as not very hardworking, lacking discipline, reluctant to perform manual labor, reticent to form partnerships, inclined to outward ostentation, with a taste for liquor, and subject to social hierarchies favoring inequalities.

In his research, Hamerly wrote that, in the Province of Guayaquil in the early nineteenth century, diseases were treated empirically due to the "lack of doctors and pharmacists," the poverty level, and the "credulity and ignorance of most of the population."[110] For the Italian Osculati, the residents of Guayaquil had a "sweet nature" but were little inclined to study and, therefore, not very well-educated, and devoted to idleness and gambling."[111] One historian from Guayaquil attributed the collapse of the shipyards, which had been so important during the colonial period, to the port inhabitants' inability to form partnerships and thus raise the capital necessary to improve the facilities and be able to compete with other countries by transforming the traditional factories into modern shipyards.[112] About 1847, Osculati found the shipyard "completely in ruins" with "only a few barges to repair," alongside "almost inexistent commerce because of political discord and civil wars," an industry less advanced than in the interior, a city without buildings or institutions "worthy of note."[113]

With respect to Esmeraldas, Kolberg wrote that "it displays the most fantastic wealth of vegetation, as almost nowhere else on earth," alongside a population of six hundred "lazy and incomprehensible" inhabitants who are "content with the dirtiest rooms and the poorest rags," who have not laid out even one road to penetrate the interior, and who only plant what is needed "for their own use" and so as not to "starve to death" and "to buy liquor."[114]

Even though bountiful nature, the port activities, and the cultivation and exportation of cacao gave Guayaquil families sources of employment that allowed them to build houses and purchase food, clothing, furniture, and other goods, Guayaquil continued to be an unhealthy city. The houses were all wooden and cane structures that had external supports that allowed the neighbors to take shelter from the sun and rain. During the rainy season the streets became "pestilent mud holes" due to the mixture of mud and garbage; and the city's inhabitants lived with all sorts of insects and animals—scorpions, lizards, and snakes, among others—which made it necessary to use stilts to cross the streets. "There is no sewage system nor trash cans, and the greatest neglect of cleanliness and pulchritude that can exist is here," wrote MacFarlane.[115] Kolberg added that the streets had been turned into a sewer despite the cleaning done by buzzards and he did not understand why the residents of Guayaquil "have cared so little about cleanliness." He criticized the dirt and grime in Guayaquil and "the lack of order and cleanliness that extends to everything: dress, chambers, kitchen, house," even in the case of the "well-to-do and rich" that "fear energetic discipline."[116] In mid-century Holinski did not find an inn worth staying at, but he solved this problem thanks to the "sentiments of hospitality that distinguished the businessmen of Guayaquil."[117]* In Whymper's book

---

*He added that "a traveller could not find along the way a sweeter generosity than that of the society of Guayaquil," which was "extremely affable."

Travels Amongst the Great Andes, there are drawings of thirty-five insects that the author found in the bedroom he occupied in Guayaquil,[118] from whose bites the residents of Guayaquil protected themselves by using mosquito nets. Nevertheless, when travelers left the highlands and reached Guayaquil, they felt relieved.

In any case, unlike the highlands, where there was no change in the inhabitants' cultural habits with regard to those that had been common during the colonial period, the people who visited Guayaquil found that there were fewer prejudices against commercial activities and that the port residents had an enterprising spirit. Although still incipient, it was beginning to have a positive impact on economic activities, encouraging their development and diversification. Terry describes them as "sociable, quick and lively."[119] Wiener, who was a French consul, pointed out that even though the "golden youth" did not have a very active imagination, they did possess a "quite well-developed and lucid mercantile spirit."[120] Kolberg found that, unlike "the Ecuadorians of the highlands" the residents of Guayaquil were "vivacious, open spenders and liberals" and that the commercial exchanges that took place on the Guayas River and the fifteen to twenty steamboats and hundreds of other boats that navigated along it gave the city "an animated life."[121] One contemporary researcher said that Quito was a city with "little conspicuous consumption" due to the difficulties that it had in transporting imported goods and because of the stagnation that limited economic possibilities, whereas Guayaquil was a "very vital" city whose inhabitants could consume all sorts of foreign goods, given the significant income that agro-export activities provided them.

Thanks to their mercantile spirit and the possibilities offered by their rich tropical soils, the residents of Guayaquil increased the production and exportation of the popular "golden seed," to which they added tobacco, wood, leather, straw hats, casacarilla, hemp, and asphalt.[122] Wool, furs, cotton, sugar, rye, corn, agave, and gold dust would also be added later.[123] Some of these came from the highlands. In addition, for some years Guayaquil maintained the naval industry of the shipyards. Eventually, they also built sawmills, rice huskers, small and large sugar mills, and flour mills; and they formed companies for the production and exportation of cacao. They worked to recover from the economic losses caused by fires and yellow fever, popularly known as "brown vomit." They financed the urban spread of a city that grew rapidly due to immigration and rebuilt it several times following fires that left the city devastated. In the early years of the fourth decade, Rocafuerte rebuilt the Guayas River boardwalk with durable materials,[124] but the ships nonetheless preferred to remain at sea or cast anchor in the middle of the river.

By the end of the century, Guayaquil had inns, taverns, cafés, clubs, and also some "beautiful buildings," water pumps to fight fires, and a banking system in which the Banco Comercial y Agrícola was notable. In the twentieth century it became the major government lender. An Italian traveler found the main streets to be paved with cobblestone, and [the city] fairly clean and supplied with potable water, gas lighting, and a streetcar, although the houses and main buildings were still made of wood.[125] Another visitor noted that the city, despite having raw materials, did not have "factories of any kind" except for a brewery "of considerable size."[126]

Peasants, artisans, and workers also benefited from the economic boom of Guayaquil and the coast. Toward the end of the 1850s, De Avendaño found that in Guayaquil all social classes, businessmen, proprietors, clerks, and day laborers, enjoyed well-being and "even luxury" because the "scarcity of workers raises the price of labor too much."[127] Mountain-climber Whymper was surprised that the workers charged "exorbitant prices for their services" and that laborers earned "wages equal to those of the small English bishops."[128] These appreciations were confirmed by a contemporary researcher. Clark considered that the high remunerations received by agricultural workers on the coast allowed them to earn up to nine times more than farmworkers in the highlands.[129] Hamerly noted that since labor was scarce "there was a notable tendency toward vagrancy" since, due to the high salaries, with two days of work one could subsist for a week.[130] This labor scarcity was due to the fact that the abundant highland workers could not travel to the coast because of the lack of roads and also because they were tied to the haciendas by the bonded labor system.

CONSOLIDATION OF PATERNALISM

In the nineteenth century the authority of the large landowners was consolidated when agriculture became the major economic activity; large properties (latifundios) took shape; and elements came together to give rise to the institution of the hacienda. Hacienda owners became the most important players in Ecuadorian society because more than two-thirds of the population lived in the countryside, and the national economy depended on the fortune of agricultural activities. This was also true of the well-being of individuals, including those who lived in the cities, but particularly those who lived in the area of influence of the large property owners: relatives, family friends, compadres, peasants, workers, artisans, businessmen, and intermediaries, as well as civil, military, and religious authorities.

Some hacienda owners stood out and managed to gain political preeminence when they rose "above the rest, acquiring large properties and exerting economic, social and political arrogance not counteracted by any other power, especially in small villages."[131] The family organization inherited from the colonial period contributed to this process. According to one author, family and kinship "constitute the most deeply rooted and esteemed institution in the country's social structure," due to the fact that [both] the Indian and Hispanic traditions emphasized them.[132] The family structure went beyond the nucleus formed by parents and children and extended to sons-in-law, daughters-in-law, grandchildren, close family friends, and close and distant relatives. All of these and many others depended on the landowners for their upkeep, employment, favors, or benefits, in exchange for which they offered their unconditional loyalty. The landowners took advantage of the extended family to organize, exercise, and spread their influence in their own locality or as a cacique in a broader area, and as a caudillo within the country. Having become such, they led revolutionary movements, headed conspiracies against the government, proclaimed themselves dictators and, exceptionally, were elected to office by a vote of the citizens, representing the Conservative, Liberal, and Progressive parties.

In the domains of the latifundios, the hacienda owner's authority was not limited to strictly economic tasks related to property management and farming and livestock-raising, which were usually performed by administrators or foremen. He was also responsible for functions that corresponded to the social, political, and religious spheres, some being of personal concern to every citizen, and others proper to state officials and the Catholic Church. As one latifundio historian pointed out, "the *patrono* not only exercised the authority proper to rural society, but on occasions [played the] role of judge, police officer and lawmaker."[133] In effect, he administered justice, applied sanctions, settled disputes in families and between neighbors, controlled private morality, preserved religious observances, determined work schedules, defined standards of behavior, established procedures, sold staple goods, provided basic health care, granted credits and compensations, and represented those subordinate to him before political and religious officials.[134]

Those who benefited from the favors and compensations granted by the "lord" of the land were obliged not only to work in farming and livestock-raising activities but also to provide occasional services and to reciprocate with loyalty, fidelity, and submission. These obligations had nothing to do with the economic activity carried on at the hacienda. These ties between the large landowner and those that depended on him were of a personal nature, because the formal authorities of the state did not intervene, nor were these relations derived from laws where responsibilities were established, obligations were demanded, and noncompliance was sanctioned, as Crawford pointed out.[135]* These personal relations between the hacienda owner and those that depended on him were grounded in a custom repeated during centuries. Furthermore, because the positions of latifundio owner and government official were usually combined in one same person, they were so broad and so strong that they prevailed over those that were regulated in legal provisions, and they marked individuals' conduct in their economic, social, and political activities. Limited access to education, scant means of communication, ideas favorable to maintaining the existing order, and weak state institutions favored the survival and spread of personal relations.

These particular relations of power in daily life, maintained over generations, led people to identify authority and understand its attributions through the orders that the hacienda owner gave his subordinates, the decisions that he made in matters submitted to his consideration, and the concessions that he made at his discretion regarding those who depended on him.[136]† Historian Pedro Fermín Cevallos wrote that, after the republic had been founded, "for the people, interest in the country consisted of interest in their protector and back then it would have been craziness, not a vain desire, to preach thinking about oneself, about one's own rights and those of the collective; craziness to think about the enemies of the country and not those of their *patrono*, a sort of feudal lord with some restrictions."[137]

The family-oriented socioeconomic structure shaped by the hacienda, the relations of a personal nature that it incubated, and the prolongation of colonial cultural habits favored the rise and spread of paternalism. If the benefits that a person sought to obtain did not depend on his merits and the efforts that he could make, but rather on the discretionary will of the hacienda owners and *patronos*, individuals' demonstration of merits and

---

*Crawford noted the following remarks by a hacienda owner: "When a young man wanted to get married, he asked his patrón for money for the celebration. For the construction of his house, the patrón sent over the hacienda carpenter and his helpers. The patrón even gave the worker a horse; and for every child that was born, the patrón gave him additional sums of money." Farther on, she indicated that "Protection also meant that the patrón would offer some type of home remedy if he were hurt and would send him to a doctor in Guayaquil for a serious accident."

†The author wrote that "the hacienda came to form a subsystem within the country's political structure, carrying out activities without any link to the State."

aptitudes or their fulfillment of responsibilities was worth little or nothing. In the future what would really matter was the possibility of having influences, connections, and leverage to open doors—directly or through intermediaries. As a popular saying goes, "If you don't have a godfather, you can't get baptized."

The social and political relations shaped by haciendas in the nineteenth century, alongside the adoption of a democratic government and the presence of authoritarian caudillos, accentuated colonial paternalism. The new citizens expected authorities to attend to their needs and solve their problems without having to contribute anything in exchange except for personal adherence and the consequent political support. The paternalistic nature of Ecuadorian society thwarted citizens' development of a sense of community and responsibility, awareness of their civic obligations, willingness to resolve difficulties through their own efforts, and the conviction that they should only seek assistance from the state when they were not in a position to help themselves. To the extent that personal political relations were worth more than institutional relations, the authorities, instead of preserving public interests and serving the common good, responded to private interests and claims of individuals or groups of varied nature, to whom they granted favors and privileges. A political society dominated by paternalism, such as the Ecuadorian society of the nineteenth century, eliminated the possibility that public power would promote the development of the incipient republic and would create conditions for the citizens to forge their economic future.

WEAKNESSES IN EDUCATION

The ideological role that the Church played during the colonial period was legally recognized in the republic because the Constitution of 1830 provided that the Apostolic Roman Catholic religion would be "the State religion" and established the government's obligation of "protecting it by excluding any other." This privileged position was maintained until the establishment of a secular state in the early twentieth century, years after the Liberal Revolution of 1895. Thanks to the "rights and prerogatives" granted to it, the Church was in charge of educating children and youth in schools and universities, operating the civil registry, and preserving the principles dictated by the Catholic orthodoxy so that they would be respected by individuals and institutions in their public and private acts. The Constitution of 1869 even went so far as to demand the Catholic faith as a prerequisite for citizenship.

The clergy in charge of teaching and orienting education were not distinguished because of their academic merits, intellectual openness, and use of reasoning. Two foreign observers noted that the "monks of Quito are ignorant in the extreme"[138] and that the instruction they imparted suffered from "a particular vice" that hindered any development "whatsoever of the child's intelligence, but rather only [his] memory" according to the style of the sixteenth-century European school.[139] Historian Van Aken considered that in the early years of the republic, "The clerical monopoly over education had much to do with the wretched condition of the schools, for most ecclesiastics were poorly trained in seminaries of mediocre quality at best."[140] Only the Jesuits were exempt from this general mediocrity, since, according to several authors, the Company of Jesus was a religious order of austere habits with an inclination to serious scholarship and a vocation for teaching. Orton attributed to them having "infused new life into the fat indolence of the Spanish system,"[141] and MacFarlane described them as "sincere and honest men inclined to save the country and reform the Church," and as "incomparably superior" to the rest of the clergy, morally, culturally, and intellectually.[142] However, in the republic they could not contribute to the economic modernization of Ecuador because they were not in charge of the important entrepreneurial activities that they had administered during the colonial period.

Hassaurek noted that schools were not free, since the government bestowed "very little attention . . . upon elementary education" whereas it supported secondary education and universities. Primary schools taught reading, writing, religion, and arithmetic, whereas in "the higher schools, Latin, and perhaps Greek, monopolize the time of the student." Students learned geography without maps; and although natural sciences and mathematics were neglected, much attention was paid to religious intolerance.[143] At the university, there were schools of medicine, law, theology, chemistry, and natural science. Halfway through the century there were twelve primary schools in Quito, two secondary schools, one university, one art school for drawing and painting, and another for sculpture.[144] At the beginning of the republic, there were three primary schools in Guayaquil and no secondary school, and the children of peasant farmers or workers received no education because of a lack of means or of interest.[145]

In addition to the limited scope of the educational establishments and the meager knowledge they transmitted, the teaching was of poor quality. Hassaurek affirmed that the clergy's knowledge of Latin was "terribly poor," that history and science "was unknown to them," that the libraries were in such a state of abandon that the books were "full of layers of dust and cobwebs" because they "were never consulted" since [the clergy's] "main occupation" was to amuse themselves in a very unwholesome way.[146] Theodore Wolf did a similar analysis when he said that teaching lacked method and, with only a few exceptions, it was not very worthwhile for a child to attend school when "teachers deserving of the name" were lacking. He attributed this shortcoming to the fact that no talented or capable person would have devoted himself to such a laborious trade in exchange for wretched pay.[147] Orton criticized Ecuador's pride in having one university and eleven colleges when people were not educated, the many young doctors had a "strangely dwarfed, defective, and distorted" education, and their knowledge was lacking in practice.[148]

Such opinions were confirmed by De Avendaño when he said that "in general one finds instruction to be to a great extent neglected" because "the higher [education] is in name only" since the university of Quito—from which "very obscure and mediocre people" are graduated—confers degrees of doctor in theology, canon, law, and medicine without having the candidates pass "previous academic courses and studies, according to current law." He also asserted that secondary schools "did not deserve their name" and that primary schools, "even more necessary and essential than the others, are not only not very widespread but also commonly entrusted to inexpert and ignorant people." To this must be added the absence of special schools to form technicians, an area in which there was not even any information.[149] These affirmations were corroborated by historian Gonzalez Suárez, who wrote that philosophy "was the most backward of all the sciences" and that in their studies of physics the students "spent most of their time copying notebooks" since they "never saw any instrument nor watched any experiment."[150]

With such deplorable conditions in education, it is not surprising that Holinksi, in referring to the cultural conditions in Quito in 1852, wrote that the visitors to the public library founded by the Jesuits "were rare" even though it contained fifteen thousand volumes and a selection of modern books. The habit of reading "does not distinguish itself at all among the inhabitants of Ecuador" so that "in all the country there is not even one bookstore or bookseller" and what was sold was "catechisms, prayer books and the novels of Alexander Dumas and Paul Cock." These were sold at fabric stores. He added that in Ecuador there was a one-sheet newspaper "that did not contain anything more than a list of official government acts,"[151] that there was "no desire for reading newspapers among the people of the highlands" since "the average resident of Quito does not read or have any desire to read," and the young people "are not friends of reading and studying." The events that occurred in the world of that era concerned them so little that it had been years since even people that occupied important public positions "had read a newspaper." Thus, "they knew only what they heard about events in the outside world." He ended by saying that in Ecuador there were "convents instead of printing presses and military barracks instead of schools."[152]

Not even progressive Guayaquil could escape from the widespread backwardness in teaching. Holinski contrasted the charm of the Guayaquil women—who were praised by almost all the travelers—with their neglected education, even among the members of high society.[153] Wiener noted that the "instruction of young people was incomplete" due to the lack of educational establishments and because from an early age, twelve or fourteen years old, "most of the youth spent their life behind a counter," selling all sorts of products. This activity allowed them to make a fortune very quickly. He added that in Guayaquil "there is no museum or school of higher learning" and people are not familiar with "the great art of past centuries, not the artistic movement of current times" since censorship has for a long time kept books from "penetrating in the country" and people have "forgotten what use they could make of them."[154] According to McKenzie, at the end of the century in Guayaquil there were three "bitterly partisan" newspapers that "barely published news from abroad" and had a very limited circulation and little influence.[155] The educational deficiencies were greater in other cities, as Hassaurek noted when he said that their inhabitants "live their lives in frank ignorance of the outside world, of great events and of great characters," since not even the whites who knew how to read and write were familiar with books and newspapers.[156]

The void of information and knowledge in Ecuadorian society, the awareness that teaching could not improve with national teachers, and the existence of "an overwhelmingly large number of attorneys" dedicated to litigating and undertaking revolutions for their own interests, must have weighed in the decision of President Gabriel García Moreno to recruit scholars in "modern sciences" from Germany. It was with them that the Polytechnic School was founded, with the aim of introducing students and intellectuals to scientific knowledge transmitted with the "amplitude that corresponded to a university" through the study of mathematics, physics, chemistry, and natural science. By virtue of uncommon government support, the novel educational institution attracted students and housed scientific equipment and collections that probably came to be the best along the western coast of South America. However, it ran up against the economic and cultural limitations of the era, as one of its professors attested. The influential social classes opposed it, the youth "was not accustomed to the effort" that scientific studies entailed, their "former preparation was insufficient" due to the poor quality of primary and secondary schools, and the country did not have an industry where the graduates could practice and find employment. So, many young people did not find reasons for acquiring a profession whose "application in the future seemed doubtful." To this had to be added the widespread prejudice against manual labor, which the polytechnic students considered incompatible with the "professional decorum" that other professions less related to practical activities would allow them to maintain.[157] The alien nature of the Polytechnic School to the national way of life was eloquently described by Theodore Wolf, another of its professors, in the following text:

> Ecuadorians are more addicted to letters than to serious studies; the republic has produced some notable poets and men of literature, but no physicist, chemist, geographer, naturalist, in short, no one that excels in the exact sciences, which require long studies and a great deal of patience. For the same reason that they work more with fantasy and the heart than with understanding and the head, they are fond of music, painting and sculpture, and for these arts show much talent.[158]

The assassination of García Moreno put an early end to the Polytechnic School.

These characteristics of education and the limitations imposed by the environment kept the teaching imparted in primary and secondary schools and in universities from contributing to changes in Ecuadorians' attitudes toward work and science, from improving their behavior in economic relations and productive activities, and from expanding their knowledge. They continued to be speculative beings, alienated from reality, reluctant to take initiatives, with few practical skills, without ingenuity, lacking in openmindedness, and with little sense of forethought, organization, and responsibility. With the exception of Guayaquil, economic activities continued to be submerged in lethargy, as they had been in the backward colonial period. In Guayaquil it was not because teaching had exerted a positive influence—because teaching in the port city was also deficient—but rather due to the economic boost that it had received for the aforementioned reasons.

By virtue of the fact that the social sectors not included in the group of whites did not have access to education—particularly the Indians, who in addition to being illiterate could not even express themselves in the Spanish language, or did so with difficulty—the vast majority of Ecuadorians were not in a position to take advantage of education to improve their preparation, acquire knowledge, better their conduct, and in this way become hardworking and productive. The lack of schools for Indian children, the extreme poverty in which their parents lived, the structures of exclusion to which they were subject, and the dominant groups' shared belief that if Indians had access to education they would become "restless," kept those who did not form part of the dominant society from becoming educated, acquiring knowledge, and thereby improving their economic possibilities.

Since schools did not offer all children and young people equal opportunities to be educated, teaching in Ecuador did not fulfill the role of a unifying force that it has had in other societies, where it has been a determining factor in social mobility and people's economic level. The extreme ignorance existing because of the lack of education is illustrated by Hassaurek with the following anecdote. The machinery of a cotton factory installed between Otavalo and Cotacachi produced such amazement that the Indian weavers thought that it was an "invention of the devil" and that the "prince of darkness made it move" because they could not believe that the machine could weave in an hour what took them days and weeks.[159]

LIMITED FOREIGN INFLUENCE

Colonial domination ended with independence, and the restrictions established by Spain disappeared, so its former overseas territories could have relations with other nations. Nonetheless, Ecuador continued to be isolated from the world, without contacts abroad, especially in the case of the highland cities. Due to the country's remote geographical location, maritime access continued to be difficult. Whoever wished to visit had to make a tiring transfer via the Isthmus of Panama to go from the Atlantic to the Pacific or sail for many days to reach Cape Horn, go around it, follow the coasts of Chile and Peru northward, sail the intricate Gulf of Guayaquil, and finally arrive at the river port located along the banks of the Guayas River. Then, whoever desired to continue on to Quito had to use the grueling colonial route, along which they suffered all sorts of vicissitudes because there were no inns, only places akin to "pigsties" where travelers could rest and regain strength to go on.

The arrival of foreigners in the capital was an exceptional occurrence that gave rise to curiosity. Travelers were lodged in the homes of well-to-do people who kindly offered them housing. Since Quito was not a destination for foreigners, the few who arrived in the capital had to seek "letters of recommendation" so that the families would provide them with a place to stay because there were no hotels where they could find lodging.

All of the visitors received by Quito in the nineteenth century coincided in saying that the capital did not have inns, taverns, cafés, a theater, clubs, public avenues, amusements, "nor any spot for public gatherings and wholesome diversion."[160] Whereas at the beginning of the second half of the nineteenth century, according to Holinski, one hundred Europeans lived in Guayaquil,[161] Osculati had estimated some years before that some twenty Frenchmen, Englishmen, and Italians were living in the capital.[162] Two decades later, Hassaurek calculated that Quito had scarcely a dozen foreigners in addition to the diplomatic representatives of France, England, Spain, and New Granada, and occasionally from Peru and Chile.[163] Orton said that the highlanders, enclosed in the territory of each province, had no accurate idea of the world and not even of their country and that even "the most enterprising merchant" was ignorant of "every thing but Quito and the road to Guayaquil." He added that the first coach, pulled by mules and not horses, was introduced in 1859.[164] This absence of the international world led the people—even the upper classes—to believe that every foreigner was French since the common people did not know of the existence of other countries.[165]

The Ecuadorians' pastimes were playing cards and dice, dancing, drinking alcohol, and going to cock fights, masquerade balls, processions, and funerals, which continued to be characterized by great pomp. Playing Carnival, where people threw all types of liquids and flour on each other, was also popular; and even more so, the bullfights introduced by the Spanish in the colonial period. These took place in improvised bullrings in public plazas and "they were received and viewed not with enthusiasm, but with fervor," according to an Ecuadorian historian.[166] Alcohol was present at all these festivities. According to Graff, "life in Ecuador is a long rosary of parties" at which aguardiente played "a major role." A party "meant no more than an excuse to drink until reaching a blessed state of oblivion, within which what happens in the world outside does not bother them at all." And if "a week goes by without a public festivity, a private one is organized based on dates in the Holy Calendar."[167]

In addition to being the place where the faithful gathered for Catholic religious services, the churches were the most important and most frequented social hub, where the inhabitants of towns and cities came together in the highlands and in Guayaquil. Hassaurek confirmed this when he remarked that since the people of Quito "have nothing to do, and nothing to see, they look upon church as on a theater or a concert room" and "with the same thoughtlessness with which they hum and prattle away at their rosaries and litanies, they pour forth their compliments and assurances."[168]

Parishioners gathered in the churches to see each other, greet each other, chat, comment on political events, show off their outfits, and court.

The geographical isolation was aggravated by a certain xenophobia expressed in silent resistance to foreigners. The travelers who arrived as tourists or to do scientific research were welcomed with notable courtesies and attentions that they had not found elsewhere in Latin America. However, this did not occur in the case of those who were living in Ecuadorian cities, despite the widespread opinion that immigration was beneficial due to the knowledge, experience, capital, and cultural habits that foreigners brought with them and that were so necessary for the country's progress. Ecuadorians, aware that they were not in a position to compete with better prepared and more hardworking people, feared that the foreigners could profit from the wealth of resources they considered their own.

In the early years of the republic, Hall considered that, despite the fact that citizens from other countries had contributed to independence, to the organization of the military forces, and to the development of trade, "in light of the current inhabitants' failure to tap the immense advantages that their very soil offered them," he was not certain that the immigrants would be welcome if they finally arrived in the country. He added that in the event that a foreigner came to discover a mine, introduce a lucrative business, or create an invention that would allow him to access "a new sphere of revenues" and replace an old one, the real or imaginary victims "would not especially view the intruder with favor or satisfaction."[169]

In mid-century, Holinski affirmed that immigration had been rejected "for a long time due to a stupid lack of tolerance."[170] A contemporary researcher added that authorizations requested of the government to permit the hiring of Chinese laborers at the end of the century were refused; and that prohibition became law in 1889 and was confirmed for the next four decades, even during the liberal administrations, at the insistence of Ecuadorian merchants fearful of competition from hardworking Asians.[171] In these old xenophobic, provincial sentiments are found the prejudices against foreign investment that are still alive among Ecuadorians in the twenty-first century, for many view such investment as an instrument of exploitation rather than progress. So, when it finally arrives, it seems "all well and good" that contracts are not honored and that their rights are trampled on.

The closed-minded and dogmatic character of Ecuadorian society also influenced the reticence to anything foreign. The Catholic Church looked suspiciously on ideas taken from other cultures, censored books that it considered inconvenient, persecuted those who dared to voice viewpoints that contradicted its creed, and condemned as heresy any idea that was not in line with Catholicism, and as heretics those that disseminated it. A Protestant minister told the story that, some years after Ecuador had been established, all of the copies of the Bible that he had distributed were gathered up, and their reading was banned under the threat of severe punishment. Years later, at the end of the century, another evangelical pastor said that in the cathedral of Quito a priest threatened to have those of his faith "taken away and destroyed" if they did not convert. Such preaching led to a mob's invasion of the house where the pastor lived with his colleagues, attacks on the street, and on one occasion their being "used as footballs."[172]

Guayaquil, on the other hand—despite its not being located on the major maritime routes of the nineteenth century—due to the cacao wealth, the advantage that it had as a port, and the opportunities offered by the import-export trade, continued to have relations with the world, to receive immigrants and foreign visitors, and to benefit from their influence. These people contributed to changes in the inhabitants' cultural habits, to the appearance of a previously unknown enterprising spirit, and to the introduction of entrepreneurial initiatives, due to which the city progressed at a faster pace than the Andean interior. Nonetheless, around 1880 there were fewer foreigners in the open port of Guayaquil than in "the other large cities of South America," according to the American consul in that city.[173] Despite the small number, they had a positive influence on the progress of Guayaquil. According to one author, "almost all of the modern advances were introduced by North Americans"; for example, the steamboats that navigated the Guayas River and its tributaries, the Daule and Babahoyo Rivers.[174] Noting this beneficial influence led to the recommendation that an emigration society be set up in Paris or London to provide the "professionals that are needed" since "the local environment cannot do so."[175]

The geographical isolation in which Ecuador lived in the nineteenth century kept it marginal to the major migratory flows of that era; and consequently, to the benefits that the immigrants took with them to other Latin American countries, where they introduced ideas, knowledge, and advances that were flourishing in Europe and the United States. The absence of positive European influences kept Ecuadorians from learning sound economic practices, adopting healthy ways of life, acquiring knowledge, assimilating technologies, and becoming infused with a spirit of hard work. Such contributions would have been very useful for modernizing the country, as in fact occurred, to a small extent, in Guayaquil. This absence was seen as detrimental by the travelers that visited Ecuador in the nineteenth century, for one of whom immigration was "the country's greatest need, on a much larger scale than foreign capital."[176]

Guayaquil's relative progress, its openness to the outside world, and Quito's delays due to its confinement were noted by Terry when he said that "relations abroad have done less to modify the customs and manners of the citizens of Quito than those of the citizens of Guayaquil." Therefore, unlike what was happening in that city, the people that lived in Quito were "lagging behind the world by a century."[177]

REDUCED ROLE FOR THE LEGAL SYSTEM

The democratic and republican political system that Ecuador adopted following Independence, despite being radically different from the system of the colonial period, did not contribute to the creation of legal conditions that would induce changes in the behaviors of the inhabitants of the newly founded state, despite the fact the public power was divided into executive, legislative, and judicial functions and that the new institutions were discussed and approved by the citizens themselves, who were recognized as equal under the law and given the right to elect officials and oversee their performance.

The liberties, rights, and guarantees consecrated in the first constitution, and broadened through the eleven that were issued in the nineteenth century, had little practical significance for the majority indigenous population, which continued to be subjected to situations of exploitation and exclusion similar to those of the colonial period. Since legal provisions were not in effect for the Indians, they could not enforce their rights, obtain protection from the authorities, or create conditions that would allow them to overcome poverty, escape the domination to which they were subject, and become citizens capable of exercising free will. Instead, if the content of colonial legislation was compared to that of the era of the republic, they were at a greater disadvantage since the first was broader and more explicit regarding protection of Indian rights. Under the theoretical premise that all Ecuadorians were equal—which did not correspond to reality—the principles of protection contained in the Laws of the Indies gradually disappeared. Whites, on the other hand, strengthened their domination by adding the political power they did not have during the colonial period to the economic power that they still held. They used this situation to maintain their privileges, impose inequality, and increase their abuses. In this way they conserved a social structure that hampered the progress of private economic activities and sound public efforts at national development.

The facts that authority originated in the will of the voters and was subject to the law and to periodical renewal, and that the citizens had legal instruments to enforce their rights, did not mean that the style of authority of presidents, dictators, supreme chiefs, officials, ministers, governors, and intendants was different than the power exercised by those who had governed the Audiencia of Quito in representation of the Spanish king—not even in the brief periods in which a constitution was in force and there was formally a state of law. For this reason it was not possible for the legal system and those that represented it to create conditions for modifying the attitudes that were shaped regarding work and enterprise during the colonial period and transferred to the republic; and worse yet, to organize a society that would offer individuals equal opportunities to construct their own economic future.

Ecuador's first constitution contained only one reference to the Indian population. The "founding fathers" of Ecuadorian democracy, instead of recognizing the legal equality offered by the new political system and establishing guarantees for it to materialize, expressed the pejorative deprecation that the white society felt toward their Indian countrymen. This concept was not modified during the rest of the nineteenth century, and it was permanently evident in the economic, social, and political relations between the two ethnic groups. In effect, Article 68 attributed to the Indians an intrinsic and irrevocable inferiority with respect to the other groups comprising the new republic, by providing that the parish priests be their "guardians and natural parents and imploring their charitable ministry to this innocent, abject and wretched class." If the constitution itself consecrated a provision of this nature, it should not be surprising that horses and mules were called "major baggage" and donkeys and Indians "minor baggage," which according to Hassaurek meant that the Indians were considered inferior to pack animals, "finding themselves only at the same level as a donkey."

In reality, Indians were viewed as "the most important and cheapest beast of burden"[178] that existed on the market. De Avendaño shared a personal experience, when his daughter was transported on a litter by a group of Indians that put together an improvised hammock so that she would not tire when climbing a hill five leagues long.[179] Indians also carried Whymper on an improvised litter from near Riobamba to Ambato, a distance of some sixty kilometers, so that an injury he had suffered on one of his excursions could be treated.[180] "On the back of an Indian" was the term used in that era. Fragile and expensive items were also carried to the highlands from Babahoyo; for example pianos and mirrors and other heavier items such as a bronze statue of General Sucre, which weighed three tons and was transported to Quito on a platform carried by Indians.[181]

The founders of Ecuador wrote constitutions, enacted laws, and represented the state, but they were not men of democratic thought and sentiments. The whites in whose hands those responsibilities lay did not consider Indians and mestizos their equals, that is, the majority of the country's inhabitants. Since the constitutions did not provide for equality before the law, legal principles were not in a position to offer men and women of color the same opportunities that whites had. This meant that the rigid social hierarchies of the colonial period were maintained without any changes whatsoever, along with the discrimination inherent therein.

According to Orton, in the Ecuadorian society of the nineteenth century, politicians made "laws for other people to obey" and under this concept "hatched revolutions when a rival party was in power."[182] Hassaurek said that there was a widespread belief that legal norms had been defined "for people of low social status—Indians and cholos—but not for persons of rank," who, because of their standing "had the right to make laws but not obey them." This lack of the rule of law led him to conclude that Ecuadorians had "established a republican form of government without being republicans."[183] Terry also noted that a republic had been founded "without meeting the basic requirements of that form of government."[184]

The weight of the power structure was so great that the measures that some governments took to improve the living conditions of the poor did not produce the desired effects. When slavery was eliminated in 1851, the blacks, to obtain an income that would allow them to live, had to become bonded laborers because that arrangement was the one means by which they could find a steady job. This actually worsened their economic situation with respect to when they were slaves, since it was much cheaper for the plantation owners to give a credit to a black laborer than to buy him.[185] The suppression of the protectorates in 1854 contributed to alleviating the economic burdens to which Indians were subject, as did the suppression of tributes in 1857, of compulsory work for road construction (as a subsidiary to the cash tax) in 1895, of the territorial contribution, and of the tithes and "first fruits" in 1898. However, these measures did not change the subordination, dependence, and exploitation to which Indians were subject on haciendas by the haughty whites and the mestizo intermediaries, the foremen, and administrators. Attorneys were appointed for the Indians, so that in each province someone would watch over their rights and appear before the authorities to defend them legally. Instead, the attorneys conspired to do the Indians harm since they [the attorneys] were the "most libertine and despicable" professionals in the community.[186]

Not only did people's cultural habits and behaviors keep them from complying with the law, but they also ended up perverting legal principles and putting them at the service of private interests. Throughout the nineteenth century, those who had power used their influence and their personal relations to impose their interests over public interests. For most people, the harm done to the state did not matter, and neither did the fact that individual benefits prevailed over collective ones, as the foreign travelers noted in their chronicles.

Historian Van Aken assured that in the government of President Flores, with whom the republic was inaugurated, "dishonesty on a monumental scale was undoubtedly the most important cause of budgetary deficits." He added that "the extent of graft and theft will never be known, but it is generally recognized that the malfeasance of tax collectors and treasury officials was horrendous." Despite causing the government losses of "enormous sums of money," such "improper" practices did not draw attention because they were "rooted in human nature and honored in Ecuador by custom."[187] Onffroy de Thoron affirmed that Ecuador was governed by men who were "incapable, [and] sof narrow ideas that always sacrificed the nation's general interests for their personal ones."[188] Holinski noted that the authorities "absorbed in political struggles almost did not occupy themselves with settling social disorder" since justice was "venal and corrupt" and the police force "a lucrative industry" that struck agreements with thieves and murderers and "benefited from large sums."[189] Crawford also wrote that ingenious smugglers, taking advantage of their political connections, constantly evaded the customs law in the port of Guayaquil, causing economic damages to the state that nobody was surprised by since contraband was seen as a "respectable" practice.[190] Hassaurek pointed out that the payment that the former slave owners were supposed to receive once their slaves had been freed was only paid to "individuals that had the favor of the government" whereas the others received certificates that, just as in the case of domestic debt, could never be redeemed.[191]

3

CULTURAL CHANGES
IN THE FIRST HALF OF
THE TWENTIETH CENTURY

In 1901, at the start of the twentieth century, *New York Times* journalist Andrew McKenzie, who had been brought to Ecuador by railroad builder Archer Harman, considered the country "one of the most backward in the world" despite being the "richest of the small countries." He believed that this was because its resources "lay sleeping" due to the inhabitants' indolence, which was so blatant that the sheep "died without being sheared." The country's bounty of agricultural resources was such that "no man needed to make much of an effort to feed himself" since "harvesting followed planting all twelve months of the year" and the "grains multiplied three times a year." Nonetheless, the country did not have "trade or scientific farming, [and] no manufacturing," except for those "of ancient times when every man had to provide for himself as best he could." The only resource lacking in Ecuador was mines since, according to the author, the findings of the geologists and engineers "of great prestige" that Harman had brought in were not encouraging. McKenzie's opinions on the national character were so negative and his doubts about the possibility of modifying it so numerous, that he went to the extreme of affirming the country "will never be developed by the Ecuadorians."[1]

Independence, the era of the republic, and democracy did not manage to rouse Ecuador from its centuries-long economic and cultural lethargy. However, the country began to react in the first half of the twentieth century, thanks to economic growth, the Liberal Revolution, modernization of communications, the end of geographical isolation, the Juliana Revolution, and the arrival of immigrants and foreign capital.

The moderate growth of the economy in the nineteenth century, based on cacao, accelerated and reached its peak during the first two decades of the twentieth century, when the average annual value of

Ecuadorian exports doubled over preceding years. According to researcher Crawford, this period of previously unknown prosperity allowed the entrepreneurs involved in the cacao business to bring to the country "more gold than any other group in the history of Ecuador."[2]* In the years after 1920, the economy collapsed abruptly, when cacao production fell by two-thirds as a consequence of the drops in volume and the amount of its sales. At one time, cacao had accounted for 70 percent of exports. This debacle was due to the *monilia* (pod rot) plague (1916); a decline in quality; trade restrictions imposed by England and France (1917); the entry of African (Gold Coast), Brazilian, and Venezuelan products on the market; and the devastating "witch's broom" plague (1922). Other maladies followed, such as the reduction of trade because of World War I, a decline in demand due to international deflation in the 1930s, and the acute political instability into which the country sank between 1924 and 1948, when governments lasted an average of one year.

For these reasons, when the third decade of the twentieth century began, the economy embarked on a deep recession that lasted for more than twenty years. During this time it reverted to the levels of the end of the previous century. Thanks to new export commodities (rubber, balsa wood, oil, gold, and cascarilla) promoted by foreign investment and propitiated by World War II, the economy recovered slowly as of 1942.[3] Despite the improvement experienced by the foreign sector, insofar as per capita exports (US$13) between 1945 and 1949, Ecuador placed behind Guatemala, Bolivia, and Paraguay,[4] countries that it now surpasses.

The Liberal Revolution implemented important legal reforms between 1895 and 1908, especially in the Constitution of 1906 and in the governments of General Eloy Alfaro and General Leonidas Plaza. They curtailed the economic power of the Catholic Church, reduced its political influence, and weakened the control that it held in all fields of knowledge, thanks to which, the minds of the Ecuadorians could open up to modern scientific and philosophical ideas. For the liberal positivists, it was science and reason—not theology—that should orient knowledge and dictate people's conduct. The laws that they enacted separated the Church from the State, to whose authority the Church was subordinated. They also consecrated secular education, reserved management of the civil registry for public institutions, recognized freedom of conscience and religion, determined that religious beliefs should not condition the exercise of political

---

*Cacao exports totaled 310,318 quintales (one-hundred-pound sacks) per year during the first decade of the century, but attained an annual average of 817,706 during the second.

and civil rights, prohibited clergymen from holding public office, eliminated their rights and privileges, and confiscated the religious communities' haciendas.

In addition, the reforms sought to correct social injustice. One constitutional principle ordered public powers "to protect the Indian race." For this purpose, provisions were dictated to prohibit demanding contributions and extra work from Indians, making them serve as stewards in celebrations and ceremonies for Christ-child figures, and charging them fees for administering the sacraments. In 1918, they revoked debtor prison, which was the basis for the bonded labor system and which the hacienda owners had been able to use to their advantage because judges and police officers exercised their authority to ensure that the system of domination and exploitation established by the hacienda owners would not be undermined.

Guayaquil, Quito, and other cities in the highlands and on the coast managed to connect with each other through modern systems of transportation. At the beginning of the century, the use of steamboats to navigate the Guayas River and its tributaries became widespread. This made it possible to reduce travel times to Babahoyo and facilitated the transport of cacao. The road from Quito to Riobamba connected with the railroad that left from Durán, a settlement separated from the main port by the Guayas River. The completion of the railway promoted by Eloy Alfaro and executed by U.S. entrepreneur Archer Harman made it possible for the first train to arrive in Quito on June 7, 1908. A comment in the newspaper *El Comercio* described the transcendental event in the following terms: "A passenger train appeared suddenly, decked out with festoons, palm branches and flags, among which it was possible to distinguish the lovely express car of Mr. Archer Harman. It is impossible to describe the wave of emotion, the joyous awe that invaded everyone, upon seeing the divine monster. It was solemnly and delightfully moving."

In 1918, Guayaquil and Quito were connected to Cuenca, in part by rail and in part by road. Despite their deficiencies, the telegraph and telephone services that were installed in these cities, in those located along the train route, and in some others, allowed Ecuadorians to communicate across large distances for the first time ever. Bemelmans recounted that "only a specialist could handle" the only telephone existing in the settlement of Baños. This called for the telephone operator to "turn the crank for a long time" and go through "a thousand contortions, gestures and shouts that left her exhausted, before she could finally transmit a message."[5] Later on, the rails were laid as far as Cuenca in the south, Ibarra in the north, and La Libertad, which was Ecuador's seaport at that time. These overland transportation advances were complemented by the startup of weekly air transportation between Quito and Guayaquil, in 1929. This later became a daily service and led to the construction of "airfields" in the country's major cities. These were actually rustic landing strips with a little building alongside them that also served as the air terminal. Meanwhile, the first two radio stations with daily nationwide programming were installed in Riobamba and Quito in the 1930s.[6]

Railways, roads, bridges, airplanes, telephone and telegraph communications, and radio transformed the economy in terms never before seen—and with that, certain behaviors of the people as well. The new means of transportation encouraged the installation of industries, the startup of mining and oil activities, greater agricultural production, and the spread of commerce. Transportation of goods and passengers between provinces and regions no longer depended on horseback, muleback, donkey, and Indians, which had worked, unchanged, for nearly four hundred years.

Using the new means of transportation, the few vehicles that existed in Quito and Cuenca were shipped disassembled, along with tons of gasoline so that they could operate. Four centuries had to pass until the train and automobiles finally made it possible to incorporate the millenary technology of the wheel into economic activities. The country had not been able to take advantage of the wheel during the colonial period and the republican period of the nineteenth century due to the total absence of routes that could be transited by carts. However, automobiles could only be used outside the cities and in rural areas as of the 1920s, as roads were gradually built. Even though these roads were dusty in the dry season and muddy in the rainy season, and sometimes impassable, they permitted transit by automobiles, trucks, and buses. The Amazon region continued to be isolated, as did the provinces of Esmeraldas, Manabí, El Oro, and Loja—or served only by precarious communications system. A report by the U.S. consul said that in Esmeraldas there were no automobiles providing transportation services and that "the age of roads had still not arrived in this part of the country. The current means of locomotion were walking, horses or canoes."[7]

A change of enormous economic significance occurred outside the borders of Ecuador when the Panama Canal was inaugurated in 1914. This new maritime transportation option allowed Ecuador to have direct access to the Atlantic Ocean, thereby breaking the inveterate international isolation in which it had lived during 379 years. However, at La Libertad travelers continued taking ships that served international routes and those that arrived in Guayaquil anchored in the middle of the Guayas River, which travelers accessed with help from a boat that they took on the Island of Puná because the port city had no wharf able to receive them. Thanks to the Panama Canal, the country's trade with Europe and the prosperous East Coast of the United States was facilitated, as was the entry of large contingencies of immigrants and foreign capital.* In the 1930s, international air transportation between the United States and Latin American countries was added. All of these were engines for progress that Ecuador had been lacking previously.

In 1925, young members of the military overthrew the government and proclaimed the Juliana Revolution, whereby they put an end to thirty years of liberal domination based on election fraud. They also proposed to deal with the economic crisis originating in the decline in cacao exports and to curtail the abuses and privileges of the "bankocracy" to whose interests the state had been subjected. The governments that followed the military coup, especially between 1925 and 1931 and then 1935 and 1938, undertook profound political reforms that granted the state important responsibilities in national development. For that purpose, the public sector was strengthened and expanded through the creation of oversight agencies for private-sector activities, improved revenue-collection systems, and protection of the rights of workers and employees. The founding of the Central Bank, the Superintendency of Banks, the Social Security Institute, public banking and customs, and tax and budget offices corresponded to this period. Numerous laws were also enacted, notably the ones for banks, currency, taxes, the treasury, social security, and labor. These economic and political changes also created conditions for workers to found the first labor unions.

The new means of communication, the opportunities offered by export agriculture, a certain liberalization of Indian labor due to the elimination of debtor prison, and the ongoing commercial progress of Guayaquil led to massive migration from the highlands to the coast. This in turn led to a decrease in the traditional demographic weight of the first, and an increase in that of the second, which in 1950 came to account for 41 percent of the population of Ecuador, according to the census for that year. Guayaquil outnumbered Quito in terms of inhabitants, and became the country's largest city. Thus, when adding its economic weight to its demographic influence, Guayaquil became a highly significant factor in political decisions as well as in electoral processes. The absence of roads that crossed the eastern Andes, on which construction began in the 1940s, kept the Amazon

---

*Since Ecuador's straw hats left Panama to go to European and U.S. markets, they earned the name of "Panama hats."

region, known as the Oriente, from becoming settled. There, the natural life of scattered Indian ethnic groups was only occasionally disturbed by the presence of daring missionaries and a few military outposts.

The country finally received immigrants from Lebanon, Italy, Spain, Germany, Syria, and China, which were later joined by an important contingent of Jews that came to Ecuador fleeing from the Nazi persecution at the onset of World War II. Even though these immigrations were less numerous than those that arrived in other Latin American countries, Ecuador benefited from their industrial and commercial entrepreneurship. The first investments from the United States, England, and Germany also arrived, for the construction of railroads, the installation of electric power plants, the hanging of telephone and telegraph lines, the exploitation of gold mines and oil reserves, the construction of roads, the provision of urban trolley-car services, the founding of industries, and the development of domestic and international air transportation. A resident of Guayaquil spoke of the foreign presence in the 1930s in the following terms "The North Americans brought development to this country. Our automobiles were North American. The Yankees established the first gas factory here; the locomotives for our railroad were North American, the trolleycars, the first boat that went up the river, and now the power plant, all North American."[8] The Guayaquil and Quito Railway Company built the railroad, the South American Development Company exploited gold in Portovelo, Ancon Oilfields extracted petroleum from the Peninsula of Santa Elena, Dutch Shell Co. drilled for oil in the Amazon region, Cotopaxi Exploitation Co. found gold in Macuchi, and a subsidiary of the German firm Lufthansa (Sedta) and the U.S. firm Panagra started air transportation. Nevertheless, foreign investment was not that significant overall, since, for example, of the nine hundred million dollars that Germany invested in Latin America in 1914, Ecuador received only four million.[9]

Despite the changes mentioned above, in the first half of the twentieth century, Ecuador continued to be a rural and agricultural society in which poverty was widespread and even well-to-do families lived rather modestly in terms of their food, housing, and dress. In 1950, 71 percent of the population lived in the country, and agriculture continued to be the main economic activity, accounting for 39 percent of the GDP and employing 53 percent of the economically active population. Highland agriculture remained plunged in backwardness, as a foreign traveler graphically described it at the turn of the century: "Wooden plows and manual scythes are still used," cereals "are threshed with the hooves of animals," people "throw them into the wind to clean them, using rustic pitchforks, as in the times of King David," and women "spin and weave their cloths as in the days of Solomon."[10] With few exceptions, these practices continued to be present in the agricultural world until the middle of the century, and in some areas for longer. And in the early decades of the century, poor peasant farmers still bartered because they did not have money to pay for their purchases.

PROGRESS ON THE COAST
AND DELAYS IN THE HIGHLANDS

Albert Franklin, a traveler who visited the country on several occasions during the 1930s and 1940s, affirmed that "Ecuador stood still" and that its people "advanced not a step from where they had been during colonial times when they had been visited by Jorge Juan and Antonio [De] Ulloa, the encyclopedist La Condamine, and the geographer Alexander von Humboldt, and during republican times when they had been visited by Whymper, Hassaurek, and Enock."[11]

It really was like that in some senses, especially in the highlands and the coastal interior, but not in Guayaquil, which progressed at a faster pace in the first two decades of the twentieth century than it had in the previous century, thanks to the cacao boom, the opening of the Panama Canal, its favorable geographical conditions, its greater social homogeneity, and its hardworking inhabitants, among other factors.

At the turn of the century, Meyer found in Guayaquil reasonable sanitary services and observed that "the wide street that runs along the banks of the river" (the boardwalk or Malecón) is "worthy of a large Latin American city." However, toward the interior, he noted that "the magnificence disappears," abandonment begins, and garbage appears.[12] Twenty years later, another traveler described Guayaquil as "a clean and modern city" with "wide and open streets," "tasteful, sober buildings," "an air of spaciousness and activity," and hotels "crowded with people."[13] In the early 1920s, a North American physician, R. S. Perry, found that the city had new buildings, urban telephones, some factories, some banks, cable to communicate with the world, electric light, motorized vehicles, movie theaters, and numerous shops that offered "all sorts of merchandise and fine products." In subsequent years, automobiles, trucks, and trolleycars replaced horse-drawn carriages; streets were paved; a sewer system was installed; and thanks to Japanese scientist Hideyo Noguchi and the cooperation of the Rockefeller Foundation, the yellow fever that had inveterately afflicted the residents of Guayaquil was eliminated. In addition, a "spirit of partnership" had developed that led to "forming collegiate bodies to link interests or contribute to public interests with disinterested work."[14]

The case of the highlands was different. There, due to its economic stagnation and the maintenance of the social organization that the hacienda had articulated in the nineteenth century, people's day-to-day life continued to be as in the days of old. For this reason, the ideological openness, greater presence of the state, a certain territorial integration, the migrations, and new entrepreneurial activities were not modified in their essence; and generally speaking, neither were the economic behaviors of the highlanders. Something similar happened with the inhabitants of the coastal interior, where fewer changes occurred due to the barriers imposed by geographical isolation. It can therefore be concluded that in the area of cultural values, except in Guayaquil, the first half of the twentieth century was a prolongation of the nineteenth century, for beliefs and cultural habits gestated in the colonial period and maintained in the early years of the republic continued to condition people's lives and to limit Ecuador's possibilities for advancement.

Several singularities of the city of Guayaquil explain why the cultural changes had greater influence on the inhabitants of the port city. The city maintained its status as the only port, which, according to Franklin, made it possible for it to continue benefiting from the import-export business and to receive a larger contingent of immigrants, attracted by the opportunities offered by its prosperous economy, even though this situation posed military risks and economic difficulties for the country. For this reason, the "ideas and information from abroad were introduced in the port more easily than in the highlands."[15] The first foreign investments in electric power plants, urban transportation, and industrial facilities were made in Guayaquil or surrounding areas. This was also the case with oil extraction in the Peninsula of Santa Elena and the railroad tracks whose construction began in the 1870s. The notable economic growth generated by cacao promoted diversification of economic activities and offered opportunities for jobseekers to find employment and for those that took initiative to start businesses. Guayaquil was a city that grew explosively and was transformed daily, with the number of inhabitants doubling between 1892 and 1919.* It also had less of a social hierarchy since during the colonial period it had not had noble families and had been inhabited mostly by outsiders composed of people from different social positions, ethnic backgrounds, and geographi-

---

*It went from 46,000 inhabitants to 89,771 (Crawford de Roberts, *El Ecuador en la Época Cacaotera*, 106).

cal origins. This was auspicious for more open social relations than in the highlands.

The newcomers' shared desire to make a fortune favored entrepreneurship, encouraged competition, and made economic activities more dynamic. The demand for labor generated by the abrupt growth of cacao production, alongside the labor shortage, made it possible to improve working conditions and raise the wages of peasant farmers and urban wage-earners. The sentiments of independence, freedom, and dignity that animated the character of the montubios made the coastal peasants more open to cultural changes.[16*] Meanwhile, the limited presence of the Catholic Church in Guayaquil, expressed in a small number of convents and clergymen, and the explosive urban growth made "religious indifference thrive"[17] and made the Catholic influence weaker in shaping the economic mentality of the residents of the port city. According to Clark, the clergymen were recruited mainly in the highlands; and of the 458 churches that existed in Ecuador at the end of the nineteenth century, only 53 were located on the coast, and of the 47 convents, only six were there.[18]

These unique features of Guayaquil were not evident elsewhere among coastal cities, where progress was slower. The other cities remained relatively isolated due to the absence or precariousness of communication routes, which were mostly usable only during the dry season, especially in the case of the provinces of El Oro, Manabí, and Esmeraldas. The settlements of Los Ríos could at least communicate with the outside via the Babahoyo River and its tributaries, and those of the interior along the Guayas and Daule Rivers.

The railroad was conceived of to integrate Guayaquil and Quito and not to connect the cities of the coast, the region where the only notable train station was the one in Milagro. There were fewer along the seacoast because of the fear of pirate looting during the colonial period. Also, founding of such settlements had been limited due to the fact that they lacked port services and were only in a position to receive small ships for coastal trade. The relative isolation in which the coastal inlands found themselves, their difficult tropical jungle setting, and the limited domestic and international migration that reached them limited the possibility that the aforementioned changes could modify their inhabitants' behaviors in a way similar to what

---

*The author wrote that montubios were relatively independent "compared to their Andean counterparts" and that they used the term "patrón" more out of a sense of obedience than humility. She added that they "had never been subject to strict terms of bonded labor" and were accustomed to a certain amount of mobility. McKenzie (*Las adventuras de Archer Harman*, 111) found a "marked difference between the servility of the plains Indians and the insolence of the mulattos in the cacao and rubber districts."

happened in Guayaquil. One exception was the small cities that grew up around the area that produced gold (Zaruma, Portovelo, and Piñas, the first a charming city) and oil (Santa Elena and La Libertad).

In the highlands, there were fewer cultural changes due to the region's different socioeconomic characteristics, the idiosyncratic nature of its people, and the limited effects produced by the new means of communication. The roads for carriages and the railroad facilitated relations among individuals, the exchange of goods, and the circulation of ideas. On the other hand, the region's general backwardness, the rural population's subsistence economy, and the relatively high prices of train freight (twice as high as prices in the United States) limited the beneficial economic effects because they had not managed to "link the nation in a large reciprocal system of domestic trade," as Clark noted. And despite the sales of articles produced in the highlands and sold in their natural state on the coast, the same thing did not occur with those transformed industrially, such as flour. Therefore, the great expectations aroused in highland farmers were not fulfilled. Only the mountain town of Alausí could receive a positive cultural influence from Guayaquil. The residents of the port city not only stimulated "projects of civic pride but also new forms of social life" in Alausí, due to the fact that hundreds of families spent their rainy-season vacations there.[19*]

Even though freedom of conscience allowed ideas to circulate freely, the power of the Catholic Church was reduced by the implementation of secular education and a secular state, and large ecclesiastic properties were expropriated, the Church maintained a significant influence due to the widespread religiosity of the highlanders. The economy continued to be primarily agricultural, the population mostly rural, and the haciendas' power to organize economic and social relations remained almost unchanged. Since there was a delay in extending the railroad to Cuenca and Ibarra, the provinces of Carchi and Loja (especially the latter) continued to be relatively isolated. The same was true of the interior areas of all the Andean provinces. The Indians' sentiments of passivity and resignation, shared by mestizos and whites in the countryside and in rural towns, continued to determine the behavior of a significant percentage of the population. The limited economic possibilities that the highlands offered did not favor the arrival of immigrants, and the few who arrived mostly settled in Quito, as occurred with the Jews. This affected the positive influence that people with innovative ideas, determined to do business and anxious to make a

---

*The author noted that the importation of foreign products, including foodstuffs, increased more than five-fold between 1908 and 1918.

fortune, might have had in the provinces. In fact, Franklin noted that Loja had received so few foreign visitors that its inhabitants could remember the names of all of them since Independence.[20]

At the end of the 1920s, Michaux did not find in Quito any trees other than eucalyptus trees, he did not see "wheelbarrows," he did not hear "the rattling of wooden wheels," and he did not see "hauling of any kind."[21] A German traveler considered that the hotel at which he stayed in Guayaquil, despite the fact that it was modest, was "paradise" after having lived in the "awful" Quito.[22] A French traveler had similar feelings of relief when he arrived in Guayaquil and was surprised by the "strange phenomenon" of finding in Babahoyo "a clean bed with white sheets" in a hotel that belonged to a Spaniard.[23] Ecuador's capital continued to be so backward that in the early decades of the twentieth century it was seen by the ministries of foreign affairs of other countries as "a kind of penal colony" to which the diplomats that had committed faults or indiscretions were sent.[24]

Toward the middle of the century, Quito and the highlands showed some progress. The capital and almost all the cities of a certain level of importance had paved or cobblestone streets and had incipient basic services (sewage, potable water, and electricity). They also had urban crank telephones and could communicate by telegraph and telephone. However, Quito did not have international telephone services, and telegrams took three days because they had to go through the North American oil company that operated in the Peninsula of Santa Elena. For this reason, the minister of foreign affairs who signed the Rio de Janeiro Protocol in 1942, establishing the border with Peru, was unable to consult the president of the republic regarding his instructions.

A Jewish immigrant who arrived in Quito in 1939 indicated that the city limits barely went past the colonial part of the city, two-story houses with balconies and courtyards predominated, economic activities were concentrated in the center "where the rich people lived" with an economic level that "contrasted enormously" with that of the poor, there was no middle class, the population used trolleycar transportation and perilous buses, the number of automobiles "was very limited," the dark shops did not have display windows and were lit by "a light bulb without a shade." Furthermore, except for "a few textile plants there was almost no industry worth mentioning" and "skillful craftsmen of all kinds were able to repair the oldest, most worn-out items."[25]

The different paths taken on the coast and in the highlands and the different character of their inhabitants have been noted by Ecuadorian sociologists, researchers, and travelers. Belisario Quevedo cited two types of Ecuadorian people, highlanders and coastal inhabitants, whose differences in character "in the area of the struggle for life is evident." The first type is "concentrated, distrustful, indolent, not very communicative, and more a friend of curves than straight lines." He lives in the "paradise of idleness" so that his chores can be done "any time" or never, or "little by little and badly, anytime." The second is active, free, energetic, straightforward, self-confident, persevering, provident, and practical, "generous and expansive as an individual, very focused, and even egotistical as a collectivity."[26] Alfredo Espinosa said that the highlander "tiringly works soil that is not very fertile" and gathers products that are "not worth much" and that are difficult to transport and thus limited to satisfying local consumption. On the other hand, even though they work lands that do not require much effort since nature "does most of the work," the coastal inhabitants are more daring than the highlanders, but more irregular and improvident.[27] According to an Ecuadorian who at the beginning of the 1890s promoted, in Europe, the construction of a railroad in Ecuador, the people of the coast (i.e., Guayaquil) were "hardworking, advanced, prosperous, full of life," apt on their own "to take any company to the top," full of "confidence and faith in tomorrow" and in "possession of almost all the advances of the century." Highlanders, on the other hand, were unproductive, complaining, unmotivated, sluggish, and not keen on work, so they lived in a wretched state.[28]

The wealth of Guayaquil promoted a virtuous [as opposed to vicious] cultural cycle of beliefs and behaviors among those who went to the port. At the beginning of the century, a French traveler found that "the inhabitants of the warm region were much more hardworking than those of the temperate region."[29] And a Protestant author wrote that "the highlanders—and there are many here—assume a new attitude and lose their fanaticism, stop fearing the clergy, and are willing to be instructed in the way of life. Thus, many, after living in Guayaquil, return to their places of origin in the highlands with a knowledge of the truth that they perhaps would not have acquired if a missionary had gone to their own settlements."[30]

UNEQUAL OPPORTUNITIES

Despite the important economic, social, and political changes that occurred in the first half of the twentieth century, the rigid social hierarchies established in the colonial period and maintained in the early republic continued to be present, above all in the highlands. One manifestation of this was the fact that the Indians continued to express themselves in Quechua and to speak Spanish with difficulty. Spanish was not known by the women, almost all of whom were illiterate. The white oppression was such that there were haciendas on which whips, stocks, and corporal punishment were still in use.

Espinosa affirmed that, just as had happened in preceding centuries, social class was determined by ancestors and skin color, so that it continued to be beneath a person of white race to "occupy himself in ignoble chores." The "superiority of the whites was so widely recognized that the peons in the field used to refer to their master or patrón as 'the white man,' even if he was not a member of that race and was sometimes as much a mestizo or mulatto as they were."[31]

At the turn of the century, German traveler Meyer described the Indians as melancholic, distrustful, submissive, irresolute persons that lived surrounded by filth and did not do hard work without coercion and alcohol, the use of which led them into an unconscious state.[32] Michaux found an indigenous family in its century-old, one-room hut built with compacted mud, covered by straw, and without a vent to extract the smoke from the place where they cooked their food.[33] Franklin noted the custom of the Indians known as *anejos* (or "Indians proper") of kissing the hands of those that did them a favor or gave them a gift. He also cited their subservient responses of "Yes, boss" or "*Arí*, boss," or "Thank you, little master." In addition, he observed that they did not understand "the concept of equality under the law" and were exploited by "members of their own race, even their own community who had learned to read and write and thus gained an ascendency over them" within the system of power created by the hacienda. He recounted that "no smile . . . no gesture . . . no word" with which he tried to approach the Indians allowed him to establish a relationship of "human equality" since he always found servile attitudes that took him back in history to the Middle Ages. He also remarked that in the highland areas, where Indians dominated, "a look at the attitude of each individual" was sufficient "to identify the place he occupied in the rigid and crystallized class system," which in the case of the Indians was possible to perceive with the simple observation of their stature, manner of speech, and "low social standing."[34] In the country's capital city—and worse yet in other highland cities—the same thing occurred. According to a Jewish immigrant, the Indians "greeted one submissively and stepped off the sidewalk to let the 'mister' or the 'gringuita' go by, for they considered them members of the race or class to which they had had to pay respect for centuries."[35]

For their part, the whites, just as in the colonial period, continued to view Indians as inferior, contemptible beings. So, whenever they wanted to debase someone with the worst of insults, even a person of their same social status, they called him a "so-and-so *indio*" or *mitayo, rocoto,* and *verdugo,* which were demeaning, hurtful adjectives considered appropriate for those who belonged to the Indian race. [36] The Indian that redressed his dignity and demanded to be treated as other Ecuadorians was considered an *indio alzado* ("an Indian with airs"); and when some white person did not respect social conventions, he heard disparaging remarks such as "*indio comido, indio ido*" (referring to someone with such poor manners that he would just "eat and run") or "el indio si no la hace a la entrada la hace a la salida" (meaning that an Indian would either "get" you coming or going).[37] The mestizos' conduct was no different, nor was that of the Indians who had managed to improve their economic and social position and who also insulted members of their own race by calling them *indios.*

Bemelmans noted that all of the Quito policemen were mestizos and that the Guayaquil policemen "had never arrested a white man" because whites were people they treated as if they were lords.[38] The same thing happened with the armed forces, where the ranks of soldiers, corporals, and sergeants were reserved for Indians, mestizos, blacks, and mulattos.[39*] So was the obligation of going to fight on the border with Peru since everybody who "had money and good relations knew how to get out of the compulsory military service."[40] Franklin noted that "decent people" of Quito wore shoes (no Indian did) and ties; and they made fun of, and spoke "patronizingly of the quaintness and simplicity of the Quito of the people." They set themselves apart by saying that "decent people do not do that" or by affirming their status with the boastful phrase "after all, we are decent people." He added that, while he was sailing along a river on the coast, the longboat pilot identified him as a foreigner by the mere fact that "he did not speak to him as to a servant" and to the contrary "was courteous and quiet" and did not express a distaste for the food, did not give the impression of believing himself superior to his surroundings nor to his traveling companions, and had seen to "his necessities without complaining about the lack of facilities."[41] Around mid-century, a Jewish visitor affirmed that social rank defined people's behavior, since nobody was surprised "to see Indian women working hard" but on the other hand "it was annoying" for

---

*The author indicated that lower military ranks were held by artisans, peasants, and young people from the middle class who had left school or abandoned their business activities.

European immigrants to "cook, sell sweets door to door, go out into the streets alone, do their shopping at the markets and carry heavy baskets."[42]

These observations by foreign travelers were confirmed by Ecuadorian sociologist Belisario Quevedo: "In our masses there is no sentiment of human equality; inequality does not bother them, and they are content with their luck." So, they did not aspire to "enjoying the comforts that the wealthy classes enjoy." In fact, he had often heard humble people say that something would be "good for the masters to use," which implied that it was not good for them.[43]*

The continuation of such rigid social hierarchies meant that a small group of Ecuadorians maintained their old privileges and added new ones, whereas the majorities continued to be subject to all sorts of obligations. Social differentiation was not perceived of as important because people on both sides continued to view it as natural. For this reason, despite the changes that occurred at the beginning of the twentieth century, it was not possible to form a society composed of citizens sharing similar rights and obligations and enjoying equal opportunities. Those who occupied lower positions on the social scale because of their skin color, surname, or economic condition did not have any kind of opportunity to obtain an education or a good job, or to progress in conditions equivalent to those of privileged people in higher social positions. The force of the social hierarchies was so great that not even the laws issued with the aim of correcting inequalities—in terms of access to goods, services, and rights—produced the desired effect. The old segregationist socioeconomic structure took precedence over them and, with its power, ended up leaving them without effect or accommodating them to its conveniences.

A society in which birth determined people's social and economic position, and during the course of their lives closed doors to some and opened them to others, deprived its members—even those that occupied positions of privilege—of incentives to introduce business innovations or perform jobs requiring hard work that would allow them to get ahead. Those who had a fortune did not see the need to make an effort to conserve their economic status or increase their wealth, and those who did not have a fortune were convinced that their sacrifices were not very useful for improving well-being. This passivity deprived Ecuadorian society of an element that is fundamental in the economic progress of individuals, companies, and

---

*The author explained this fact by the deep feelings of inferiority implanted in the Indians as a result of the Conquest, a complex that affected 80 percent of the population.

countries: the desire to get ahead and the ambition to make one's fortune through hard work.

INFLUENCE OF TRADITIONAL VALUES

Despite Guayaquil's progress and the hardworking attitudes adopted by its inhabitants, in the first half of the twentieth century Ecuador was no different than it was in previous centuries in terms of the citizens' cultural habits and the country's level of development.

At the beginning of the century, Delebecque considered that "the state of sanitation in Quito was so bad that it was better not to mention it," that the "filth in Ecuador, at least in the highlands, surpassed anything that one could imagine," especially in eating and sleeping areas. Referring to the important Chiquipoguio stopping-place or resting house that had horrified Whymper, the French traveler added that he doubted "that there is a real desire to progress in a town that would allow" such wretched, flea-ridden lodging.[44] Almost all of the houses in the highlands continued to be plagued by these insects, so that the unpleasant habit of hunting, trapping, and killing fleas on other people—mentioned in the previous chapter—continued.

Years later, Bemelmans confirmed the absolute lack of hygiene. At a Riobamba hotel located near the train station, there was no soap and the towel that hung on the wall was the size of a sheet of newspaper folded into fourths, and it was "filthy and gray." Along the way, people, even first-class passengers, got out of carriages at rest stops to eat at improvised dining rooms covered by a canopy installed by the side of the railway, where food was served on plates "that have been licked clean but never washed."[45] The often quoted Espinosa said that not only the cleanliness of bodies and clothes "left a lot to be desired" but also of rooms, since there was a habit of dry-sweeping them and spitting on the floor, which contributed to the transmission of infectious diseases such as tuberculosis, especially on the coast. This lack of hygiene was repeated on streets and squares, which had heaps of trash and waste that had not been collected in a timely, efficient manner. He added that in the highlands, "there was horror at the water, and baths were taken with an unbelievable frugality," since some people came to consider them detrimental to their health.[46] After speaking about the poor hygiene that he had observed in Riobamba and in the villages of the plains, Meyer wrote that the filth was "cultivated with love and perseverance." According to the German traveler, this could be explained by the fact that in Ecuador "the Spanish Creole and the Quechua Indian live and work together, [both] peoples disinterested in day-to-day cleanliness."[47]

This widespread lack of personal and environmental hygiene continued to be a "petri dish" for bacteria and parasites that led to diseases and epidemics of all sorts, among them, tuberculosis and the feared bubonic plague. To the population's scant interest in personal hygiene, upkeep of their homes, and clean public areas must be added the lack of potable water and sewage services. For this reason, even in the major cities there were no bathrooms or latrines, and not even well-to-do families had them. To substitute for these, there was the corral, the backyard, or the garden, where those who did not have an umbrella got wet on rainy days.[48] The absence of sanitation services only began to be corrected toward mid-century.

Franklin's tales were similar. Like other coastal cities, Babahoyo was a group of "bamboo houses on piles" that were lacking in comfort and hygiene. Despite being located on fertile lands, the "modern village" of Ibarra, like other cities, lacked sanitation and cleanliness, so the threats of infections were constant. They did not have good communications, and the railroad provided only a weak contact with the outside world due to its scant use. There was no market for agricultural products and the "handful of telephones" that existed were almost worthless, since they did not make it possible "to obtain the rapid assistance of a good doctor" or close a business deal. In the construction of a highway in the province of Azuay, tractors, rock crushers, cement mixers, and bulldozers were not used because manual labor was cheaper. The farmers in the area did not select seeds for cultivating corn; they planted the same grains that they ate, which, because they had "run out" long before did not allow them to have good harvests, according to the comments of a Minnesota farmer that was there building a road.[49]

As had occurred in previous eras, the survival of old practices, beliefs, and attitudes insightfully described by two Ecuadorian sociologists influenced Ecuador's backwardness in the first half of the twentieth century.

Belisario Quevedo characterized Ecuadorians' attitudes and behaviors as follows:

> Nonchalance, indecisiveness, dismay at the thought of great effort, especially continuous effort; a propensity to restless laziness resulting in more noise than work; preference for fierce, short-lived spurts of work over relaxed, long-lasting effort made in equal doses; waiting to do business until the last minute and always relying on chance and luck, because they do not foresee the most inevitable contingencies, or do not want to.

Further on, he added that his fellow countrymen were more instinctive than reflective, slaves to traditions, individualistic, self-centered, "alien to social discipline, cooperation, [and] solidarity." He also said that they demonstrated "aversion to sustained and persevering effort," admired and sympathized with those "who spend and sterilely waste their fortune," expressed a "kind of disdain" for everything that was "foresight, order and personal effort," and acted "in bad faith with different nuances." He remarked that such conduct was not to be put past merchants, artisans, members of the military, policemen, politicians, clergymen, officials, Indians, ultimately everyone—no one was exempt from such conduct. Referring to Indians, even though the observation was also valid for whites and mestizos, he repeated what foreign travelers from previous centuries had written: "they lived in [an] alarming [state of] drunkenness."[50] Niles described a scene that was common in cities, villages, and roads in the highlands on Saturdays and Sundays after the open-air market activities: drunken Indians lying on the ground, solicitously cared for by their wives, who had abstained from drinking to protect and care for their husbands.[51] Michaux considered that Indians "like to get drunk like nobody else in the world, not just getting drunk one or two nights, no." During religious celebrations, they were "drunk for three weeks."[52]

Alfredo Espinosa Tamayo confirmed what Quevedo said. Ecuadorians were always disposed "to easy enthusiasms rapidly snuffed out." So that they undertook projects "that they abandon the next day," forgetting them after they have been launched and received "with great passion and fervor." Bureaucrats, military men, professionals, and members of the middle class in general sought "occupations easy to perform," "hated work, lived pretending to work, nourished false luxury" and when they emigrated to the coast, "they failed due to their lack of preparation for life's struggles." They were lazy, verbose, melancholy, arrogant, suspicious, distrustful, [and] improvident; and their volubility made them "easy prey for enthusiasm and discouragement, especially in the case of the highland *chullas*,* whom he described as "incorrigible bohemians" and people that "want to and can't." Since there were no amusements, both the peasant farmers and the city-dwellers were "very contaminated by the vice of alcohol, which was more widespread than in other countries." As for the Indians, he indicated that, despite their undeniable laziness, "they are much more hardworking than the mestizos and whites of the cities." However, he characterized them as indolent, servile, distrustful, impassive, resigned, set in their ways, alcoholic, and given to theft.[53] As an example of their lack of flexibility,

---

*A Quechua expression used to describe those that had only one suit but many social pretenses.

one author mentioned the Indians' resistance to making furrows against the direction of the slope, which was necessary to avoid erosion and the loss of soil quality.[54]

Researchers, travelers, and immigrants reiterated much of this. Clark cited an official report at the turn of the century, which spoke about lethargic young people who refused to work, and about educational and repressive measures taken by the liberal government against vagrancy. He added that, when construction was undertaken on the railway in the foothills of the Andes, it was necessary to import four thousand Jamaican workers because of the national labor shortage or the labor force's poor performance.[55] Around the same time, Meyer found in Ecuador "good elements in the population" and "a large number of very honorable men" who were unfortunately helpless to impose their good habits "among the great majority" who acted otherwise. He added that "even the high social classes" bragged about a culture of "varnish and whitewashing." They only provided a service when "it does not cost them effort and money." He went on to say that they spoke a lot "but for energetic action they are lacking in strength" and are overdue in the payment of their debts. He also thought that becoming "rich without working is their ideal" and that "their ineptitude to compete with the steady and upright work of Europeans and North Americans"[56] gave rise to these practices.

Later on, in the decade of the 1940s, Weilbauer noted that, even though there were no robberies in the ceramics factory that he installed in Quito, the workers were characterized by their lack of "compliance and sense of duty," although both of these concepts seemed basic to the German-Jewish immigrants. He was surprised that when they were absent from work they would make up "the most incredible excuses instead of telling the truth," that "well-educated people" did not "fulfill their contracts and commitments, or did so late," and that arriving on time for an invitation was "considered impolite."[57] Around the same time, Franklin noted that in Loja "there are no games, almost no sports, except for drinking, murmuring and politics"—in addition to being "a population where almost no one works." He indirectly suggested that Ecuadorians did not realize that mere words, promises, and good intentions were not enough. They lost resources and wasted their energies and efforts trying to do everything at the same time. In addition, they were not very willing to make personal sacrifices to join forces and attain common objectives that it was not possible to achieve individually.[58] Kreuter wrote that Ecuadorians did not understand why Jewish immigrants did their chores "in such a hurry" if there was always a tomorrow to do them. At the same time, the Jews were surprised that the responses of "coming right up" ("*ya mismo*") or "tomorrow" did not mean that something would actually happen "right away" or the next day, but rather "some day in the more or less distant future." Likewise, it was difficult to receive an unequivocal "yes" or "no" as a reply to a request or "timely notice" from a person that "was not going to be able to keep an appointment."[59]

As had occurred in preceding centuries, the lack of respect for property rights continued to mark relations that Ecuadorians established with each other or maintained with public institutions. What happened with materials used in building and operating the railroad illustrates this. Even though the railroad belonged to a foreign company and was the state's, sticks of dynamite, telegraph line wire, crosses and nails from the rails, wooden posts, and telephone insulation were all stolen by peasants, artisans, merchants, and, in general, all kinds of people, in complicity with scheming authorities who acted with those implicated, or protected them when they were discovered. Even a bridge disappeared overnight. Because thefts were repeated and uncontrollable, they became "endemic" both on the coast and in the highlands.[60] These losses caused the railroad service to become paralyzed and caused economic losses for its users, some of whom were from the same region as the transgressors.

In one of his reports, Professor Kemmerer, an advisor to the Ecuadorian government, noted that a senator who was entrusted with buying ten thousand saddles from the United States for the Ecuadorian army's cavalry regiment, bought them at US$7 apiece and billed them to the state at US$40. His earnings were so significant that later "he was very pleased to enjoy permanent residence in New York."[61] Sociologist Belisario Quevedo affirmed that "the public works contract in which a more or less sizeable mischief is not involved must be rare" and that "fraudulent contracts with the State; monopolies created by venal or complacent lawmakers, or authorized by corrupt officials; [and] timely variations in customs duties, are the origin of many fortunes, and all of these bear the stamp of plundering."[62] Franklin attributed the collapse of several buildings during the 1942 earthquake that affected Guayaquil to the fact that the builders, to increase their earnings, had reduced the proportion of cement in the reinforced concrete.[63] Weilbauer recounted that public employees, due to the poor salaries they earned, even "at the highest spheres" sought "additional income in any form." This corruption included buying off judges and witnesses "for a few sucres." Since in commercial relations, "debts were paid as late as possible, on principle" and the risk was run that the value of the merchandise sold on credit would not be collected, he decided to forego expanding the operations of his factory.[64] If he had gone ahead with the expansion, the community would have benefited economically and socially, because he would have needed to hire more workers and buy larger volumes of raw materials.

The case of contraband was another illustration of how prevalent corruption was. A French traveler who visited the country in the early years of the twentieth century wrote that customs employees in Guayaquil had the "annoying habit of collecting a fee in advance on the merchandise that passed through their hands," in addition to switching the contents of goods with no declared value through "marvelous tricks of prestidigitation."[65] According to Crawford, the practice begun in the colonial period of "unloading imported products at a prudent distance from the wharfs of Guayaquil" continued during the twentieth century since, for many, "deceiving customs officials has always been respectable" since contraband was seen as a "special privilege of the commercial oligarchy." Those involved in the devious act took advantage of connections, special customs arrangements, and a "price," that is, a bribe paid to the customs official that had expedited the "little operation." Contraband and the intricate network of interests and complicity to which it gave rise made the mechanisms that the liberal governments wanted to establish to persecute customs fraud "last little." These controls were viewed by everyone as "odious." In 1910, coastal merchants rose up for the "purpose of redressing their rights," and with this forceful measure they managed to cancel a contract signed with a foreign company to inspect customs transactions, thanks to whose effective management it had been possible to "put an end to contraband and increase revenues in a surprising manner."[66] The citizens did not see smuggling as an act that went against the law or public interests, or as discriminatory against those that paid duty on imported goods, but rather as a privilege to which certain people were entitled because of their social position or political influence, or as retribution for services provided to the government during election campaigns. Quevedo confirmed this when he mentioned that many had gotten rich from contraband, "even leading men in politics, heads of the (Conservative) party of *order and legality*."[67]

"And who thinks it is wrong to steal from the State?" inquired Belisario Quevedo.[68] Alfredo Espinosa passed judgment as follows: "If people are accustomed to considering the administrators of public funds swindlers, it would seem that the latter believe that they are obliged to justify the popular belief."[69]

Ecuadorians' behavior in their private relations and business relations was no different. The lack of trust even in the word of people from the same social circle, partners, and counterparts was illustrated by Michaux when he said that "all those around him" lied with the "greatest naturalness." This circumstance led him to do the same, even though lying had not made sense to him before that.[70] Espinosa said that in the highlands, to avoid the losses caused by stealing from gardens, farmers were forced to sell their fruits before harvest-time, and buyers had to pick them before they ripened in order not to lose them.[71] Franklin wrote that along an unknown road "he could not receive assistance from an Indian boy because his father would not allow it," thinking that since he [Franklin] spoke "Christian" the father ran the risk of losing his son. However, had he known that Franklin was a foreigner, he would have "obliged his son to help him." And when he asked for directions to visit the castle of Ingapirca, the peasant whom he asked believed that Franklin, like the other "gringo" who had come before, was looking for gold and not the Inca ruins.[72] An Adventist missionary in 1934 recounted that "many times" Indians approached his church "with the hope of obtaining material assistance" and that they left as soon as they realized they would receive no economic benefit.[73]

Just as Hassaurek had noted in the nineteenth century, Weilbauer underscored the beneficial influence that Protestantism had on people's morality. A servant who worked in the home of his family denied that she had stolen his wife's jewelry but returned it fifteen years later, prompted by the requirement of the evangelical community that she had joined that, before adopting the new religious creed, she had to "free herself from all the sins committed in her life."[74]

Foreigners, as before and still now, were viewed as easy prey for all sorts of deceit. One traveler told the story of how the person who was selling her a hammock in Guayaquil tried to trick her once she had paid for it by giving her one of "inferior quality and size."[75] Bemmelmans wrote of a hotel in the province of Imbabura where they tried to make him pay for a newspaper that was distributed free of charge to guests; however, since he was a foreigner, they had taken him for a "moron."[76]

In Guayaquil, there was no change in the propensity to unproductive, sometimes ostentatious, spending devoted to pastimes and buying imported items, some of them lavish. This inclination was shared by broad segments of the population, not only well-to-do cacao growers and exporters. This spending was sizeable in the case of the hundred or so large landowners who moved to France to live, or spent long periods in Paris, enjoying the good life that their fortune permitted, while it lasted. Some resources, undoubtedly not enough, were allocated to financing the expansion of the plantations, but not to improving production systems, whose increased output was due, rather, to the expansion of agricultural frontiers through the incorporation of unused land. There were cases in which the emigration of affluent residents of Guayaquil served to improve their cultural knowledge and for them to learn new techniques that would yield benefits for urban and rural economic activities.

Despite the economic changes, just as had occurred in previous centuries, some people who managed to accumulate capital in the highlands continued to keep money and jewelry in "trunks hidden inside walls and floors or simply inside mattresses."[77] Indian peasants wasted the few economic resources they had on unproductive activities, especially alcohol and religious festivities. Residents of Quito, and highlanders in general, were described less as spendthrifts and more as savers than coastal residents—and even as stingy, especially those that were less well-off. On the other hand, the families that had fortunes were "wasteful and splendid," but only in the "ornamental and external" since their houses lacked comforts.[78] Michaux told of how a foreigner could travel with merely the label of "a gentleman" because Ecuadorians were incredibly hospitable and so generous that he had met "more than one" [Ecuadorian] who, having been an "arch-millionaire," had for that reason lost his fortune.[79] Crawford cited a report that affirmed that rich residents of Quito sold their jewelry and mortgaged their homes to buy elegant evening gowns and attend the opera that came to Quito. He added that the railroad, by allowing merchants to reach the highlands, increased the propensity to consumption and reduced the capacity for savings.[80]

There were highland hacienda owners who, like their coastal counterparts, moved to Paris accompanied by their families, where they lived off the earnings of their haciendas. These earnings were periodically remitted to them by their administrators. In some cases the high costs of Paris and the economic damage caused by those left in charge of their properties left them in poverty. I once met a widow in Quito who owned a huge piece of agricultural land, among other properties; she moved to Paris and many years later returned to Quito in the most abject poverty. She told me that she and her three children, accompanied by a servant, had traveled to Guayaquil by train and then continued to the port of La Libertad by *autocarril* (a bus-like train that traveled along a single rail). A boat took them to the ship that was anchored at sea—and they wore yellow shoes, which they had been told would be good to avoid getting seasick. While abroad, they only became familiar with Paris and the surrounding areas, and no other European city.

Despite the fact that the first banks that managed to last were founded in Quito and other highland cities, the people who saved, because of the inveterate lack of confidence, continued to stash their money away instead of investing it in productive activities that would have made it possible to obtain revenues and contribute to the country's progress. This was noted by Alfredo Espinosa when he said that the savings "remained stagnant due to the lack of confidence," which worsened with the failure of banking institutions. This reluctance made highlanders in the working, middle, and upper classes hide their money (if they were not involved in usury) instead of keeping money in savings and loan associations or credit institutions, thus "making unproductive and stagnant a part of the wealth that in other countries was a driving force for commerce and industry."[81] However, highlanders were more likely to save than the coastal residents; and when the banking system developed toward the middle of the century, their savings helped to fund the aspiring businesses of the coast instead of the economic activities of the highlands, which were still scarce.

In the first half of the century, paternalism began to find expression in the political field, as more people were incorporated into public life. Freedom of suffrage, women's right to vote, urbanization of cities, the radio's mass media role, new communication networks, and modern transportation systems all contributed to this. Thanks to these transformations, people could be informed about public matters, attend political meetings, vote in elections, and take their demands to authorities.

The political influence that people attained through their votes, and the need for the candidates to obtain votes to win an election, contributed to the expression of paternalism not only in patron–client relations and personal relations in general, but also in political ones. Since the Ecuadorians' mentality was impregnated by paternalistic culture regardless of their social position, their behaviors were driven by their values when they had to act in public life, attend political meetings, participate in political parties, intervene in electoral processes, cast their ballots, and demand attention to their needs.

In the words of Alfredo Espinosa, "a mass of people" with limitations "for understanding ideas that are abstract and too subtle and complex," with little democratic experience, accustomed to "caudillo systems and military governments," upon encountering "demagogic excesses" incarnated "their ideas in one man and concentrated all of their aspirations in a providential being that they surrounded by a halo of glory, with all of the exaggeration and all of the vehemence that tropical imaginations lend to their passions and their affections."[82] This analysis was shared by Quevedo when he noted that "we Ecuadorians feel an innate need for protection by the government, a caudillo, a savior, a hero; we always want to find a man to whom to give all of the powers, and all of the liberties that we gladly renounce for ourselves."[83] José María Velasco Ibarra was the first caudillo that took on this role in the 1930s, and he played it so well that he led Ecuadorian politics for almost half a century and left behind followers that periodically resurged until the twenty-first century.

Whereas the citizens who took part in politics in the nineteenth century and the early decades of the twentieth did so driven by ideological motivations, as liberals or conservatives, those who became involved in public life later on were driven by their needs and frustrations. The migrants who came to the cities from the countryside, in droves, discovered that their participation in elections could be profitable if they could get neighborhood leaders and local caciques to intervene with authorities for their demands to be met. In addition, in the backward Ecuador of those days, where there were few economic activities in the private sector—and these were weak—government offices, municipal offices, and other public institutions became important sources of employment. Alfredo Espinosa referred to this when he said that the distribution of public-sector positions followed the criterion that "it is necessary to keep friends and party members of the Head of State content, without consulting the aptitudes that they have to perform." Such positions were considered "prebends and sinecures" (benefits) with which unconditional political adherence was rewarded.[84]

In this way the patron–client roots of the paternalistic society inherited from the colonial period and the early years of the republic were maintained and deepened. Just as in previous centuries, but with a broader scope, social ties of family, friendship, and party were worth more than laws, merits, or prerequisites if a citizen desired to obtain retribution, a benefit, or recognition. The fact that personal ties weighed so heavily in the destiny of individuals reduced the incentives that are usually needed for people to educate or train themselves, take initiatives, and work with effort since their future would not depend on their virtues but rather on the possibility of influencing those who could do them favors and grant them benefits. Crawford mentioned that "the inhabitants that lived along the railroad demanded expensive electric power installations and tracks to their localities. And they got them."[85]

CULTURAL ELEMENTS IN
CONSERVATION OF THE STATUS QUO

The institutions established by the Liberal Revolution reduced the Church's economic and political power, but not its cultural influence, which remained in force, especially in the highlands. Since Catholicism continued to be the religion of almost all Ecuadorians, broad sectors of the rural and urban populations continued to explain natural phenomena, political positions, and their economic conditions through religion.

In referring to the early twentieth century, Espinosa said that even though new ideas and the triumph of the liberals had taken away from the clergy "a great deal of their old influence," it had not ceased to be "quite powerful, especially in the Sierra" since the "popular class" had been marked "by its religious fanaticism and the domination that the clergy had exerted over it." He added, "The convents have not produced anything in many years, and the religious laymen are more of the 'go to mass and eat out of the pot kind.' They are not concerned about one another except in the outside religious ceremonies, to inflame the piety of the faithful, without undertaking any social mission whatsoever or using their influence in benefit of the moral education of the people."[86] Well into the century, Peralta affirmed that "fanaticism in our republic has all of the [same] awful traits as it did in the Middle Ages."[87] Clark sustained that the Catholic Church was opposed "to the kind of economic motivations that would lead to increases in agricultural output" as well as to valuing earnings. Had such attitudes flourished, they would have contributed to "improving the productive systems." He added that "the immigration of non-Catholics was not looked well upon" and that the Church "aimed to keep those people" in their places of origin so that the faithful could not be exposed to new ideas if they traveled and had contact with people from other latitudes. He concluded by saying that the law that expropriated the haciendas of the religious orders (eighty-six in eight highland provinces) was called the "Law of Dead Hands" because the lands that were affected lay fallow.[88]

Despite the fact that the Liberal Revolution was determined to modernize education by introducing the study of sciences and technical education, it continued to suffer from the limitations of previous historical periods that had kept education from contributing to the formation of practical mentalities capable of tapping the economic possibilities offered by the country and encouraging individual and collective progress. Espinosa established this in his classic work, mentioned above, and in a study on problems in teaching. Even though he recognized that public education had improved, he believed that it continued to be deficient, backward, and incomplete because, generally speaking, it did not develop "the pupils' minds perfectly" since "the sciences, particularly the exact sciences, were scarcely cultivated and therefore scientific literature [was] rare, with the exception of works of law and history."[89] The teaching of arithmetic was reduced to "students memorizing the rules and mechanically doing the operations without its occurring to them [the teachers] to take advantage of this teaching to make them [the students] see the practical applications for using it, nor awakening in the children the spirit of observation and logical reasoning and discernment." The same thing happened with grammar, whose rules students knew perfectly well, yet they spoke and wrote Spanish very badly. He lamented the fact that education did not inculcate "constancy, energy, personal initiative, an enterprising spirit, a sense of duty and obedience, a spirit of solidarity" and compliance with the law.[90] These opinions were shared by Belisario Quevedo, when he wrote that "The university student is brilliant when he memorizes the text, the dogmatic manual of official science, which never speaks of life's pressing realities nor knows how to awaken a critical sense and does in no way address old and new national issues."[91]

According to Espinosa, this deficit in scientific education led empiricism to be in force in politics, economics, industry, and agriculture, that is, in all activities and in those that performed them. So, "high and superior" ideas could not be transmitted, whereas, on the other hand, those that were "easily accessible to intelligences little accustomed to analysis and perception" were the ones disseminated. The lack of an appropriate environment and suitable means, in other words, incentives and instruments that would favor scientific efforts, made such efforts practically nonexistent. All of Ecuador's scientific culture was therefore owed to foreigners, and "the studies of greatest interest for the country—geographical, ethnographic, geological, and mineralogical ones—had been done by them." Referring to the "wealthy classes," Espinosa mentioned that a large number of their members were "empirical or rudimentary in their procedures" since, though they were not ignorant, one could not say they were instructed either since they had had a "frivolous and superficial education, distant from any administrative or professional skills, a weakness that kept them from influencing the country's progress." The professions were reduced to law and medicine, and the attempts made to establish technical careers were just beginning to bear fruit.[92] In that regard, it is worthwhile to note that in Loja, a city that had ten thousand inhabitants and 1,500 attorneys, Franklin observed "a concentration of knowledge and culture" superior to that of the largest cities in the United States, but that, nonetheless, did little for the country's progress since they were people "unskilled for practical manual labor and financial matters."[93]

At this point it proves useful to share an experience of a German traveler at the beginning of the century, since it is revealing of the fantasies in which Ecuadorians lived and the widespread ignorance about basic scientific concepts. Upon returning to Quito after climbing the Cotopaxi volcano, as he rested at an inn he encountered a group of Ecuadorian army officers who "recounted in all seriousness" how the last eruption had shot out "a wooden table with the name of a ship that shortly before had sunk off the coast." This "proved with unquestionable evidence the connection of the Cotopaxi with the [Pacific] Ocean." Meyer added that the fact confirmed a similar experience of his fellow countryman Stüben, who in 1873 was asked in Quito by "a number of people," including a high government official, "if he had seen in the Cotopaxi crater the large ship anchor that the volcano had expelled a long time before."[94]

If the knowledge of those that had some education was so limited, one can imagine what occurred among those that had none at all and lived in isolation in the countryside or in certain provinces. For this reason, if one of Franklin's anecdotes is believable, many were not even aware that they were members of a political society called Ecuador. About forty years ago, a small-scale farmer in the province of Azuay thought that Ecuador bordered France; "had no notion of any of the [country's] last three presidents"; gave the impression that he was not sure that he was Ecuadorian; thought that Franklin was a mason since he was a foreigner; and when he learned that Franklin was from the United States, asked if "that was in Peru."[95]

Just as in previous centuries, legal norms continued to carry little or no weight in the daily life of Ecuadorians; and when they were enforced, it was in a lax and biased way. The failure of the laws is evident: "they are in writing," said Quevedo.[96] Along the same line of thought, Espinosa considered one of the vices of public life to be "the lack of respect for the law, the facility for failing to abide by it, and the frequency with which it is infringed upon by the very ones entrusted with enforcing it" since "any individual given authority" places himself above the law "without detriment to applying it harshly to those that are under his authority."

Thus, those governed saw the state as "a despotic force, always willing to restrict their rights" and viewed authorities as a source of "abuse and exactions."[97] An author who studied Indian issues rightly affirmed that "neither yesterday nor today, never, has the Law met Indians on the terrain of justice and with the clear intention of seeking their welfare."[98] In 1922, a respected socialist jurist came to the following conclusion: "We have many laws, and theoretically very well thought-out: the Eight-Hour Law, the Traffic Accident Law, the Law for the Instruction and Protection of the Indian Race, etc., but which one is enforced? None of them. Wage-laborers, peons, and masons work ten and twelve hours a day. There is still no example of a monetary indemnification for work-related accidents, and the ignorance of the Indians could not be any greater, nor the slurs with which they are treated."[99] Quevedo attributed this persistent illegality in the day-to-day life of Ecuadorians to the belief that legal norms "can do anything, and create anything," a belief derived from Latin education.[100]

Just as in the nineteenth century, those who had government responsibilities believed that the issues submitted to their consideration would be resolved by simply enacting laws. They did not stop to reflect on the laws' relevance and applicability as a function of the economic and social realities in which they had to operate and the power factors that would interfere to undermine them; or on the fact that in the minds of the citizens, the law was not usually present to orient their everyday acts.

The abolition of debtor prison in 1918 is just one example of the many that could be cited. Even though hacienda owners could no longer take advantage of personal pressures in order for peasant farmers to fulfill their labor obligations, farmworkers could not freely negotiate the value of their labor due to the stratified and paternalistic society that existed at that time, and the fact that the haciendas were the main source of employment—and in some places, the only one—except during the cacao boom.

Albert Franklin wrote that Ecuador's "laws in matters relating to social legislation are often more advanced" than those of the United States.[101] Despite the fact that this was actually true, Ecuadorians' well-being at the middle of the twentieth century was notably inferior to that of the North Americans, not only because of the failure to comply with legal norms, but also because social hierarchies and economic stagnation kept the country from offering its citizens opportunities to improve their living conditions through work.

CULTURAL ELEMENTS IN CHANGE

The freedom of thought imposed by the Liberal Revolution, alongside the adoption of secular teaching in public primary schools, secondary schools, and universities; some circulation of ideas and knowledge; and fast and modern communications, contributed to decreasing the hegemonic influence that the Catholic Church had had in shaping Ecuadorians' mentality. The founding of the Colegio Alemán (German School) in the first third of the twentieth century, and of the Colegio Americano a few years later, also contributed. These schools offered Quito's elite the possibility of accessing different worldviews and new ways of seeing individuals' social and economic roles.

With the new communications, distances ceased to be an obstacle for people's mobilization and relations and for the exchange of goods. Thus, commerce and trade were facilitated, and closer ties were forged between regions and provinces. A trip between Quito and Guayaquil decreased from two weeks to two days, and its cost to one-fifth of what it had been. So, the lack of communication in which highlanders and coastal residents had lived for so long because of the impassable mountains and dense selvatic vegetation that separated them was finally remedied. Means of communication and transportation also facilitated the broader dissemination of ideas and the extension of the state's authority to a larger proportion of the national territory. This process coincided with the strengthening and increasing of the state's responsibilities. However, except for those who could make use of trains, automobiles, buses, and trucks—which not all Ecuadorians had—transportation continued to be a risky adventure, just as it had been for travelers from previous centuries, especially on the coast, about which one foreign visitor commented that nobody embarked on a journey "without a powerful reason."[102]

The opening-up of means of communication and the new means of transportation also helped the newspapers published in Quito and Guayaquil to reach the provinces. However, the general backwardness—expressed in high indexes of illiteracy, low levels of education, scant dissemination of reading, and widespread poverty—made oral language weigh more heavily than written language. For this reason, the number of people who could actually read the newspapers and magazines was reduced to those of a certain economic and cultural level. This limitation was offset somewhat thanks to the radio, by means of which news and commentaries from the written press could reach a larger number of citizens, who for the first time could be informed about what was happening in Ecuador and in the world. This meant that the teachings imparted by the Catholic Church in its religious publications and in education ceased to be the only source for shaping conscience.

With foreign capital arrived modern means of production, previously unknown technologies, criteria of efficiency, foresight in the use of resources, and systems of work characterized by responsibility, organization, and productivity. All of this constituted a novelty in the backward Ecuador of those times. Thanks to a foreign presence and the businesses that the immigrants established, Ecuadorians came into contact with modern technologies, unknown systems of production, and efficient modes of work that led to positive changes in the conduct of the employees who worked in foreign companies or were overseen by foreigners. The demonstration effect that they generated allowed their practices to be spread widely, and this contributed to changing unproductive work and business routines that had been repeated in economic activities for centuries.

One public official in the 1930s confessed to a visitor that there was "a general opinion that foreigners had more business sense, were more resourceful, and were more daring and resilient than the natives of the country."[103] Espinosa Tamayo wrote that in Ecuador four-fifths of the commerce was in the hands of foreigners, and that the "upper class" in fact recognized their intellectual and cultural superiority and preferred their involvement "as a driving force for industries and the country's material progress."[104] Belisario Quevedo noted the fact that wealth and production were being snatched away by the "foreign element, [which was] enterprising, active and thrifty."[105] He illustrated the foreign influence in the economic arena of those times with the English term "watchman" used to designate a guard at mining, industrial, and construction sites; in Spanish, it became *guachimán*, a term still used today.*

In Albert Franklin's visit to the gold mine that a North American company was exploiting in Macuchi, it caught his attention that the mine workers, instead of having the servile attitudes of the peasant farmers on the haciendas of the coast, where they came from, were "intent upon their job," and that the "sudden appearance of their [gringo] boss did not cause them to cringe and grin in obeisance" since "they realized that all he asked of them was care and constancy in their work, and not flattery of his own personal importance."[106] The professional training and hardworking spirit acquired by the Ecuadorian workers who had the opportunity to train in English and North American companies made them much-appreciated and valued labor who easily found jobs in national companies when the foreign ones left.

In Guayaquil, as has occurred in other societies, in addition to unleashing a virtuous cycle, economic growth was an important instrument of change in cultural values. First of all, it offered opportunities, and then it demonstrated that those who made an effort, undertook a business, and worked with determination increased their earnings, improved their economic condition, and in some cases got rich. The economic possibilities offered by the port attracted immigrants, who opened new businesses

---

*Since remote colonial times, Ecuadorians always admired European foreigners, whom they showered with attentions that the travelers noted in their writings. This fact was commented on by one author as follows: "Regardless of where he comes from and who he is, the foreigner is preferred in everything, even in marriage, which is all one can say on this subject" (Peralta, *Tipos de mi tierra*, 93–94).

and introduced efficient practices. The evidence of success among those who worked with discipline and effort led others to imitate behaviors that proved beneficial. The accumulation of resources and the possibility of increasing them through investment encouraged savings and partnerships. The open competition of those who started a business encouraged the improvement of those already established. All of this produced an economic multiplier effect on agriculture, commerce, and services in Guayaquil and the surrounding areas.

The same thing did not occur in industry, however, an activity in which the residents of Guayaquil were less interested. At the beginning of the century, the port city imported all sorts of manufactured goods, since "industry was almost nonexistent" and the few factories that did exist were in the hands of foreigners.[107] Another traveler noted the presence of an "incipient industry" of beer, ice, chocolate, and fabric, to which he added print shops, a trolley drawn by animals, an electric power plant, and a small fleet of river steamboats.[108] Crawford explained the absence of industry, despite the economic resources and the existing demand, by saying that the entrepreneurial capacity and the "hard work" of the residents of Guayaquil were directed to commerce and real estate rather than manufactured goods. This conduct was influenced by their impatience to progress, a market that was better known to them, the possibility of obtaining high earnings, the easy and attractive credit available, the rapid profits they obtained, and a stable business code.

According to the aforementioned author, the inclination to commercial activities in Guayaquil was so widespread that in "each man, woman and child of upper or lower class, an almost contagious desire to buy or sell developed." For these reasons, despite the fact that economic resources were accumulated thanks to cacao, no manufacturing industry developed to permit the exportation of finished products or the substitution of imported articles that could have been manufactured domestically. For example, cacao was not processed in plants to transform it into chocolate, and not even a broom factory was established even though all the labor and materials for the production of brooms existed. The author concluded by remarking that for these reasons "the growth transfer factor was completely lacking" in the economy of Guayaquil.[109]

The early enterprising spirit of the residents of Guayaquil appeared in the highlands five decades later, after the start of the twentieth century. Thanks to the railroad, the first motorized vehicles arrived in the highlands for the transportation of passengers and freight. Machinery imported from abroad could be mobilized to cities and to the countryside for industrial and agricultural production and road construction. The importation of tractors, hoes, machetes, and other farming tools and equipment increased considerably. The twenty textile factories installed in the highlands by 1930 represented 90 percent of the national total. Of these, eighteen were founded during the first three decades of the twentieth century, most after World War I. However, even in these, the national way of life continued to hold sway, and it was not very favorable to partnerships. Most of these enterprises were personal; only seven were established as companies composed of several individuals willing to combine their efforts and their capital.[110] In addition, the factories accounted for little within the overall economy and offered limited employment possibilities. In 1914, Espinosa considered that "it was not necessary to found special technical schools since the workers that would finish there would not find jobs and would be frustrated and feel deceived, or condemned to emigrating in search of work."[111]

In 1906, the Banco de Pichincha was founded in Quito. It is the only financial institution in Ecuador that has managed to last for more than one hundred years. Later, other banks were established in Ambato, Riobamba, Cuenca, and the capital itself. About 1930, Quito "caught up with Guayaquil in the number of banking establishments" and thus the highlands could finally have the credit institutions that were so sorely needed for the development of its economic activities. Farming and livestock-raising also saw progress with the improvement of seeds, the introduction of new crops, the importation of breeder animals, and the incorporation of machinery (tractor-drawn plows), especially after World War I.[112] All this occurred in part thanks to the efforts made by the Sociedad Agrícola e Industrial (1907) and the Sociedad Nacional de Agricultura (1913). However, backwardness continued to predominate in agricultural activities: on highland haciendas, even until mid-century, grains continued to be threshed by teams of horses that were made to walk in circles on the shafts spread out on the ground, and then the chaff was separated with the help of the wind.

Nonetheless, the economic, social, political, and legal changes favorable to progress and the renovation of cultural values took on even greater dynamism in the second half of the twentieth century, as will be seen in the next chapter.

4

CULTURAL CHANGES
IN THE SECOND HALF OF
THE TWENTIETH CENTURY

A recapitulation of the cultural values shaped during more than four hundred years will help readers appreciate the scope of the changes in the cultural traits of Ecuadorians during the second half of the twentieth century.

The feudal Spain from which the conquerors, colonists, and bureaucrats came, alongside the despotic pre-Columbian indigenous societies and the abundant labor force that existed in the territory of the Audiencia of Quito, shaped a stratified society in which whites and people of color were separated by abysmal economic and social differences. Those on the one side and those on the other took for granted that their living conditions would not change, nor the place they occupied on the social scale, regardless of how they performed. During the colonial period and the republic, the rigid social hierarchies and the conviction that the inherited socioeconomic status would be maintained for life kept rights and obligations from being similar for all individuals, and kept their opportunities from being equal. Geographical isolation and the values transmitted by the Catholic Church contributed to the lack of change in this type of society.

The travelers and chroniclers who recorded everyday occurrences described Spaniards and Creoles, and later Ecuadorians, as lazy, indolent, wasteful, lacking in an enterprising spirit, and not very interested in economic progress. This attitude toward life was shared by whites, Indians, blacks, mestizos, and mulattos. Despite the changes that occurred in Guayaquil during the late nineteenth century and in the rest of the country during the first half of the twentieth, such behaviors varied only slightly. Those who worked, regardless of their social condition, were not hardworking, efficient, and persevering. To the contrary, they performed their tasks leniently, inconsistently, and routinely. Property rights were not respected, and in general individuals did not fulfill their commitments and did not adhere to the provisions of the law. Merit was not recognized, effort not rewarded, and the sense of responsibility not shared, due to the strength of personal relations and paternalistic values.

For these reasons, those who directed economic activities lacked incentives to save, invest, incorporate technologies, introduce innovations, expand markets, and thereby improve their earnings from production processes. For their part, those that performed manual labor (such as the artisans or wage-laborers) believed that the zealous performance of their tasks would not be adequately compensated for. Neither was it possible for economic relations based on reciprocal trust to exist. This led to the fact that the small amounts of savings were not invested, and meant that forming the partnerships so necessary for undertaking enterprises that could not be undertaken individually proved difficult.

All of this kept individuals from improving their well-being, kept business activities from progressing, and kept Ecuador's economy from developing.

THE COUNTRY'S NEW CONDITIONS

In the second half of the twentieth century, the cultural values of Ecuadorian society, which had been maintained for centuries, began to change as the hardworking and enterprising spirit that had appeared in Guayaquil during the previous century extended to other regions. The different kinds of transformations (mainly economic, social, and political) that occurred as of the 1950s contributed to awakening interest in work and to generalizing the pursuit of profits to thereby advance and build wealth.

The element that most influenced this cultural change was the economic growth unleashed by exports: first of bananas and later of oil, especially the latter. A phenomenon of such magnitude had never been experienced by the country, since the remote time when the Audiencia of Quito was established. In the long historical period of more than four hundred years, economic growth had been insignificant, except during the booms of textiles and cacao. This reality explained the backwardness with which Ecuador arrived at the second half of the twentieth century, in economic and social conditions that did not differ much from those of the colonial period and the early days of the republic.

Sales of Ecuadorian products abroad rose from US$64 million in 1950 to US$4.45 billion by the end of the century. Thanks to bananas, between

1950 and 1969 the GDP grew at an annual rate of 4.7 percent; and thanks to petroleum, at an unheard-of rate of 12 percent annually in the first five years of the 1970s and at a significant 6.9 percent in the next five. Three consecutive decades of unprecedented economic growth produced transformations in all spheres of national life, which allowed Ecuador to abandon the group of Latin America's least developed countries and move into an intermediate position. New forms of agricultural production appeared, industrial activities were developed, services grew, physical infrastructure improved notably, and employment opportunities increased. This economic progress was followed by important social and cultural changes.

Agriculture lost its traditional significance when at the end of the century it fell to less than 10 percent of the GDP and employed only 26 percent of the economically active population. Meanwhile, services, industry, commerce, and mining rose to the top positions. To agriculture's loss of importance must be added the liquidation of the economic and social system constituted by haciendas, in the 1960s and 1970s. This was the result of the Law of Agrarian Reform, the Law for the Abolition of Hazardous Work in Agriculture, and Decree 1001, which transferred to peasant farmers the lands on which they grew rice.

The country finally managed to achieve greater integration through a system of roads, mostly paved, that linked provinces, cities, and towns, even in the isolated Amazon region. With this, automotive transportation came to be the principal means of communication, and the railroad ceased to be competitive. The river port of Guayaquil, which had served the country for years, was replaced by a seaport; and the city could connect with the central highlands and the southern coast directly by land by means of a bridge built across the Guayas River. The ports of Bolívar, Manta, and Esmeraldas began operating, as well as new airports in Guayaquil and Quito, along with others in almost all of the cities in the country. Thanks to this, notable development occurred in maritime transportation and in national and international air transportation.

When I was in primary school in the mid-1950s, the weak light in Riobamba, which my mother called "mortecina," only provided a little more light than candles. However, when the Paute and Agoyán hydroelectric power plants were built alongside new thermoelectric power plants, they allowed industries to have sufficient energy and provided lighting to all of the cities and towns, and even rural areas. Progress was notable. In 1951, ECLAC estimated that the country had 35,000 kW of electricity supplies, which according to Germánico Salgado only made it possible to serve a small contemporary city.[1]

The memory of how Ecuador had been so cut off from the rest of the world reflects the significance of the progress made. In the early 1950s, the only road that penetrated the Amazon region went just a few kilometers past Puyo, the first town settled by colonists from the highlands. To travel from Chone to Quito, a distance of no more than three hundred kilometers, it was necessary to navigate the river of the same name, downstream toward the Pacific; continue by sea to La Libertad; and take the autocarril to Durán and then the train to Riobamba, where travelers spent the night and then headed for Quito the next day. The trip lasted a week. In the early 1960s, to travel from Machala to Guayaquil it was necessary to take a boat at the port of Bolivar and sail overnight by sea, enter the gulf, go up the Guayas River, and finally arrive at the port. In the highlands, the cobblestone roads were considered good since all the others were dirt roads. None were paved.

Ecuador experienced rapid urbanization, and city populations went from 29 percent in 1950 to 55 percent in 1990 and 61 percent in 2001. The migrations originating in the countryside and outlying provinces were directed to Guayaquil and other coastal cities, which saw explosive growth. People were attracted by the wealth that banana production had generated; and later on, shrimp-farming, fishing, and other agricultural crops, as well as the employment possibilities that the construction boom generated. Through invasions of land in peripheral cities, without potable water, sewage systems, electricity, and streets, the migrants formed squatter settlements or shantytowns.

The coverage of potable-water and sewage services extended to almost all of the country's population, as did health care, better nutrition, greater personal hygiene, and a certain concern for community sanitation. These were aspects that had been neglected in previous periods. Such progress made it possible to eliminate epidemics, reduce mortality rates, and increase life expectancy to the age of seventy-two. In cities and in the country, the size of families decreased; and in the highlands, for the first time ever, the scourge of fleas that its inhabitants had lived with for more than four hundred years—and that had tortured the travelers who had visited the country during the colonial and republican periods—was eliminated. However, the tendency to drink did not disappear, and it continued to be noticed by foreigners, visitors, and residents, as well as by the natives of countries to which Ecuadorians had immigrated or where there were large numbers of middle- and upper-class students. Another example of this are the excesses that occur in Quito during the Founders Day celebrations held every December, and in other cities with similar festivities. According to a survey conducted by the firm Informe Confidencial (2007), 76 percent of the residents of Quito and 63 percent of the residents of Guayaquil felt that alcohol consumption was a "very serious" problem in their city.

Thanks to first the invention of transistors and later the extension of electric power services, all of Ecuador's inhabitants could listen to the radio. This was followed by the appearance of television, which by the 1980s had reached all urban households, even the poorest ones. This made it possible for exponential growth in the citizens' capacity to stay informed. Illiteracy was reduced to less than 10 percent of the population, and primary-school services extended to all school-aged children. Notable quantitative advances ensued in secondary-school and university education. The Constitution of 1979 recognized illiterate people's right to vote.

Foreign companies and investments appeared in numbers and volumes previously unknown to Ecuador.* Among these, the companies that began producing and exporting bananas and oil were noteworthy. These two sources of wealth were the basis for the country's progress in the second half of the century, and for the improvements in the standard of living of millions of Ecuadorians. The U.S. firm United Fruit undertook the initial development of banana production on the coast. Its exports came to account for 60 percent of sales abroad. The U.S. consortium Texaco-Gulf began drilling the first oil wells in the Amazon region, and their exports amounted to almost 50 percent of the total for a number of years. Other foreign companies incorporated new oilfields in the 1990s and built two costly oil pipelines between the Amazon region and the Pacific Ocean; the state was not in a position to finance these from its own resources.

The economy reaped the benefits of the ventures undertaken by the immigrants who arrived in the country around mid-century. The foreigners who visited the Audiencia of Quito and Ecuador, after noting the inhabitants' scant interest in individual and collective progress, had coincided in noting that the country would not emerge from its backward state if it did not receive immigrants from European countries. Even though the immigrants who came to the country were not as numerous as those who went to other Latin American countries, they had much to do with national progress, for they founded successful industrial, commercial, tourism-oriented,

---

*In the 1950s, the average annual foreign investment was US$4.9 million; in the 1970s, US$68 million; in the 1990s, US$470 million; and between 2002 and 2006, US$651 million. During those periods, the average ratio between foreign investment and GDP was 0.7 percent, 1.5 percent, 2.7 percent, and 2.1 percent, respectively. Banco Central, *Memoria del Gerente General* (Quito, 1959); Banco Central, *Sesenta y cinco años de Información Estadística: 1927–2002* (Quito, 2002).

and agricultural enterprises that contributed to Ecuador's leaving behind the centuries-old immobility.

New and refreshing ideas were brought to the country from abroad and were adopted by some Ecuadorians. From different ideological perspectives, they questioned the old order of things, stressed the importance of economic matters, and promoted the pursuit of progress. Among these should be noted those derived from the Marxist line of thought, those originating in Catholic social action, those recommended by international organizations, and those preached by Protestant churches.

Political parties, labor unions, intellectuals, and journalists framed within European Marxist thought disseminated socialist ideas and struggled to implement them by criticizing the old agrarian society represented by the haciendas and promoting laws and reforms geared to correcting the unfair economic and social relations that still existed. Even though socialist ideas reached the country in the early decades of the century, it was only with the Cuban Revolution (1960) that they managed to extend beyond the ideological "chapels" in which they had been secluded. This spread allowed them to influence a broader spectrum of Ecuadorians, even some who did not call themselves Marxists, especially those who worked in the social sciences. However, these ideas on occasion became a stumbling-block for the country's development. For example, the construction of a revenue-producing second oil pipeline, necessary for the exportation of heavy crude oil found in the Amazon Region, was postponed for nine years due to opposition to foreign investment from self-proclaimed leftist nationalists (technocrats and members of political parties, unions, and even the military). They demanded that the work be done by the state, even though the latter lacked the economic resources.

Popes John XXIII and Paul VI redefined the economic doctrine of the Catholic Church in the encyclicals *Mater et Magistra* (1961), *Pacem in Terris*, and *Populorum Progessio* (1967), and in the documents issued by the Second Vatican Council in 1965. In these, Catholicism delegitimized the belief held for centuries that the socioeconomic order in effect was immutable because it was "desired by God." They also recognized the importance that individual advancement, economic progress, and national development held for human realization. And they valued material needs; accepted the autonomy of earthly realities; legitimized scientific research; acknowledged freedom of conscience; and granted importance to enterprise, the market, economic creativity, and the business world. In keeping with these ideas, the Catholic Church undertook a program of agrarian reform on its haciendas and promoted financial and technical assistance services for peasant farmers, such as the Ecuadorian Populorum Progressio Fund (FEPP).

Evangelical churches, first from Europe and then from the United States, composed of Methodists, Lutherans, Anglicans, Presbyterians, Baptists, and Pentecostals, constantly increased the number of their followers in the second half of the twentieth century, especially the last two denominations. In 2006, Protestants came to represent 11 percent of the national population, with an upward trend.[2] This percentage is as high as 65 percent in the areas in which their religious activities began in the early 1920s.* The first important missionary group was set up in the Indian canton of Colta, in the Province of Chimborazo. A testimonial community project in education and health (in 1956, bilingual schools were established; in 1958, a pioneering hospital for Indians), the habitual use of Quechua, the startup of a local radio, and the reading and discussion of the Sacred Scriptures from the standpoint of everyday problems allowed them to penetrate the world of Andean and Amazon peasants and later to make inroads among working- and middle-class sectors in cities. This expansion of Protestantism was accompanied by changes in the followers' behavior, and these changes made them abandon habits incompatible with personal economic success and collective progress.

In the 1960s, ECLAC and the Alliance for Progress, created by the United States, promoted structural reforms aimed at strengthening the State's involvement in national development and redistributing wealth. Among them, the agrarian reform is noteworthy. These policies were adopted and promoted by the Junta de Planificación (1954), the technical body that had a significant influence on the government's decisions for thirty years. In keeping with such ideas, the state took on a decisive role in the creation of conditions favoring development, through planning, project implementation, public investment, creation of institutions, constitution of companies, and the issuing of protectionist measures. It built infrastructure, regulated production and distribution processes, established incentives and subsidies, improved the taxation system, modernized the administration, increased tax collection, expanded public services, began social programs, granted production credits, expanded agricultural frontiers, and implemented the agrarian reform. These tasks were facilitated by the state's control over the oil wealth and the sizeable revenues from rising oil prices. Thanks to this, the public officials' decisions could obtain a certain degree of autonomy with respect to private interests.[3]

---

*The first Protestant missions were the Evangelical Missionary Union (1896) and the Christian and Missionary Alliance (1897). Susana Andrade, *Protestantismo indígena: procesos de conversión religiosa en la provincia de Chimborazo, Ecuador* (Quito: FLACSO, Abya-Yala, IFEA, 2004), 27. The Adventists arrived in Colta in 1921 and opened a mission house near the lake. Alvin M. Goffin, *The Rise of Protestant Evangelism in Ecuador, 1895–1990* (Gainesville: University Press of Florida, 1994), 85.

Later on, toward the end of the century, the Inter-American Development Bank, the World Bank, and the International Monetary Fund promoted structural reforms. Even though these were of a different ideological orientation, they were also geared to the country's development. They sought to liberalize the economy, reduce the scope of the state, and promote a market economy, in keeping with the recommendations summarized in the Washington Consensus. Although they were not applied with the depth proposed by foreign and national ideologists, the state granted the private sector some of its responsibilities in construction or administration of physical infrastructure (roads, airports, ports), in the exploitation of natural resources (oil, hydroelectricity), and in the provision of certain services (communications, potable water, air and sea transportation). They also propitiated laws and policies oriented to reducing protections and subsidies, favoring foreign investment, and encouraging the action of market forces. They granted the market responsibility for allocating resources, setting prices, and creating incentives for the implementation of economic activities.

In recent decades, knowledge, attitudes, ideas and behaviors brought in by the numerous young people who traveled abroad to study have also come to Ecuador. In the middle class, this was due to scholarships; and in the upper class, it was because of economic resources provided by the country's progress. Many were educated at prestigious universities in the United States, Europe, Chile, and Argentina or in the centers for higher learning of Monterrey in Mexico, INCAE in Costa Rica, and the Zamorano in Honduras. Thanks to the Internet, newspapers, magazines, books, and technical reports, those who did not have the opportunity to study abroad had daily contact with the world through reading and thereby managed to broaden their cultural and informational horizons in a way that their parents and grandparents could not.

There has been significant improvement in the equipping of the cities. In this area, it is important to note the progress made in the port of Manta. Guayaquil has consolidated its economic, demographic, and political influence; recovered its deteriorated sanitation, potable water, and sewage services and its streets; built a more elegant and comfortable airport and a better bus terminal; and improved urban beautification. This process began with the construction of a beautiful boardwalk area (Malecón) along the banks of the Guayas River. All of this has made it possible for residents of Guayaquil to recover the self-esteem that they had lost.

The backward and provincial capital also changed as of the 1970s, thanks to the appearance of oil wealth from the Amazon region, which it controlled to a great extent, and to the cultivation of flowers and the production of foodstuffs and industrial goods for export. By the end of the century, Quito had become a modern, cosmopolitan metropolis that had grown toward the north and toward the south and spilled over into neighboring valleys. International hotels; a variety of restaurants, theaters, bookstores, concert halls, avenues, parks, and amusements; a trolleybus; and the restoration of the colonial part of the city left behind the inadequacies that had caught the attention of foreign travelers. Quito's progress, accelerated in the early years of the twenty-first century by a new oil boom, attracted thousands of emigrants from the coast. This was an unheard-of demographic phenomenon that occurred for the first time in hundreds of years, for it had always been the highlanders who left their region to go to the coast in search of employment.

ECONOMIC AND SOCIAL EFFECTS

Such numerous and profound changes in all aspects of national life led to economic, social, and cultural transformations that Ecuador had never before experienced.

Agriculture lost importance and other economic activities carried on in urban areas, or related to those, gained significance. Services, commerce, industry, and mining notably reduced the traditional influence that farming and livestock-raising activities had had, and the influence of those who had controlled them: the hacienda owners.

Traditional haciendas in the highlands produced for domestic consumption; and those on the coast produced cacao, coffee, and rice, part of which was exported. They suffered from the infiltration and competition of agricultural/livestock companies. Among these, the banana and sugar plantations and the ones established to produce better breeds of cattle for milk and beef production should be mentioned. In the last decades of the twentieth century, these activities were joined by shrimp-farming (shrimp became the third most important export commodity); fishing; and in the highlands, food and flowers for export, using greenhouses and modern technologies.

The agrarian reform and the elimination of hazardous work in agriculture, in addition to redistributing land and allowing peasants to own the parcels where they lived, freed up a labor force that for centuries had been tied to haciendas through the *huasipungo* system in the highlands and *sembraduría* or *finquería* on the coast. As of then, the peasant farmers—who had been subject to the haciendas in a relationship of dependency—could decide where it was most convenient for them to work, in keeping with their interests and as a function of the remunerations they were offered.* Thus, a labor market that had traditionally been controlled by the hacienda owners came to be determined by wages. Especially significant was the economic, social, educational, and political advancement of the indigenous population that, as seen in previous chapters, had lived in poverty and marginalization for centuries.

In the process of redressing indigenous rights, important steps were: the formation of the Confederación de Nacionalidades Indígenas del Ecuador (CONAIE), an organization that became the most influential political pressure group of the 1990s; improved education, sanitation, and health care for the Indian people; recognition of their collective rights in the Constitution of 1998; creation of public organizations to promote their development; and the notable positions that Indian leaders occupied in the federal government and the National Congress. Just thirty years before, no one would have imagined that they could attain such political power. However, perhaps the most important transformation for the indigenous peoples was the recovery of the cultural values of their race and a sense of personal dignity.

A description of the oppressive social conditions in which the indigenous world found itself immersed in the early decades of the second half of the twentieth century helps one to grasp the magnitude of the transformations that occurred. For North American anthropologist Casagrande, "Racism in Ecuador is institutionalized to a degree that would shock many oppressed peoples elsewhere."[4] Ecuadorian anthropologist Burgos, referring to Riobamba, the capital of a province with a strong Indian presence, wrote that it is "expected that the roles assigned to mestizos will not be performed by Indians, so that it would cause surprise if a cultural Indian, in other words one wearing Indian dress, were to be seen driving around Riobamba."[5]

Currently, not only do many Indians drive vehicles, but they also own them. The donkeys that used to be part of rural landscapes in backward countries have disappeared in Ecuador's countryside, and horses, bicycles, motorcycles, and in some cases pickup trucks have taken their place. It is a shame to have to admit it, but only fairly recently—for the first time in hundreds of years—Indians can wear shoes [instead of their traditional cloth

---

*In 1954, independent wage laborers accounted for 54 percent of the coastal peasant farm workers. Comité Interamericano de Desarrollo Agrícola (CIDA), *Ecuador: Tenencia de la Tierra y Desarrollo Socioeconómico del Sector Agrícola* (Washington, DC: Unión Panamericana, 1965), 409, ff.

sandals] and can have more than one change of clothes. In early 2000, a journalist from the French newspaper *Le Monde*, who resided in Lima and was very familiar with the backwardness of Peruvian Indians, told me of his surprise at having seen CONAIE leaders using cell phones in Quito. I explained to him that not only they did, but many other Indians did too, even those who lived in rural areas, because of the progress that they had experienced.

Economic growth and the state's development efforts—through the physical infrastructure provided, the new legislation enacted, the institutions created, and the sources of financing that opened up—favored the formation and advancement of a number of enterprises. To implement their initiatives, Ecuadorians finally had basic services such as ports, airports, roads, bridges, electric power, [more reliable] postal service, and telephones, many of which had been lacking for those that wanted to undertake industrial activities. Many companies were formed because of laws that favored partnerships, such as the Law of Companies, or those that shielded them through subsidies, tariff protections, and tax exemptions.* The scarcity of capital was in part remedied through the expansion of the operations of the development bank, the Banco de Fomento, and the opening-up of credit lines under special conditions of terms and interest by the Corporación Financiera Nacional, the Banco Central, the Banco de la Vivienda, and the Banco de Desarrollo; this last one for public-sector projects. The state itself assumed business responsibilities through the creation of public organizations for the exploitation of air and sea transportation; the production of goods; and the extraction, exportation, and marketing of petroleum and petroleum products. The state oil company (CEPE and its successor Petroecuador) became by far the country's largest enterprise.

Companies also benefited from private-sector contributions to the modernization of the economy. The growth of the private-sector financial system and its expansion to the provinces, cities, and towns was of such magnitude that it relegated to second place the Banco de Fomento, the state institution that in the 1950s had attracted most of the deposits and become the major credit provider. Banks and insurance companies furnished businessmen with instruments that they had been lacking, thanks to which the management of productive, commercial, and service activities was facilitated. Technological advances that occurred in the last two decades provided accessible, instant, and affordable communications; for example,

---

*Laws were issued in the areas of industrial development and the development of crafts, trades, and small industry; agricultural/livestock activities; forestry; and tourism.

first the telex (which no young person nowadays would have ever seen), the fax (now obsolete), and later on the "magical" services of Internet and cell phones.

The following anecdote illustrates the magnitude of the country's transformation in the area of communications. It must have been 1983 when dozens of journalists, photographers, and cameramen met in my office to record the moment in which the President of the Republic was going to call the Ecuadorian ambassador in Washington without the intervention of an operator, by dialing the number directly on a rotary phone. Afterward, the Ecuadorians who had access to the service marveled at the fact that they did not need to shout to be heard, and that they could clearly hear the voice of the person with whom they were speaking, anywhere in the world.

Internet and cell phones caused a revolution in economic activities and proved especially advantageous for small-scale farmers, informal businessmen, artisans, and service-providers, who had the opportunity to be in contact easily and directly with customers, even abroad in the case of small exporters. These novel means of communication opened up to companies—but above all to those who, without means or resources or influences, wanted to undertake businesses—a gamut of opportunities that they had never had previously, despite the institutions that had been created, the laws that had been issued, and the efforts that governments had made to open doors.

Advances in the provision of services by the private sector, which had been inveterately lacking in the country and its productive activities, even those that were indispensable, contributed to facilitating industrial, commercial, agricultural, and mining operations. They obtained financing, covered the risks of unforeseen losses, modernized machinery, supplied themselves with inputs, and marketed the goods they produced, both inside and outside the country, even in the case of small personal or family-run businesses. The opportunities opened up by economic growth, the incentives created by the state, and the new technologies were tapped by traditional businessmen and by foreign immigrants. The former awakened latent initiatives, and the latter were encouraged to expand their activities and undertake new projects. Those services also benefited entrepreneurship among groups that had been excluded from business activities because of their poverty or marginal position.

Globalization, economic openness, the action of market forces, the withdrawal of the State, and technological advances in the field of communications contributed to the opening up of opportunities for new small and medium-sized businesses. Among these, it is worthwhile to mention the modernization of the commercialization systems used by supermarkets; overland transportation cooperatives; and the production and exportation of nontraditional products, which between 2000 and 2007 increased at an average annual rate of 15.2 percent.

The generally well-paid jobs created on modern agricultural plantations made it possible for peasants to improve their standards of living in terms that they had not attained through the agrarian reform, for which those who had wanted to transform the backward rural world had had such high hopes. This is what happened, for example, with workers, mostly women, in the flower and food enterprises of the highlands. They not only bettered their personal well-being (food, housing, health, clothing), but their higher income also fostered notable progress in the surrounding impoverished towns that nowadays, in addition to having basic services, have hair salons, bars, all kinds of shops, amusements, and Internet services.

The large amounts of capital that were necessary for the acquisition of machinery, technologies, and other inputs made it necessary to save and provided incentives to partnerships. The appreciable amounts of capital committed, the need to maintain them without running risks, and the desire to make profits called for the efficient organization of production processes. The growing number of Ecuadorians who—as workers, employees, or professionals—earned regular wages or professional fees, made it possible to form a consumer market. This opened up the possibility that the companies that produced for domestic consumption could prosper because they had sustained demand for their articles or services. The large concentrations of population in Guayaquil and Quito and the growing urbanization of the cities facilitated the commercialization of goods and services produced or provided by the companies, which thus had more than half of the potential consumers within their reach.

Workers and employees involved in such activities were recruited for their skills and not their influences. In addition, they received a salary and social benefits that gave them a certain economic independence. All of the obligations that they had to their boss lay in doing efficient work, unlike what had occurred in the traditional paternalistic agrarian society. The creation of state organizations and the development of private-business activities offered employment and good remunerations to professionals recruited for positions as directors, managers, or consultants freely working in their areas of expertise. This made it possible to form a middle class, which the country had formerly been lacking.

The new ideas contributed by Marxism, Protestantism, and international organizations did away with the ideological frameworks that had supported the old socioeconomic order, aroused people's interest in improving their economic condition, led the state to assume a decisive role in promoting the country's development, and later promoted liberalization of the economy and encouraged private enterprise.

Protestantism deserves special mention due to the emphasis it placed on the value of the temporal life and because it encouraged its followers to abandon practices contrary to individual and collective progress, and instead promoted the adoption of attitudes that favored such progress. Unlike Catholicism, whose preaching was originally conformist and merely doctrinal but became repleviable and militant, Protestantism emphasized personal economic success, which in no case should be viewed as incompatible with eternal salvation. In the faithful was instilled the idea that they were capable of meeting their needs, solving their problems, and defining the future of their lives through their own effort. They were urged to rid themselves of the fatalistic idea that the economic conditions into which they were born could not be changed, and they were called to construct their own destiny through their actions. To this end, they had to work hard, save part of their income, lead a frugal life, respect others' property, abstain from drinking alcohol, obey the laws, honor their commitments, pay taxes, tell the truth, be attentive to their personal hygiene, and keep their homes clean.

Even though these new cultural values are orienting the conduct of all the evangelicals, regardless of their social status, the change among Indians is particularly significant. In that regard, a scholar in this area wrote: "The Protestant Indians reject their old beliefs and customs. Catholicism, for them, represents a sign of backwardness, a state of savagery overcome. Traditional beliefs and practices are considered superstitious, a product of ignorance. They cannot explain how they could have wasted so much money on festivities and pilgrimages (*romerías*), at the expense of their health, nutrition, and the education of their children, and the sale of lands and animals."[6] Another author noted, based on statements made by Indian converts and their behavior, that they rejected the exploitation and abuse they had suffered previously; that they had recovered a sense of dignity that allowed them to look whites and mestizos in the face and consider other Ecuadorians as equals, speak without complexes, and, avoiding confrontations, ask authorities to improve public services; that they valued education, health, and housing, to which they allocated a good part of their savings; that they acted as good citizens; and that they were reliable, honest, and serious.[7]

The Protestant practices of reading the Bible daily and permanently studying and discussing its content have contributed to the fact that evangelical Indians have improved their knowledge of Spanish, improved their comprehension of oral and written language, and learned to express their thoughts correctly. This makes it possible for them to perform economic activities with greater efficiency than other Ecuadorians who have not managed to improve their skills because they do not perform mental exercises. The possibility that they can interpret the scriptures for themselves gives them a sense of freedom and independence in their day-to-day family and civic life and at work. This makes it possible for them to organize their activities in keeping with their own viewpoints, and not in response to directives, which they used to receive from their bosses, Catholic priests, or other paternalistic figures.

Voluntarily giving up alcohol, whose consumption is so widespread in Ecuador, especially among indigenous people, has allowed converts to save money that they would have previously wasted on drinking. They have used this money to improve their own well-being and that of their families (education, housing, health, clothing) and to accumulate small amounts of capital that, invested in businesses, have generated additional income; this has enabled them to economically surpass those who have squandered their money on getting drunk. The results of such a radical cultural transformation can be seen in many Indian communities in which evangelicals have surpassed the living standards of those of the Catholics.[8] A recent personal experience of mine reflects this. While I was traveling along a rural road, across the plains near the Ozogoche lakes (Province of Chimborazo), an Indian woman asked me to give her a ride to the main highway. During our conversation, she commented that she had left Catholicism and adopted the Protestant faith, just like the rest of her family. When I asked her if the change had been beneficial, she responded, "Of course, sir. My husband no longer beats me up on Saturdays because he doesn't get drunk."

ECONOMIC SUCCESS

The country's territorial integration, economic growth, modern communications, international opening-up, urbanization of the cities, certain public policies, foreign investment, liberalization of the economy, renovating ideas, immigration, market economy, and the demonstration effects produced by the pioneers who decided to undertake new businesses created conditions for Ecuadorians finally to abandon attitudes that were contrary to individual, community, and national economic progress.

In the second half of the twentieth century, the pursuit of economic success extended everywhere, to rural and urban areas and to different social classes. Ecuadorians sought to take advantage of the opportunities that opened up due to the country's new conditions; and they were convinced that if they worked hard, saved, invested, took risks, started companies, established businesses, installed services, improved their workshops, or looked for a job, they would get ahead. The peasants who obtained lands under the agrarian reform became interested in using them to the greatest advantage, an attitude that they had not had when they cultivated the lands of their masters, which they had not viewed as their own and did not devote much effort to. The influence that the new ideas made people abandon the belief that their inherited economic condition was a misfortune that could not be changed; instead, they assumed stances consistent with the need to transform it. This behavior contributed to the expansion of the virtuous circle that economic growth had unleashed, the result of which was the country's continuous growth between the 1950s and the 1970s, the intermittent growth of the following decades, and the promising growth of the early years of the twenty-first century. Thanks to this, millions of Ecuadorians emerged from the poverty that their ancestors had lived in for centuries. The most fortunate ones managed to accumulate capital and improve their well-being at levels that their parents would never have dreamed of.

Idleness came to be looked down upon; prejudices against manual labor decreased; commerce gained prestige; and Ecuadorians, rich or poor, did what they could to earn a living and get ahead through their own effort. Only fifty years ago, no one would have thought that young people from the middle or upper class could study cooking and work as chefs or in other manual trades. Some dared to set up their own businesses, and the most enterprising ventured into new and innovative fields such as the shrimp-farming companies on the coast or the flower plantations in the highlands. Of the many that can be cited, these are only a few: Supermaxi, Mi Comisariato and Fybeca, in the area of commerce; Pronaca, Confiteca, Sumesa, Nirsa, and the Vilaseca Group, in the food industry; Pinto and La Internacional, in the textile industry; Andec, Andelca, Ideal Alambrec, and Indurama, in the metal mechanics industry; Plasticaucho in shoe manufacturing; and the Noboa and Wong Groups, in bananas.

Nonetheless, the bounty of a country rich in natural resources that can be exploited with little effort, a varied and permanent supply of foods that even poor people have at their disposal, the survival of certain segregationist social hierarchies, the absence of economic relations based on reciprocal trust, the state's inability to enforce the law, the low levels of savings and investments, and the appearance of different forms of populism, meant that the awakening of a hardworking spirit and economic initiatives was not accompanied by changes in Ecuadorians' other behaviors.

More time will need to pass to appreciate the economic and cultural effects that the emigration of about one and a half million Ecuadorians to developed countries in North America, Europe, and Australia will produce. Almost all of them have done well, thanks to the fact that they live in societies that progress daily, offer equal opportunities, and are less discriminating than Ecuadorian society. This is a reality that those who speak of the "tragedy" of emigration refuse to admit. After covering their own necessities, educating their children in schools and colleges with high academic levels, ensuring the family's health care, and—in the case of the luckiest ones—buying a home, the emigrants save sizeable sums of money, part of which they send to Ecuador. These sums totaled US$3 billion in 2006, and they are producing significant changes in the living standards of the family members of those who left Ecuador and are making an important contribution to the country's development.

Immigrants are gradually adopting the good habits of the inhabitants of the developed countries where they live, with regard to working hard, obeying the law, respecting commitments, and honoring interpersonal, community, and public relations. They are also developing a certain financial culture that helps them manage the family assets better. The children who could not accompany them receive these values through regular conversations that they have with their parents thanks to modern electronic means of communication, as well as books, didactic materials, and useful information of different kinds. The families that receive remittances from abroad are forced to render accounts and make productive investments in businesses or improvements in the family home, or to purchase a new one. When the emigrants come to Ecuador for vacation, they broaden these positive cultural influences among friends and relatives by telling them how democracy and the economy work in Europe and North America, and informing them about how their success is due to the efforts they have made and how some of their fellow countrymen have failed to prosper because they have not done a good job. These positive influences will be more enduring in the case of those who return to their homeland. And this number will increase over time if the Quechua expression "*la sangre llama*" (meaning that "blood calls you home") is true.

ENTREPRENEURIAL CONSTRAINTS

An enterprising spirit and the desire to earn money led Ecuadorians, formally or informally, to establish small, medium, and large enterprises. In implementing them, they took initiatives and ran risks to take advantage of the opportunities opened up by economic growth, greater consumption, international openness, and globalization. However, equivalent changes did not occur in other attitudes that have to do with the productivity of economic activities, the seriousness of businesses, and long-term business development.

Despite the fact that work has come to form part of the daily life of both rich and poor, it is not always conscientious, enterprising, persevering, diligent, and effective. Often it is indolent, irregular, routine, and listless. So, the companies and businesses that are established are not always productive,* innovative, and competitive. Ecuador occupies one of the lowest rankings in Latin America in this area.† This constitutes a severe constraint for the successful insertion of the country and the companies in the contemporary globalized world, where commercial freedom rewards those who are competitive and punishes those who are ineffective. The lack of interest with which work is done is most notable among those who work as employees, especially in the public sector, "keeping their seat warm" in ministries, municipal offices, provincial councils, and other government offices. There are rural teachers who arrive at school to teach class at noon on Mondays and then stop working on Thursdays.

Since there is no concern about the economical use of time, few consider it a productive good that must be used minute to minute. There is a persistent tendency to do things without dedication, eagerness, and speed, unlike the hardworking Asians who do everything fast, and many times, in a rush. Many Ecuadorians continue to leave things for later, instead of doing them immediately; and what can be done today is still left for tomorrow. The old sayings that refer to this tendency date back a long way and in reality mean that a task, a project, or a commitment will be completed someday, or maybe never. The poor sense of responsibility and the tendency to transfer it to others is expressed in ambiguous language that leaves

---

*Between 1997 and 2000, whereas Costa Rica's banana yield was forty-two metric tons per hectare, Ecuador's was thirty-two; whereas Brazil's coffee production was 7.5 kg per hectare, Ecuador's figures were less than half; and whereas Colombia's cacao production was five kg per hectare, Ecuador's was only 2.3 (Source: http://faostat.fao.org).

†According to the Growth Competitiveness Index prepared by the World Economic Forum regarding fifteen Latin American and Caribbean countries, Ecuador placed among the bottom three between 2001 and 2005, with a downward trend in its position in more recent years.

blame in limbo. When an object is broken or misplaced, the responsibility is lessened with expressions in passive voice, where no agent is responsible for the occurrence. When someone misses a plane or a bus because he or she arrived late, the event is justified by saying that the person "got left." When highlanders want to ask someone to do something, they say the equivalent of "bring this to me" or "do that for me."

The absence of a practical attitude toward life makes for: time lost in useless discussions, unspecified objectives, hindered agreements, more accent on ends than means, a lack of perseverance in the face of great difficulties, and projects abandoned when they are only halfway done. Instead of propitiating constructive positions that will make it possible to reach an objective, solve a problem, or settle a conflict, negative attitudes are encouraged. In the face of good ideas and positive initiatives, the people involved express all types of "buts" instead of making contributions to perfect a suggestion or find a solution. The force of personal relations, especially in the case of coastal businesses, leads people to make decisions, make purchases, and hire services thinking about the ties of family or friendship they have with the people offering something rather than quality and usefulness. In the business world of the highlands, it is not easy to know with certainty what speakers are thinking, due to the fact that they tend to hide their true intentions. In transactions, the customer's or the counterpart's interests are not taken into account, without anyone realizing that the businesses that last are those that leave both sides happy.

Those who form part of a private enterprise or a public institution at the different levels of direction, administration, and implementation do not identify with them nor do they cooperate loyally to achieve their success. They do not link their interests to those of the institution they serve, nor to those of the country they live in, so they are not willing to cooperate by renouncing something, making sacrifices, and doing extra work when critical circumstances arise. Underlying such behavior is the selfish belief that the problems of the institution or company where they work, the community where they live, and the country where they were born are none of their concern.

Just as during the cacao period, the lack of interest in saving and the tendency to unproductive spending worked when the country received sizeable capital revenues from petroleum. Even though the state invested part of these resources in equipping the country with physical infrastructure, better communication, and a variety of public services, another part was wasted on unproductive spending on works that were unnecessary, poorly executed, or never finished; subsidies for influential groups in acts of corruption; a cumbersome, and in some cases privileged, bureaucracy;* socially regressive subsidies that in 2007 exceeded 5 percent of the GDP; and heavy military spending originating in the border conflict with Peru.† For these reasons, in 2002 savings represented 20 percent of the GDP, whereas in Chile it was 27 percent and in the successful economies of Singapore, China, and Malaysia it exceeded 40 percent.[9]

The upper classes were also spendthrifts, but they were not the only ones. They spent a significant part of their income on excessive consumption that was sometimes lavish,‡ left part of their export business earnings abroad, and deposited in foreign banks funds produced by the national economy. The lack of confidence caused by the chronic political and economic instability of recent decades influenced this capital flight. Such instability also led to the failure of banks in 1999, when thousands of Ecuadorians lost part of their deposits. The slight inclination to savings has led businessmen, especially on the coast, to set up their businesses with large percentages of debt. This has made their operations more expensive and in some cases has led them into bankruptcy. For the well-to-do upper classes, especially those in Guayaquil, who have their own houses and apartments in Miami, that city became the place to which they traveled regularly to shop and spend part of the year.§

Instead of inspiring admiration, wealth built up through personal or entrepreneurial effort leads to suspicion. It is not viewed as a fair reward for work, initiative, sound decisions, talent, and sacrifice. One example of this is the informal merchants and small shopkeepers who work from dawn to

---

*According to INEC, in 1972 there were 115,000 public employees; and ten years later, 337,000.

†In 1969, military spending was 2.2 percent of the GDP; between 1975 and 1988, it fluctuated between 3 percent and 4.6 percent. Samuel Fitch, *The Armed Forces and Democracy in Latin America* (Baltimore: The John Hopkins University Press, 1998), 80.

‡In 1970, consumer goods accounted for 13 percent of total imports; in 2002, for 28 percent.

§A good illustration of this is an anecdote told by a woman from Guayaquil's highest social circles. To escape from the innumerable creditors whose loans she had squandered, along with her assets, she vanished from Guayaquil one night and fled the country across the northern border. In her memoirs she recounts that on one of her numerous trips to Miami, where she had gone "to bring back Christmas presents for the children," when she was about to return, she saw an enormous stuffed animal, a cat the size of a person, in a mall store window. Her husband wanted to buy it because it was one of the few Hello Kitty figures that their daughters did not have. However the store clerk told them that she could not sell it because it had been manufactured to attract the attention of potential customers. Given their insistence, the clerk consulted the factory, which responded that they could make another one in fifteen days. So that they could take the cat back with them, they extended their stay in Miami for two weeks; and when they arrived at the airport to fly back to Guayaquil, they bought a ticket for the stuffed animal, so that it could travel comfortably beside them in a first-class seat "with a seat belt and everything," and not be damaged in the luggage bins. Marta Muñoz de Arosemena, *Marta Muñoz solamente*, ed. Rosa Guzmán (San Juan, Puerto Rico: 1996), 57, 60–61.

dusk, including weekends. This attitude leads to viewing with envy those who are successful and get rich, and few feel and express admiration for those who have triumphed in life. With imagination, intelligence, and hard work, there are many Ecuadorians who have come up from nothing. The most notable case is that of Luis Noboa Naranjo, who as a child sold lottery tickets and trinkets in the streets of Guayaquil, and as a young man and mature adult ran multiple companies, among these a multinational banana company (the only Ecuadorian one), which made him the richest man in Ecuador. A similar case is that of the descendants of English immigrant William Wright, who started a small grocery store in Quito and introduced supermarkets. Under the name Supermaxi, his heirs have transformed these into one of the most modern, prosperous, and useful business conglomerates in Ecuador. There is usually a similar begrudging attitude toward successful professionals, intellectuals, artists, and politicians, whom few are willing to acknowledge and commend, much less publicly.

LACK OF TRUST

The sense of distrust that Ecuadorians have traditionally had continues to manifest itself when it comes time to make a deal, set up a company, grant credit, reach an agreement, and undertake different kinds of activities. There is reluctance to tell the truth, and people are frequently late in arriving at their appointments, fulfilling commitments, implementing a contract, performing a task, submitting work, providing a service, and paying a debt.*

A "yes" cannot be considered a real "yes" due to the lightness with which people respond positively to a request and due to the widespread reservations about saying an uncomfortable definitive "no." What people consider right and convenient in the way of principles does not correspond to what they do in their practical life, so there is a clear difference between what they say and what they do. This conduct means that there is widespread suspicion that when a person gives his word it will not be honored, that agreements will not be fulfilled, and that the money or goods contributed to a business will not be looked after, even when the commitments have been legalized through public documents, contracts, IOUs, checks,

---

*The outstanding debt index for the Ecuadorian financial system is 6.1 percent of the total portfolio, whereas in Chile it is 1.6 percent (Ecuador: Superintendencia de Bancos y Seguros, www .superban.gov.ec, *Reporte Gerencial*. Chile: Superintendencia de Bancos e Instituciones Financieras, www.sbif.cl, *Índices de provisiones de Riesgo de Crédito de Colocaciones*).

and guarantees. The fear of receiving bad checks, without sufficient funds, explains why this form of payment is not accepted at hotels, restaurants, and business establishments when it is a personal check. To ask a friend, relative, or colleague at work for a loan, with the unkept promise to pay it back right away (*sablazo* or "sponging"), forms part of everyday life. When a foreign author warned that "theft is so pervasive in Ecuador that everything is literally nailed down or fenced in,"[10] he was not exaggerating if we stop to think about the high property walls, alarms, iron bars on windows, guards, and watchmen that the owners of houses, apartments, vehicles, and businesses use to protect their belongings.

The so-called *viveza criollo* is an example of the admiration that unscrupulous conduct causes. The person who, like a con artist, astutely or shrewdly deceives others is seen as clever; and the one who acts seriously and in good faith, as naïve or dumb. Since ingenuous foreigners are easy victims of the *viveza*, when an Ecuadorian thinks that someone wants to "take" him, he responds in an annoyed voice, "What do you take me for? A gringo?" It is with that moral stance that the many children and youth who cheat on tests, homework, papers, and theses without being caught by their teachers are treated. In recent years the names of top-level government officials who plagiarized entire chapters of their dissertations from other authors—including even an Attorney General and a general in the police force—have come to light. Since such conduct is not uncommon and is thus not seen as reproachable, the people who do it are not sanctioned morally by friends, classmates, neighbors, partners, and colleagues. Hence, as though nothing had happened, they continue participating in the family, social, institutional, or community circles of which they formed part before their misconduct became known.

A Jewish immigrant has told of how he formed a partnership with Ecuadorian businessmen to produce limes. Some of them paid for their shares with bills of exchange "that were never settled." Such conduct made him learn fast that in this country such documents were readily signed but proved hard to collect.[11] Another wrote: "Those of us that trusted everybody, very soon learned to resign ourselves and realize that with that mentality here we would not advance at all. We did business and made deals without signing any contract or any document, just trusting that the person was upright. We were really foolish, totally naïve; and little by little, with everyday incidences, we gained experience and learned how to behave here and whom to trust." He added that over time he learned "that the parameters of honesty in Ecuador were minimal and they deceived us gringos awfully."[12]

Preceding chapters have noted that the phenomenon was common to all social classes, and the following experiences confirm this fact. When

I built my house, the mason who I reprimanded for an error "got back at me" (another national habit) by installing a bathroom drain with holes in it, which led to a continuous leak. On two occasions, water ruined the wood floors, until finally, after several years of coping with the problem, I managed to discover the hidden cause of the persistent moisture problem. A foreigner who has lived in the country almost all his life told me about a plumber who did repairs in his home for many years; he did them halfway so that they would call him back and he could charge them again. This deceit was discovered when the plumber slipped up and told a maid in the house about it.

Ecuadorians' lack of trust is reflected in a 2007 Latinobarómetro survey, according to which only 12 percent of the people interviewed believed they could trust others. The economic damages that this distrust has caused the country, companies, and individuals cannot be quantified.

The lack of transparency in people's acts has led to the failure of business initiatives to materialize, delays in businesses, a lack of entrepreneurial operations, and inability to achieve objectives. The fear that the parties will act in bad faith means that many companies are family-owned and operated, and few open up to participation by multiple shareholders. This business structure limits capital accumulation; hinders transparency in the payment of taxes; propitiates noncompliance with laws, statutes, and regulations; and leads directors to be named because of personal considerations rather than capabilities. Evidence of this is the fact that in 2006 of some 37,297 companies, only 142 sold shares on the Quito and Guayaquil stock exchanges.[13]

The lack of trust also affects efficient, honest public administration. The businessmen who have contracts with the state or are associated with it are not certain that the agreements they sign will be respected; and in the event of disputes they doubt whether the authorities and judges will reach a fair decision or settlement, in keeping with the law and without accepting any political interference or seeking improper compensations. For this reason, speculative businesses that yield immediate earnings are more attractive to investors than the long-term projects that are so important for national development. Others protect themselves from the high risks run in Ecuador by raising the prices of the goods they sell or the projects they build. Meanwhile, in light of the magnitude of the contingencies, the large corporations—whose transparency is controlled by their countries' governments and laws—postpone or cancel their projects and opt to invest in safer countries. Since honest businessmen avoid signing contracts with the state, it is the corrupt ones that end up becoming its collaborators. Thanks to political, family, or friendship influences or the payment of bribes, they sign contracts at inflated prices, obtain unjustified contract readjustments, do work of poor quality, or simply abandon the project without finishing it. When the state turns to the international market to procure credits, it must pay high interest rates and must sell the bonds that it issues with large discounts. These are means by which the market reflects economic agents' distrust in the seriousness of the country.

A PERMISSIVE SOCIETY

The expansion of the public sector's sphere of action, the multiple attributions it took on, but above all the sizeable oil wealth that it administered, made the state the subject of malicious interest to which many sought access so that its decisions would favor them. For those who think and act in this way, the state is not the body to which it corresponds to protect public assets, defend general interests, respond to legitimate rights, demand obligations, seek the common good, and guarantee enforcement of the law, but rather an instrument whereby individuals, social organizations, public labor unions, economic groups' directors, political leaders, and private businessmen can obtain favors, benefits, or privileges and get rich, by assuming public functions or influencing the decisions of government officials. This permissive mentality had led to a tight-knit network of interests, complicity, bribes, and cover-ups that have been used to carry out unlawful operations and the immoral appropriation of public goods and resources, many times with impunity.

The oldest, most widespread and incorrigible form of corruption is smuggling, where operations, influences, and complicity are still the same as over four centuries ago.* It is so integrated into national life that thousands of merchants make a living from it, and many more benefit from shopping at La Bahía in Guayaquil and La Ipiales in Quito, huge markets that sell all types of merchandise introduced illegally into the country without paying duty. Fraudulent connections make it possible to steal electricity, telephone time, potable water, and fuels; and at night, pipes, electric cables, and telephone lines disappear. With the collusion of police chiefs and the lead-

---

*According to research conducted by Prófitas regarding imports brought into Ecuador illegally from Argentina, Bolivia, Brazil, China, Colombia, Panama, Paraguay, and Peru between 2000 and 2003, the state failed to receive US$457 million from customs duties and value-added taxes. This represents 12 percent of the total revenues earned from such sources during the same period. Prófitas, *Estudio de estimación del contrabando* (Quito, 2005, unpublished printout).

ers of professional drivers federations, thousands of illegal driver's licenses are issued annually.* Commissions have been paid on weapons bought by the Junta de Defensa, as during the border conflict of 1995 when corrupt military chiefs did not even care that the country's territorial integrity was at stake.† Those involved in lawsuits in courts know that the judges who charge for the verdicts or sentences they reach are not an exception; and if "tips" are not paid to judicial employees, proceedings are not expedited. This is illustrated by the dismissal of dozens of magistrates in recent years, even from the Supreme Court.‡ The leniency of the judicial system in pursuing and punishing corruption is so great that in some cases the sanction has come through the U.S. government's cancellation of its visas for the citizens involved.

In government offices, municipal offices, provincial councils, and other public institutions the presence of *pipones* ("fat cats")—payroll employees who collect a salary without working or even without going to the office—is frequent. In the National Congress there are habitually hundreds, and estimates are that five thousand teachers (4 percent of the total) are also *pipones*, some even residing abroad. This fraudulent practice would not be possible without the complicity of authorities at the Ministry of Education and the national teachers union (UNE).§ In Manabí and other coastal provinces, important politicians and wealthy businessmen have fraudulent electric power connections or owe large sums on overdue power bills. However, unlike what occurs with small consumers whose payments are overdue, they are not deprived of the service and their debts are not collected.¶ In 2006 it came to light that since 1998, with the connivance of officials, technical experts, and directors at Petroecuador, a system was operating in the oilfields that allowed production to be recycled to conceal the incompetence of the state company. Fictitious figures were presented on the number of barrels of oil extracted. Articles stolen from homes (*cachinerías*) are sold from store to store under the tolerant eye of the police. A European business advisor who complained about the widespread

---

*In 2005 the Inspectoría de la Policía Nacional determined that in the previous three years eight thousand fake licenses had been issued. *Diario Hoy*, June 12, 2006.

†On February 10, 1995, during the conflict on the country's southern border, the Junta de Defensa Nacional bought useless weapons and ammunition from factories in Argentina.

‡According to an Informe Confidencial survey covering the years between 2000 and 2007, on average 45 percent of the inhabitants of Quito and Guayaquil did not trust the Judicial Branch.

§The investigation was ordered by Minister of Education Consuelo Yánez in 2005 but did not continue when she left office.

¶The April 29, 2006 newspapers published a list of people with outstanding debt. Provided by the Fondo de Solidaridad, that list included some ten businessmen with debts of between US$100,000 and US$900,000, as well as two congressmen who owed US$22,000 and US$57,000.

corruption in the public sector of Latin America remarked to me that there are countries like Ecuador where corruption is not "honest," in the sense that certain officials, after receiving a bribe, did not fulfill the commitments made.

Another form of corruption is the gratuitous transfer of public funds from the Banco Central and other institutions to private individuals. This occurred in 1984, during the government of President Leon Febres Cordero, when he softened the conditions of securitization of the foreign debt, which had been resolved by the previous government. He eliminated exchange-rate risk commissions and froze interest rates.[14] Then, he authorized banks to compensate for their debts with the issuing institution, and authorized certain companies to capitalize by purchasing Ecuadorian debt on the international market, at up to 30 percent of its nominal value, and immediately selling it to the Central Bank at 100 percent, which meant a gratuitous benefit of US$396 million.[15] On numerous occasions, governments and congresses have forgiven interests and commissions that farmers with overdue debts owed to the Banco de Fomento. Labor unions for public enterprises obtain immoral privileges—and their directors, costly indemnities—thanks to gracious concessions made by their administrators in the collective contracts that they irresponsibly signed.

In the private sector, there has also been permissive economic behavior, although to a lesser extent than in the public sector. However, since these examples are held in reserve and not published in the mass media, citizens are not familiar with them; for example, the swindles perpetrated by managers and employees. Personal and family expenses, sightseeing trips, and maids' salaries are charged to companies; and the cases in which it proves to be an odyssey to collect an invoice—for instance, in condos and exclusive clubs—are not rare. There are managers who charge commissions on the transactions that their firms carry out, repeating the custom that the officials of some banks in Guayaquil and one in Quito had until the early 1970s of charging "interest under the table" paid "secretly" by the customer who received a credit.

The timely and fair payment of taxes, which is the citizens' main obligation to their country, is seen by a large majority of citizens as a naïve rectitude. Since the word "taxpayer" is not part of the national language, citizens are not usually bothered by the fact that the taxes paid to the state are wasted. To avoid paying taxes and to be able to transfer a part of their profits abroad, there are companies that have two sets of books, underbill exports, overbill imports, or have their partners set up companies in fiscal paradises. Through confidential agreements, businessmen who manufacture similar goods set uniform selling prices to keep the market from setting them through free competition. Greedy citizens have been swindled by supposed financiers, to whom they handed over their capital as a loan in exchange for usury interest payments, so high that those that actually managed to collect them before the improvised bankers "flew the coop" obtained, in a little more than a year, sums equivalent to the capital originally invested.* In quite a few companies, the employees are obliged to return used pencils, pens, erasers, and other items when requesting they be replaced by new ones.

There are figures to illustrate this. According to ECLAC, in 2006 the tax burden in Ecuador was 10.4 percent of the GDP whereas in Chile it was 17.1 percent. This low figure can be explained by the tax evasion that, according to Internal Revenue Service (SRI) officials' estimates, could be as high as 25 percent of the value-added tax and 30 percent of the income tax. According to research done by CORDES, in 2001–2004 the provincial tax burden in Pichincha was equivalent to 22.2 percent of the GDP, whereas in Guayas it was only 9.4 percent,† despite the fact that the latter was the richer of the two provinces. In 2004, according to the Superintendencia de Companies, 52 percent of the new capital contributed to companies came from Panama, the Virgin Islands, the Grand Cayman Islands, the Bahamas, and other foreign tax havens. The financial crisis of 1999, during which thirteen banks either failed or were taken over by the state—some due to the corruption of their administrators—represented a cost to the state of about 25 percent of the GDP in the year 2000.

A public opinion poll requested by the newspaper *El Universo* established that 67 percent of the residents of Guayaquil and 25 percent of those of Quito admitted to having paid someone to expedite some bureaucratic process.[16] According to other research of a similar nature done in 2006, 21 percent of the country justified the payment of bribes, the highest percentage being in Guayaquil (37 percent) with a lower rate in Quito (14 percent). There were no differences in the behavior of the interviewees because of socioeconomic or educational levels; however, unlike what one might have thought, there were differences according to age. A large percentage

---

*The largest embezzlement occurred in 2005 and was perpetrated by Machala notary public José Cabrera Román, who received around US$500 million from a wide variety of citizens, including members of the military, the police, political leaders, government officials, judges, and others with some affluence.

†These figures were calculated on the basis of statistics from the Banco Central (Central Bank) and the SRI (Internal Revenue Service). To avoid distortions, state-owned companies, oil enterprises, and foreign firms in Pichincha and Guayas were excluded, as well as those that paid income tax and value-added tax in Quito and Guayaquil even though they were from other provinces.

of young people justified the payment of bribes, which would lead one to think that dishonesty will worsen in the future.[17] Transparencia Internacional, in its 2005 report, pointed out that 18 percent of those surveyed in Ecuador admitted to having paid a bribe within the last year. In Latin America, this percentage was only surpassed in Paraguay, Guatemala, Bolivia, and Mexico. In another survey, the same organization established that the sum of US$177 was the average that each family paid in bribes in 2007, which would imply that Ecuadorians allocate US$533 million per year to that item. If the payment of "little tips" is so widespread, it is reasonable to deduce that the payment of sizeable bribes must be much more frequent when contracts worth millions are signed with public institutions.

These data and the analyses of foregoing paragraphs explain why Ecuador has figured among the group of the world's most corrupt countries since 1996. This is according to the corruption perception index prepared by Transparencia Internacional, where Ecuador is number 139 among 163 countries, surpassed in Latin America only by Venezuela and Paraguay. Moral permissiveness tends to be higher on the coast, for instance in terms of tax evasion and payment of bribes. Evidence of this fact led the author of the aforementioned research to affirm that "the entire coastal region seems to be more tolerant of the payment of bribes than the highlands and the Amazon Region," especially the inhabitants of Guayaquil.[18]

Due to the broad scale that corruption has attained in Ecuador (and not the lack of organizations and laws to tackle it, which are actually abundant), politics, the state, and the sectional governments cannot escape from its pernicious presence. Therein lies the reason that the laws issued to curtail it have not produced the desired effects, that the organizations created to control it have not met their objectives, and that the successive governments' promises to eliminate it have failed. Beyond the norms, the institutions, and the authorities, what ended up imposing itself was the moral blandness that dictated the day-to-day behavior of numerous Ecuadorians. Honest societies have honest politicians and public officials, while permissive societies, such as the Ecuadorian one, give birth to corrupt politicians and officials. However, there is apparently no awareness of this reality in our country, according to a survey conducted by Transparencia Internacional in 2007, according to which only 21 percent of those interviewed considered that "there is much corruption among the citizens."

The absence of ethical principles is so great and has such a long history that national language has adapted to it. To attenuate feelings of guilt, euphemisms such as *llevar* and *coger* are used, with which the action of appropriating someone else's property is made to seem lighter. The person who dishonestly profits from state money, "*lo lleva*"; and the person who takes something during a visit to someone's home, a party, or a trip to the supermarket or a store does not steal it, "*se coge*."

UNEQUAL OPPORTUNITIES

The rigid social hierarchies of old have become somewhat attenuated, as a result of agriculture's loss of its traditional importance; the disarticulation of the hacienda system; the "awakening" of the indigenous community; the predomination of urban economy; the liberation of peasant labor; the agrarian reform; the action of the state; the expansion of education; and the ideas spread by Christianity, Protestantism, socialism, and international organizations. These changes opened up opportunities for individuals of color (mestizos, Indians, blacks, and mulattos) to be educated, take care of their health, work, negotiate their remuneration, and undertake any type of activity—notably, agriculture, commerce, transportation, artisanry, and sports, thanks to which they have managed to improve their standards of living.

Even though the stratified society shaped in previous eras weakened in the second half of the twentieth century, it did not disappear since family descent and skin color continued to carry weight in the social differentiation of Ecuadorians. It is curious that things are like that if one recalls that in the 2001 census a large majority of Ecuadorians declared themselves mestizos (77.4 percent) and only 10.5 percent considered themselves whites.* It is not easy to find an explanation for this strange duality except for the possibility that those who accept their Indian blood in everyday life prefer to forget their heritage and in their social and economic relations act as if they were entirely white, an ethnic label that leads them not to consider as equals those who have distinct indigenous facial features and, worse yet, those who preserve their Quechua culture.

Despite the economic and social progress of recent decades; the advances made by Indians, blacks, mestizos, and mulattos; and the fact that the society has become more open and permeable, at the end of the century Ecuadorians with a skin of color continued to suffer concealed forms of discrimination, and belonging to a given race continued to determine people's destinies. Almost all the Indians and blacks are poor, but no whites are. In

---

*According to the 2001 census conducted by INEC, 77.4 percent of the population called itself mestizo, 10.5 percent white, 6.8 percent Indian, 2.7 percent mulatto, 2.2 percent black, and 0.3 percent other races.

discotheques in Quito and other cities, young people's physical appearance determines whether they will get in or not. This discrimination is handled by the doorkeepers of the establishment, some of whom are blacks. Among the reasons that Quito's middle and upper classes were mobilized in 2005 for the purpose of overthrowing President Lucio Gutiérrez—in addition to his abuses of power—there was a racist element that few accept and that was ignored by those who commented on events in newspapers, magazines, and books. According to a contemporary North American researcher, "class consciousness permeates every facet of life in Ecuador," since those who form part of the elite, or aspire to be part of it, are distinguished by their family name, the club they belong to, the school where their children study, their business connections, and the way they treat others in their day-to-day life.[19]

According to Latinobarómetro (2007), 71 percent of those interviewed thought that equal opportunities were not guaranteed in the country, 81 percent thought that access to the justice system was not equal for all, and 45 percent believed that connections were more important than effort in attaining success.

Ecuador's development has been limited by a society with manifest ethnic differences, composed of individuals who do not consider each other equals and that, in fact, are not equal in exercising their rights, fulfilling their obligations, and obtaining opportunities.

Neither was it possible for the country to construct a national identity, which has always been lacking and that is so necessary for constituting a community committed to its destiny and willing to fight to attain it. To the contrary, social and economic margination provoked sentiments of exclusion that unleashed social and political conflicts that in the 1980s were led by a workers federation (FUT) and in the 1990s by the Indian confederation (CONAIE). Through protests and strikes, these organizations kept the governments from making decisions aimed at promoting economic growth and, consequently, social welfare.

The inequalities caused by social hierarchies kept those who were situated at the bottom of the social pyramid from having the same opportunities as those located at the top enjoyed when facing the challenge of finding employment, starting a business, undertaking an economic activity, and getting an education. Whereas the children of working-class families attend deficient public establishments, those from well-to-do families are educated in private schools and universities of a better level. This is one of the reasons that public education and health care services have been left to their luck. Since members of the middle and upper classes use their own resources to provide themselves with education and health care, they have done nothing to detain and invert the deterioration of the corresponding public services. In that regard, one scholar has reflected as follows: "Disparities in the distribution of health care and education, for example, have had a clear impact on social behavior. The Ecuadorians that have the means to avoid public facilities are seldom concerned about improving them. Insufficiently staffed and poorly equipped hospitals, clinics and schools become 'simple matters' in a society that has created parallel institutions for the haves and the have-nots."[20]

Finally, the social hierarchies make personal relations prevail over institutional ones. Decision makers think about the person or the group that will be benefited or harmed, and not about the merits that the person seeking something might have and the needs that would deserve to be taken care of, especially in the case of the public sector. When government officials find themselves with the opportunity of providing retribution or sanctioning an individual, instead of bearing in mind the person's capacity, experience, and responsibility, what frequently counts is friendship, kinship, and the relationships between someone and his or her godchildren's parents, as well as political affinities, union camaraderie, connections, contacts, and favoritisms, just as occurred in the society that preceded modern Ecuador. The aforementioned author noted that "The intricate web of relatives is of major significance, since its members have easy access to all types of opportunities in society. Personal connections are a guarantee that, when necessary, one can find an appropriate person with influence." He added, "the curt and cold behavior" of those that serve the public in government offices "quickly becomes cordial and effusive when an Ecuadorian recognizes a face or a name" since "personalism, connections and the parent/godparent relationship (*compadrazgo*) are fundamental factors that make it possible to successfully navigate a system that rewards social status and connections."[21]

In some governments more than others, just as in other national and local public institutions, nepotism and favors for "buddies" are commonly present. The relationship between relatives and friends is so strong that the person who does not accept requests and does not place them in bureaucratic positions causes resentment among those affected, to whom it would never occur to think about whether the person was deserving of the position or not. According to a 2007 Informe Confidencial survey, 52 percent of the residents of Quito and 62 percent of those of Guayaquil would appoint a family member to a public-sector position if they were Cabinet ministers. In similar percentages, they would be willing to prefer them in contracts for office supplies. In trade associations, professional associations, and the military and police corps, judicial or disciplinary bodies seldom sanction the faults of their members, and directors recur to the so-called *esprit de corps* to silence mistakes and wrongdoings.

INSECURITY IN THE LEGAL SYSTEM

There have been no significant modifications to the limited role that the law has played in citizens' everyday lives; in the exercise of authority; and in the action of governments, congresses, public institutions, and political, social, and economic organizations. The deep-rooted custom of failing to respect the law, practiced for centuries, has weighed more heavily than the innumerable laws issued to minutely regulate all of the aspects of national life, the penalties established to sanction violators, and the efforts that some authorities have made to enforce them. In a World Bank study done in 2005 to measure the rule of law in 208 countries, Ecuador was ranked 161st. In Latin America, only Guatemala, Haiti, Venezuela, and Paraguay obtained lower scores, whereas Chile was ranked 27th.[22] According to Latinobarómetro, in 2007 only 32 percent of Ecuadorians considered the people that observed laws good citizens; this was the lowest percentage in Latin America, alongside Guatemala's.

The rule of law exists in societies in which citizens regularly question whether the act they are about to commit is framed within legal provisions. There, laws have penetrated citizens' minds in such a way that naturally, and without the need for coercion, they frame their everyday behavior within the norms and do not exceed them no matter how laudable the purpose they propose to achieve. This does not happen in Ecuador, where the law is viewed instead as something unreal (an entelechy), alien to people's lives or simply a nuisance, when they work, go along the streets, do business, deal with the state, or carry out any other activity. The aphorism that "whoever breaks it, pays for it" is not the one that counts in the life of Ecuadorians, but rather "once the law exists, so does the way to get around it." This sad reality explains the multitude of laws existing in the country, some of whose provisions have been dictated for the sole purpose of sewing up loopholes.

In societies in which numerous citizens disobey laws all the time, it is impossible for police officers, judges, and officials to impose compliance. When there is the custom of ignoring the law, of violating it on an everyday basis, of interpreting it in bad faith, and of eluding it through the use of loopholes and shortcuts—as well as of taking advantage of influence and power to manipulate or bribe judges and authorities—justice is degraded, and legal norms are applied in a discretionary way, according to conveniences. A good example of this is what occurs with traffic laws on streets and highways. They are systematically disobeyed by drivers and pedestrians of all social classes, and not even the risk of dying motivates them to comply with the cautionary regulations dictated for their safety. In Ecuador, traffic accidents constitute the third-highest cause of death for men, and are mainly caused by drunk driving, excess speed, and other driving violations; and in the case of pedestrians, by not using the crosswalks.

If citizens do not care about legal norms, it is logical that the provisions of the constitution and the laws will not govern the acts of the government, the Congress, the Electoral Board, the Constitutional Court, and other public agencies. These state bodies have repeatedly violated the constitution; for example, when the Congress did away with three presidents of the republic, a Supreme Court justice, and a Constitutional Court, and when the Electoral Board dismissed fifty-seven congressmen. Violating a constitutional prohibition, the Congress has many times given itself the attribution of drawing up and submitting bills that create public spending and endanger fiscal stability. It has ignored a dozen transitory provisions of the 1998 Constitution, which orders that laws be issued to permit the application of constitutional norms. For instance, it provided that all of the magistrates and judges that depend on the Executive Branch, including the military and the police, be part of the Judicial Branch. Due to the culture of illegality existing in the country, these arbitrary actions of public powers have been approved by a vast majority of the citizens, according to a number of opinion polls.

In the absence of a culture of legality—and not the lack of legal norms or the existence of inadequate political institutions—the democratic system has functioned poorly in its duty to protect rights, ensure political stability, propitiate economic continuity, and promote Ecuador's development. Something similar has happened on an individual level. The law is not capable of offering guarantees that citizens will have equal opportunities and of demanding similar obligations. For that reason, it is not possible to recognize merit; reward effort; guarantee equitable economic, social, and political relations; and encourage emulation and competition, all of which individual and national economic advancement depends on.

The state is not in a position to provide legal security to economic activities, that is, the certainty that conflicts will be resolved in a fair way, that authorities' and judges' decisions will be in line with the law, and that the legal principles that regulate contracts signed under their protection will not change. The absence of legal security has not allowed the country to generate an environment of confidence that will favor the entry of foreign investment, which is an element that in the modern world has become a lever for national development. Furthermore, in the economic sphere it seems natural to Ecuadorians for there to be a double standard for Ecuadorians and foreigners. The cases in which the latter suffer outrages justified through nationalistic allegations that have nothing to do with State of Law regulations and procedures are not exceptional.

The lack of compliance with the law limits the possibility that it can play a transforming role in the culture of the citizens by reducing the capacity of the legal principles to change misconduct and inappropriate behavior. If those who disobey the laws do not receive any sanction, it is understandable that other citizens are tempted to follow in their footsteps, even those who are naturally disposed to obeying. The fact that the rule of law exists in the United States, Spain, and other countries explains why the Ecuadorians who reside there follow authorities' orders and comply with legal dispositions and thereby gradually adopt the correct everyday practices of the natives of the place where they live.

Nonetheless, despite the fact that laws do not count for much in Ecuador's social, economic, and political life, there is a collective obsession with resolving national, local, business, and community problems through the enactment of legal norms expressed in constitutions, laws, regulations, decrees, ordinances, etc.

FROM PATERNALISM TO POPULISM

"The patron–client relationship, highly asymmetrical and with strong overtones of dependency" in Ecuador "is the prototype for all relationships" between the people and "authority figures who are potential benefactors," including scholars and community-development agents.[23] According to this observation made by anthropologist Casagrande, to which others of similar nature could be added, paternalism continued to shape social relations in the 1970s just as it had in previous eras, even when people opposed to such practices were involved. Therefore, in the second half of the twentieth century, populism continued to be nourished, along with the leaders that reproduced the patron–client relationship in politics.

Sentiments of social exclusion among the sectors that did not benefit from economic progress contributed to the thriving influence of populism, as did rapid urbanization, the incorporation of numerous new voters into public life, the clear predomination of urban voters, the spread of radio and television, and the absence of community life in the case of coastal populations. Populist leaders intuitively realized the political potential of these new realities, and with their rhetorical demagogy touched the sensitive fiber of popular sentiments. They exacerbated frustrations; highlighted social problems; identified the ones to blame; promised to wreak vengeance on the oligarchs, mafias, and "pampered" members of society; and swore to redress the rights and needs of the dispossessed. Taking into account that, as a Spanish traveler said a century ago, the American peoples "obey sentiment more than reason,"[24] they directed their discourse to the heart of those left out. The caciques and caudillos thereby wove a net of enduring loyalty that did not seem notably shaken even when they attained the government and did not fulfill their promises.

The common people saw populist leaders as a living example of sacrifice, abnegation, commitment, and solidarity that they did not find in other political leaders. In the former, they saw people who would do away with privileges, destroy the old order, and substitute a different one in which all of the problems of the poor would be resolved because the government would finally be theirs. They usually had support from regional, local, and neighborhood caciques, who were in control of electoral groups and their political mobilization, and who were also intermediaries between authorities and the people's clamors that their needs be met. The relationship between the caudillo and his followers was so personal that when his political career ended, so did his party. However, since the country's social and economic conditions did not change and Ecuadorian's paternalistic cultural values continued to be in force, populism was soon reborn with new leaders at the helm.

The populist groups were originally nurtured by adhesion that they received in the poor outlying neighborhoods of the coast, populated by migrants from the paternalistic society of the hacienda system. Poor social sectors left to their luck in a hostile and unknown urban world—without deeds to the property that they had taken by force as squatters, living in precarious housing, lacking public services and subject to all sorts of deprivations—found refuge in the paternal and munificent populist leaders. The personal relations that marginal urban populations established with their providential benefactors, based on their electoral adhesion in exchange for political favors, made it possible for them to obtain protection and aid in covering their most pressing needs: landfills, potable water, electricity, paved streets, medical dispensaries, and in some cases, housing.

Over time, populism extended its presence to the provinces of the highlands and the Amazon Region, without managing to achieve there the majority influence it had achieved on the coast. Despite the fact that it was a fundamentally regional political expression, the importance that it acquired in public life was so great that its rhetoric and practices ended up permeating the behavior of the political parties of other tendencies, including those whose electoral base was in the highlands, as well as those of citizens who did not suffer from deprivations and enjoyed a certain level of well-being.

Populism in its different party expressions having become the principal electoral force in the country, it repeatedly won the presidency of the republic and became hegemonic in coastal provinces and cities where it regularly obtained prefectures and mayorships.* At the forefront of the populist groups were charismatic caudillos that exhibited many of the same traits that the large landowners had had. Among these, as mentioned previously, José María Velasco Ibarra stood out. Thanks to his long involvement in politics and the fact that in 1960 he defeated the modernizing alternative represented by candidate Galo Plaza, his practices served as a model of public life, and his demagogy as a model for the discourse of a good number of Ecuadorian politicians.

Populism brought with it numerous negative economic consequences. The state could not maintain its subsidiary role, and it became the first recourse to which citizens recurred to have their needs met, even those that could be resolved through individual effort or community intervention. This hindered the implementation of long-term policies on which the country's development and the people's progress depended, since the populist governments opted for immediate results, easy solutions, and political opportunism. They promoted the waste of fiscal resources, which resulted in costly economic crises that caused huge social damages, bred greater poverty, and worsened inequities. Populism obstructed the making of decisions that were necessary to reestablish the health of the economy, ensure its stability, promote growth, and increase employment. It favored attention to private interests beneficial to only a few and prejudicial to most. It encouraged the transfer of individuals' and the society's own blame to imaginary guilty parties that became scapegoats for all of the people's problems. It did not pay attention to the social programs on which the creation

---

*José María Velasco Ibarra was elected President of the Republic in 1934, 1944, 1952, 1960, and 1968. Assad Bucaram served as Mayor of Guayaquil on several occasions but never became president because he did not have the backing of the military. Other populist leaders who have won the presidency have been: Jaime Roldós (1979), León Febres Cordero (1984), Abdalá Bucaram (1996), Lucio Gutiérrez (2002), and Rafael Correa (2006).

of opportunities for the neediest sectors depended, such as improvement of deteriorated public education. It limited the possibility for individuals to gain awareness of their personal, community, and public responsibilities, and for them to feel compelled to contribute to the support of the state by paying taxes and their utility bills.

The populist policies, and the sectors that called for them or favored them, multiplied with the appearance of oil wealth, especially when because of high oil prices the governments enjoyed abundant fiscal resources and squandered them. This is what occurred during the dictatorships of the 1970s and the democracies of the early years of the twenty-first century. Many times the waste of public funds was provoked by the citizens themselves, under the premise that, since the people had so many needs and the state had such abundant economic resources, there was no excuse for their needs not to be met. In the country, it occurred to few to think about the harm that the populist policies would cause for everyone's well-being and national development. This is what happened recently in the case of the decisions made by governments and congresses, to widespread applause, to spend the savings that in recent years had been built up to see the country through bad periods—savings based on the extraordinarily high income received by the country due to high oil prices. It also occurred when the Social Security Institute decided to return to its affiliates the reserve funds that they had built up with their savings to ensure their future.

If populism continues to be present in public life, and if with its discourse and its practices it continues to foster paternalism, it will not be possible for Ecuadorians to assume their responsibilities, cease to transfer problems of their own concern to others, and view public institutions as subsidiary authorities to which they should only recur if they cannot handle something themselves. To the extent that this happens, paternalism and populism will continue, as before, to be a hindrance to national development.

5

IN PURSUIT OF
ECONOMIC SUCCESS

In preceding pages, Ecuadorians' cultural habits have been analyzed, alongside the obstacles that they posed for individual and collective progress and the way in which cultural changes beginning in the nineteenth century in Guayaquil and in the twentieth century in the rest of the country opened up the possibility that individuals could advance, entrepreneurial activities could emerge, and the country could begin to develop.

This chapter will study four cases of economic success. Even though they are not the only ones, they can be considered the most significant. In all of them, a community's cultural habits played a decisive role. In some cases the habits were brought in by immigrants who made Ecuador their adopted homeland; in others, they were embraced by Ecuadorians themselves due to the economic and social changes that occurred around them. These singular cases correspond to the city of Cuenca, to the indigenous community of Otavalo, and to the Arab and Jewish immigrations.

PROGRESSIVE CUENCA

The descriptions that travelers and officials provided of the Cuencanos' attitudes toward work, innovation, economic relations, and the law during the colonial period were similar to those referring to inhabitants of the other provinces of the Audiencia de Quito. So were the references to the hierarchical and paternalistic society in which they lived, and the backwardness of their ideas and education.

In the middle of the eighteenth century, Delaporte, a French abbot, commented that Cuenca "would be the most delightful villa of Peru given its location, the abundance of its water, the fertility of its land, and the

151

beauty of its sky, if the insuperable laziness of its inhabitants did not make all of these advantages useless."[1] In 1765, the Spanish corregidor De Merizalde wrote that whites "are lazy and opposed to work; the others live in idleness and value that as much as food." He went on to say that they did nothing to satisfy their needs and planted "only what they need to eat."[2] Historian Juan de Velasco coincided with this when he pointed out the absence of "hardworking and industrious" people.[3]

In Cuenca the French scholars who comprised the Geodesic Mission found a society that was "much more closed and apprehensive" than those of Quito and Lima, one that it was "better not to rile too much."[4] In 1804, Caldas was surprised that a priest was interested in his scientific work, given the suspicion with which he and the others were viewed in a city where "the letters were nonexistent" and there were "not the slightest notions or news" about science, "a little but poor grammar was all the public education" that young people received, and the artisans were "not as advanced as in Quito."[5] Other authors noted the presence of patriarchal families and mentioned the artisans' failure to keep their commitments, the exaggerated consumption of alcohol, the reticence to pay taxes, the disdain for commerce, and the lack of trust. Furthermore, they found a certain tendency to violence and brawls that they did not mention in their chronicles about other territories.

In the second half of the eighteenth century, unlike other inhabitants in the Audiencia, the Cuencanos were described as quarrelsome, virulent, and disorderly by a colonial official, a clergyman, and a Jesuit traveler. The first said that "they generally presume themselves to be valiant and to deserve this credit" they commit frequent murders which, instead of making them lose moral worth, give them more credit in the esteem of their fellow countrymen.[6] The second described them as contentious, violent, and vengeful. He added that, since they were always armed, "no one feels his life is safe." Hence, the governors, in light of the impossibility of exercising their authority in such a wayward, ungovernable city, were forced to abandon their positions, making it necessary to name military men who could maintain order, make justice respected, and avoid having crimes go unpunished.[7] It is also worthwhile to mention that in Cuenca, due to a dispute over a woman, a physician with the Geodesic Mission, Jean Seniergues, was victimized by two young men who were later protected by local authorities and judges, despite the pertinacious determination of La Condamine to have them put on trial and convicted.[8]

In view of the fact that the residents of Cuenca were given to social and political clashes and that the city remained cloistered until the early twentieth century—and only with difficulty managed to be in communication with the rest of the country decades later—it is important to explore the reasons why nowadays they are a peaceful society whose members work readily, conduct themselves in a manner that is inspired by ethical principles, obey laws, respect institutions, and undertake innovative enterprises.

As often occurs in the process of cultural change, in the case of Cuenca a number of elements came into play. First of all, artisans, common people, and Sephardim descended from Jewish converts were involved in its colonization. All of these were given more to work and innovation than the gentlemen (*hidalgos*) who settled in other parts of the country. Furthermore, large landownership was not widespread; instead, agricultural properties were small and medium-sized. Cultivatable land was limited and not very fertile. Obrajes were exceptional, and the hacienda system did not take shape. The existence of a less numerous indigenous population than in the central-northern highlands also meant that the whites had to work and occupy themselves with tasks that they did not perform in other settlements; for example, the manual labor done by workers in the fields and by the city's artisans and merchants.

The land shortage forced rural residents to perform nonagricultural chores in the trades. The absence of noble families and a certain ethnic homogeneity favored the development of less stratified, less discriminatory social relations, and even greater equality. This offered opportunities to those who were the best at what they did, and reduced social resentment. The people with money were not the large hacienda owners, but rather individuals who worked in the city, especially professionals, jewelers, and those in charge of exploiting silver mines, washing gold, and exporting cascarilla and hats. The export business made it possible for the residents of Cuenca to have ties to the outside world from early on; and it offered them the opportunity to train doctors, engineers, and mechanical technicians in Europe. The production and exportation of metals, cascarilla, and hats—part of which were sold on the domestic market—contributed to the development of business habits. The lack of abysmal economic inequalities made it possible to increase the number of people in a position to require and purchase goods, so that a consumer market gradually formed. Cuenca historian Juan Cordero Iñiguez adds the factors of the lower elevations of the Andes, which allowed the residents of Cuenca "to travel in the direction of all four cardinal points," along with the absence of active volcanoes that could cause periodic destruction, easy irrigation thanks to the abundant water provided by the rivers that ran through the area, and the surrounding forests that made available wood for fuel and the construction of houses.[9]

Travelers and researchers contribute evidence that this was indeed true. In the colonial periods, Jorge Juan and Antonio De Ulloa found the women to be industrious and "very given to work" since they spun wool and wove baize (flannel) of "good quality" and "finely dyed." They were also involved in business dealings.[10] Delaporte concurred with this when he noted that "they are so hardworking in their woolmaking and fabric dying that they are usually the ones" to provide their families with economic resources.[11] For corregidor De Merizalde, the flannels and cotton linens "were due to the work of the women, without exceptions among them" who "spun thread year-round, with untiring tenacity." He added that the Indians were "more diligent than the whites" and they "attained some greater comfort and rest in life" compared to those of other territories. He also noted that the mestizos, "because they were more industrious and applied to work," had obtained a plot of land, and that there were "some scarce noble families" whose "poverty and lack of funds" kept them from having the "luster and splendor that they have in other places."[12]

Even though Cicala saw manifestations of laziness and disinterest in work, he also observed that the residents of Cuenca were "very skillful" craftsmen, because they were endowed with "capability for the work and occupations that required delicate, fine finishing" in addition to having "much fondness for commerce." They also kept up the city streets with gutters and aqueducts for water to run along, which Quito did not have.[13] With the knowledge he obtained from traveling around the provinces of the Audiencia of Quito because of his religious functions, historian Juan de Velasco wrote that the administration of Cuenca distinguished itself as "being the best."[14] At the end of the eighteenth century, the region of Cuenca exported cascarilla to the world market and textiles to Peru, Chile, and Panama. It supplied its market from its own agricultural and livestock production and sent surpluses to the coast, along with fabrics.[15]

Scholars confirm these travelers' appreciations. Chacón, Soto, and Mora wrote that "titled nobility practically did not exist" in Cuenca. Through their research of wills and purchase agreements (1777–1826), they showed that small and medium-sized agricultural properties predominated.[16] Tyrer observed that in Cuenca, apparently "the haciendas were smaller; the indigenous settlements, more prosperous; and obrajes based on the Quito model, not very common."[17] Historian Jorge Núñez pointed out that between the sixteenth and seventeenth centuries "Portuguese emigrants of Jewish descent" arrived in Cuenca and "developed trade and credit." He also noted that "the small size of their properties and the lack of obrajes had deprived the large landowners of Cuenca of the opportunity to build large-scale wealth."[18] Fernando Jurado noted that in Cuenca "there were not enough Indians" and in "the era of corregidor Mechor Vázquez Dávila, the social differences decreased because the lack of labor obliged the Spaniards to devote themselves to tasks that in other places "were left exclusively to Indians."[19] This labor shortage was confirmed by Cuenca historian Juan Cordero Iñiguez when he pointed out that in the sixteenth century Cuenca's neighbors' aspiration of "receiving Indians as labor went only as far as mere hopefulness" because in the region they did not exist "in abundance." For this reason, the residents of Cuenca "had to cope with the tasks of building their houses and cultivating their gardens themselves," working as masons, carpenters, farmers, tailors, locksmiths, ironsmiths, and cobblers. He added that those involved in commerce, which was considered a "dignified activity," sent agricultural products, manufactured goods, and crafts to Guayaquil, Loja, Zaruma, and Zamora.[20]

Research done by Silvia Palomeque helps to understand Cuenca's economic process in the nineteenth century. In the region of Cuenca, "most of the population had access to having or owning land," especially in the neighboring areas in which there was "greater presence" of "small and medium-sized production units." This agrarian structure, maintained until the end of the century, hindered the formation of haciendas, facilitated commerce, and permitted a certain labor-force mobility. As of 1845, straw-hat production began, even though the raw material did not exist in the area. This craft grew rapidly due to the exportation of hats worldwide, and to the fact that domestic demand attained equivalent volumes. As of mid-century, casacarilla exports were a thriving business, but they "abruptly" ended in 1885 due to the depletion of the trees, the failure to renew them, and competition from British colonies. Later, they were apparently reactivated prior to World War II due to the demand from Germany.

Benigno Malo rightly attributed to these activities the fact that "the spirit of enterprise and partnership" had awakened in Cuenca and created "capitals unknown in other times" that contributed to improving agricultural production. Cuenca's entrepreneurs allocated their accumulated wealth to importing machinery to produce cotton fabrics, installing quinine factories to benefit from the transformation of cascarilla, and extracting silver and gold from mines and washes. To exploit the mines of Zaruma, some ten enterprising pioneers from Cuenca formed a partnership and, together with British investors, set up the Great Zaruma Gold Mining Co. Ltd.[21] in London (1880). This was an utterly unusual occurrence for the times, both because of the willingness of several people to unite their efforts and capital, as well as because of the daring initiative of seeking and obtaining partners in what was the major world economy of that era.

Foreign travelers who visited Cuenca at the end of the nineteenth century found in its inhabitants "a temperament with an industrial tendency,"[22] "quite important commerce," and a city that exported straw hats and gold dust, among other products.[23] The early flourishing of Cuenca's economy was facilitated by the fact that one could travel from Cuenca to Guayaquil in less than a week. A horse or mule trail traversed Cajas, and from Molleturo descended the cordillera to Naranjal, the "port" from which one continued along gulf waters to Guayaquil.

A North American traveler who visited Cuenca around the 1940s found that its inhabitants had "a surprisingly rich vocabulary," the houses of well-to-do people were "better kept" than in Quito, and Cuencanos were "perfectly happy" not to leave their "little world ever." Also, even though there were "rigorous class divisions," the *cholos** "in their own way" had an "equally great" pride so that they had no interest in what occurred in high society. It was as though they lived "on the other side of the ocean." It caught his attention that the Indians spoke the Spanish language and that the "standard of living among the common people" was much higher than in any other region of Ecuador. He also noted that the cholos were attentive to cleanliness; were rich, well-dressed, and industrious; and looked healthier than other inhabitants of the Andes. They also walked "erect and looked one in the eye," and in their physical appearance and stature they had "nothing in common with the subordination of the typical Andean cholo, but instead, to the contrary, showed pride in their race." He concluded by pointing out that the women "stood up for themselves" and were "clean" and always had "their fingers occupied in something useful."[24]

These opinions were shared by Jewish anthropologist Constanza Di Capua, who upon her arrival in Ecuador observed the dirtiness of Guayaquil and Quito and many of their inhabitants, as well as the neglect and poor habits. This contrasted sharply with what she saw in Cuenca in 1941. In that city she found "another world," where people were "diligent and hardworking," and the authorities "fine, dignified," and respected by the citizens. She added that among the people "great pulchritude and elegance" reigned, even among the peasant women known as *cholas*. She also remarked that her husband, a doctor in chemistry and manufacturer of medicines, was "impressed by the high professional level of Cuenca's physicians."[25]

---

*The author was probably referring to the *chasos*, who, despite being as white as the most presumptuous people of high social standing, were rustic and poor.

The beliefs and customs of people in Cuenca, as described in a study entitled "La psicología del pueblo Azuayo" ["The psychology of the people of Azuay"], written by Octavio Díaz in 1926, were similar to those cited above and completely compatible with the necessities of economic progress.

The author wrote that "the law of work has been religiously obeyed" in Azuay because "Nature, on occasion rebellious, has denied it what was necessary to preserve life," which made the citizens recur "to industry" and that "assiduous effort" of their "intelligence and their arms" to provide themselves with the necessary sustenance. This attitude meant that members of "all of the social classes," from the little girl of "the highest nobility to the lowly fieldworker," worked in the straw-hat industry. In that province the territorial division—which, according to the author, socialism should envy—was such that "everyone owns property" and it is conveyed and divided up so as to provide a "basis for future fortunes." If some material progress was observed in the cities and villas, it was "due only to their own efforts" since the "action of the central government does not make itself felt and these places do not share in the fiscal funds allocated to works of national scope."

The Cuencanos, "exposed to the approval or rejection of good and bad, never take justice into their own hands and recur to judges to declare what is right." This attitude was due to the fact that they always had "a voice of encouragement for the true good," proclaimed the "excellent quality of virtue," rewarded and commended "those that served the Homeland well," declared what was fair and condemned what was unlawful. The "spirit of partnership" that was a manifestation of the social culture of the residents of Azuay led them to establish partnerships "every day" for specific purposes with "their own existence, relative autonomy, and sufficient economic means." In shaping this mentality, "education and instruction have had a powerful influence." This was "dispensed to all the [social] classes" with regard to setting and meeting objectives.[26]

In referring to the era analyzed by Díaz, an upper-class resident of Cuenca told me how, for the construction of their house, he had often seen his father working with his hands, sometimes unloading boards and other materials from the vehicle that had brought them and carrying them on his back. This conduct was common among other people of their social level when manual labor had to be done.

To these cultural factors were added other elements, thanks to which conditions were created for Cuenca's economy to take off in the second half of the twentieth century, and thus laying the groundwork for the development of the city and the surrounding region.

Perhaps the most important element was the pioneering and systematic domestic and international migration of the populations located in the area of Cuenca. In the region there were numerous free peasants who were not dependent on haciendas. This unusual situation made it possible for them to move to the coast early on (one said that they were "going down"), starting in the early nineteenth century. This was also the route taken by professionals. The migration became more accentuated by mid-century due to the crisis in straw-hat exports. People emigrated to the provinces of El Oro, Manabí, and Guayas; and the boldest decided to leave the country. They traveled first to Venezuela and then to the United States, where the most numerous group of Azuayans have settled, especially in New York. Later, they traveled to Spain, giving rise to a diaspora of more than one hundred thousand inhabitants from the provinces of Azuay and Cañar. Thanks to this emigration, Cuenca's area of influence has been fed by permanent transfers of capital, which in 2006 totaled an impressive US$867 million, according to an unpublished CORDES study. This implies that every Azuay or Cañar family that receives remittances collects, on average, the sizeable sum of US$22,000 annually, a large proportion of which is spent or invested in Cuenca.

For its part, the state issued protectionist economic laws and founded the Centro de Reconversión Económica del Azuay (CREA), whereby it sought to promote recovery of the productive activities affected by the mid-century economic crisis, improve the network of roads, expand public services, and promote the development of industries and trades. The Paute hydroelectric power project and dam built between the 1970s and 1980s, the country's largest work of infrastructure after the railroad, created thousands of direct and indirect jobs and generated an important demand for materials and services. Cuenca also became integrated into the system of roadways that connected it with the southern and northern provinces of the inter-Andean region, as well as with the Amazon Region and the coast.

Some of the characteristics of Cuenca, its institutions, its economic activities, and its citizens explain the successful local development and the well-being attained by its population.

Cuenca has a commendable and transparent group of leaders and citizens that fulfill their civic duty and contribute to collective progress. The political struggle usually has a constructive nature that makes it possible to discuss community problems without personal and party conflicts. Public interests weigh in the decisions of the authorities, and private interests are subjected to these. Populism has not managed to catch on among politicians, officials, and citizens; so, the programs, projects, and expenditures are conceived of, and carried out, with criteria of priorities. People with a vocation for public service take part in political activities; they are prepared to perform them and are not improvised people coming out of 'show business' or only interested in getting rich.* Individuals and civil-society organizations have a favorable disposition toward assuming their own responsibilities, and there is a tradition of compliance with the law and respect for institutions and authority.

In Cuenca, the mayors, and public officials in general, have a virtuous sense of public service and of honest and effective attention to urban needs and problems. So, the local administration has higher moral and technical levels than those of other cities in Ecuador. The city is orderly and clean, and it has developed harmoniously, without marginal neighborhoods and with a supply of acceptable public services in the areas of education, health, and safety. There is continuity in the programs carried out by the municipal government; and its bureaucracy is stable, professional, efficient, and honest. The rivers that run through the city are crystal-clear. Thanks to a dual system of canals that keep wastewaters from flowing into them, the citizens do not contaminate them with garbage, and the mountain springs where they originate are protected by forest reserves. It is the only city in the country with automatic parking meters and underground power lines and telephone lines.

The public university of Cuenca managed to escape from the academic decline that the universities of Quito and Guayaquil experienced, and it is the only university in Azuay that has attained accreditation of its quality. These aspects have made it possible to train competent professionals. First, a school of arts and trades, and later the school of professional education founded and directed by Italian Salesian priests, facilitated the training of technicians that have contributed to industrial development. The city has a model public enterprise (ETAPA) which, unlike others, is innovative, efficient, and honest, and which provides good telephone, potable-water, and sewage services. The Empresa Eléctrica Centrosur has the lowest figure nationally of "black losses" (fraudulent connections), four times lower than those of the power companies of Manabí and Milagro.† The city can also rely on a dynamic group of businessmen who have fostered modern industrial and commercial production, as well as crafts and tourism; and

---

*During the 2006 elections, in almost all the provinces of the country but particularly on the coast, there was a proliferation of candidacies by citizens from the world of celebrities (singers, actors, athletes, journalists, and television stars). This did not occur in Cuenca and Azuay.

†Cuenca's power company, the Empresa Eléctrica Centrosur, has black losses of 7 percent, whereas those of Milagro and Manabí have figures higher than 40 percent (source: CONELEC).

the city exports manufactured goods—ceramics, electrical appliances, and tires, among others—whose development contributed to the creation of Cuenca's industrial park in the early 1970s. The television station Telerama is the only one in Ecuador that broadcasts cultural programs, and in Cuenca there have been athletes with important international triumphs.

Cuenca's business initiative was also demonstrated by the fact that a group of twelve small local leather industries, to compete on the U.S. market against articles manufactured in Pakistan, managed to increase their productivity in barely six months, raising their daily output of machine-made hats from eight to thirty-two and of purses from four to twenty-five.

Merchants from other provinces of the country prefer to import through the Cuenca customs office because the procedures take less time, no thefts occur, and no bribes are paid. The administration of justice is independent, reliable, honest, and timely. This is evident in how a provision introduced in the Constitution of 1998 has operated, whereby prisoners who were not sentenced within one year could be set free. Unlike what occurred in Guayaquil and Quito, due to the meticulousness and uprightness of the judges in Cuenca, no one obtained his freedom in advance.

In a letter written in 1858, a Spanish traveler said: "Cuenca is perhaps one of the largest and loveliest cities in Ecuador. Its location is awe-inspiring. Located on a broad, horizontal, and very fertile plain, it enjoys a healthy and pleasant climate and is very picturesque and joyful."[27] Similar opinions were expressed by foreign travelers that visited the city during the colonial period, when the houses had straw roofs, and also during the era of the republic. Since the privileged landscapes and the elegant architecture of republican times have not been affected by urban progress at the end of the twentieth century, the residents of Cuenca benefit from intangibles that impact their quality of life.

Socioeconomic indicators can be used to illustrate the progress of Cuenca and the well-being of its inhabitants. Following Quito, the city occupies second place in terms of satisfying basic needs.[28] The coverage of sewage, electricity, telephone, and potable-water services is better than in the other cities of the country. The rate of illiteracy (3.9 percent) is equivalent to less than half of the national average. The infant mortality rate is lower than in Quito and Guayaquil, and the rate of unemployment is 50 percent lower than those of the two major cities. Therefore, poverty as measured by unsatisfied needs (26 percent) is lower than in other provincial capitals and much lower than in Guayaquil.[29] In 2006, the per capita GDP of Azuay was US$2,916, and it was based on the contribution of industry and services. It was higher than the figure for Guayas (US$2,726) and slightly lower than that of Pichincha (US$2,983). The per capita taxes paid totaled US$168, only two dollars less than in the rich province of Guayas, which was second to Pichincha, where they totaled US$470.* Cuenca has the highest per capita rate of vehicles (ten people for every one motor vehicle) and a lower rate of outstanding debt on bank loans than in Quito and Guayaquil.

INDUSTRIOUS OTAVALANS

The Indians of the community of Otavalo, located in the Province of Imbabura, work in the areas of handicrafts and commerce and enjoy greater well-being than the members of their race that inhabit other territories. In general, Indians are Ecuador's poorest social sector despite the progress made in recent decades. However, the Otavalo Indians' income is higher than that of many mestizos in the area, and the most prosperous ones have built up a net worth that in certain cases is higher than that of the descendants of their masters of old.

Unlike what occurred among other Indian groups, the Otavalans' accomplishments have not led them to abandon their culture. They communicate with each other in Quechua, conserve their clean and elegant traditional dress, and take pride in their race; and many have not abandoned the characteristic braid that they have always worn. Their sense of dignity, according to one author, makes their manners and the way they behave with whites and mestizos different from the attitude of "submission of most highland Indians."[30] The Otavalans' originality is also expressed in other areas. They work in manufacturing and commerce more than in agriculture, travel abroad on a regular basis to market their products, set up workshops in the countries they visit, employ mestizos in Ecuador and whites abroad, correctly speak and write Spanish and even some foreign languages, and marry foreigners; and the most fortunate even send their children to college.

It seems that in the early decades of the twentieth century they began selling their handicrafts, especially textiles, at the Saturday fair in Otavalo. Upon realizing that their main buyers were foreigners, as of the 1940s they periodically traveled to Quito and other cities in Ecuador in search of buyers. The most enterprising installed selling points near the hotels where

---

*Estimates are based on figures from the Banco Central (Central Bank), SRI (Internal Revenue Service), and INEC (National Institute of Statistics and Censuses). Except for unemployment, which corresponds to 2006, the data refer to averages of annual figures for 2001–2004.

tourists stayed, and in the places that tourists visited in highland and coastal cities. Around the same time they managed to obtain employment in the textile mills of Otavalo, "first in separating, then in spinning, and finally in weaving," in all of which their work was appreciated by the owners, due to "their skills at operating the machines," their "great deal of patience, good performance and high degree of responsibility."[31] Gradually, they left the countryside and moved to Otavalo to carry on their artisanal and commercial operations more easily. The Otavalo handicrafts market, which began with selling points scattered along streets and on corners, later came together in a plaza organized for that purpose. It now encompasses several city blocks.

The interest that their manufactured goods awakened in foreign tourists, diplomats, and international employees led them to explore foreign markets, as a function of the number of buyers they could find there. First they traveled with their weavings to Latin American countries, particularly to Colombia and Venezuela, which at that time was enjoying petroleum prosperity. Encouraged by the economic success of their first "multinational" operations, in the 1960s they boldly decided to explore the North American and European markets. It is worthwhile to quote something said by one of them: "This traveling has come down from my ancestors. I myself started to travel when I was two years old. When I traveled to Holland at the age of 19, I realized that we Indians—I don't know if because of our roots, or why—are more curious, a little more rebellious, more daring."[32]

The fact that the handicrafts were made and commercialized by the Otavalans themselves, without the participation of intermediaries, allowed them to increase their income substantially. The accumulated capital served to improve the stocks of raw material, modernize the workshops with new machinery, and expand their economic activities to hotels, restaurants, and sightseeing services. They were also able to buy vehicles for use by their families and to transport merchandise; to repair and enlarge their homes; and to buy the houses of mestizos and whites in the city of Otavalo, which they made the center of their artisanal, mercantile, and tourism operations. Their urban presence has grown so much that Otavalo has ceased to be a white/mestizo city and become an Indian city.

Otavalans travel abroad for up to eight months at a time, from spring to fall, to conduct commercial operations that some of them combine with musical performances in popular areas of major cities, to supplement their income. Quite a few live in other countries, where they have built their own workshops to save the costs entailed in importing handicrafts and at the same time to benefit from having more merchandise available to be sold. The young people who have accompanied their parents on business trips abroad consider that, to expand operations and increase sales and earnings, it would be more useful to study English in addition to Spanish, instead of the Quechua that they learn in bilingual education programs in primary and secondary schools in Ecuador.

The modernity of the Otavalan Indians is also expressed in their ideas and political attitudes, which are different from those defended by the leaders of the indigenous movement represented by CONAIE and other smaller organizations. Mayor Mario Conejo, a descendant of the Indian merchants who marketed their products in Latin American countries, heads the municipal government of Otavalo without the least bit of populism, and with criteria of responsibility, efficiency, modernity, honesty, and austerity. He eliminated the potable-water subsidy that had been provided for many years, despite the fact that it was less regressive than the costly one that was granted by the state on fuels and defended by CONAIE and almost all the national political leaders, not only the leftists. The technical and social consideration that the subsidy took important economic resources away from the mayor's office weighed in his decision because his administration needed those resources to improve the quality of public services. He publicly favored Ecuador's signing of a free trade agreement with the United States because he considered commercial openness convenient for the interests of the hardworking Otavalan artisans and for the country, and he has asked his community to get training and improve production, "with or without the FTA." He considers "dangerous" the ethnocentric indigenous power that CONAIE leaders promote; they have been criticized for not having "constructed a movement of Indian citizens with rights and obligations." This means he has discrepancies with the paternalistic attitude and desire for vindication that the organization promotes in its political struggle. To provide grounds for the civic content of his affirmations, he has remarked that the Otavalans have attained greater prosperity because of their "own capacities," their "spirit of working to get ahead," and their "self-confidence"—and not because of government assistance.[33]

Otavalo has social indicators higher than those of other cities with Indian populations, such as Pujilí in Cotopaxi and Guamote in Chimborazo. For example, it has less illiteracy; higher levels of education; and better coverage of potable-water, sewage, electricity, and telephone services, even with respect to major cities such as Guayaquil. To this must be added the fact that Otavalo has a poverty level of 54 percent, as measured by unsatisfied basic needs. This figure is lower than the indexes for Pujilí and Guamote and similar to those for coastal cities, including Guayaquil (52 percent).[34] Since these figures are averages, they do not reflect the reality of many Otavalans whose standard of living is equivalent to those of the middle classes of Quito and Guayaquil—and in some cases better.

The singular cultural and economic aspects of the Otavalo Indians are not a novelty of recent decades, or even of the last century. They are the result of a process initiated hundreds of years ago for reasons that cannot be satisfactorily explained, especially if one keeps in mind that, just like other Indians in the Ecuadorian Andes, they were also subordinated to the encomienda system, obrajes, and haciendas—institutions that closed the door to progress for their peers and plunged them into abject servility and extreme poverty.

The different situation of Otavalo and the Otavaleños was perceived and recorded by foreign visitors who came to the Audiencia of Quito at the end of the colonial period. In the middle of the eighteenth century, Abbot Delaporte was "astonished" by the fact that the land was "well cultivated," that the "clothing factories were rich and numerous," and that for the first time he could see hanging bridges with handrails to cross rivers, like those that existed in Peru, as well as cable cars.[35] Von Humboldt thought that the Otavalans enjoyed "some freedom and the fruits of their labor" since they were "almost all unbound, not slaves of the haciendas."[36] Stevenson observed that they seemed to be more inclined to work in the obrajes that manufactured cotton and wool than in cultivation of the land. As for their physical constitution and personal dignity, so diminished in the case of the other Andean Indians, he pointed out that some men were "quite robust and muscular" and that he had never seen—one assumes in the South American regions he had visited—"a finer race of people than the Otavaleños on a Sunday when they are at church or attending a celebration."[37]

In the middle of the nineteenth century, during the time of the republic, Holinski mentioned that in the "fertile province of Imbabura the Indians are more industrious, more intelligent and happier than their brothers in Quito."[38] Kolberg wrote that Indians in "Imbabura are tall and handsome, not at all inferior to Europeans, not even the Germans."[39] About the same time, De Avendaño found that they were "clean and relatively more robust and skilled than the others of the republic," as well as "cheerful, hardworking and quite intelligent."[40]

Around the middle of the twentieth century, other travelers made similar comments. Bemelmans told of how some Otavalans were weavers and others were potters. He said that "their dress was clean" and that they walked, sat, and stood "with exquisite grace."[41] Franklin described the Otavalans as "clean, lovely, strong and happy" and therefore "very different from the Indians of the central provinces." He noted that many were "owners of their lands" and "famous weavers" that obtained supplementary income from the sale of their handicrafts. This money allowed them "to afford to use imported cloth," to which he attributed the fact that they had been able to resist "political and social absorption by the rest of the country."[42] Later, Lilo Linke recounted that the Otavalo market was "one of Ecuador's largest tourist attractions," that "the houses of these Indians are well built and comfortable and that among the men certain luxuries such as gold wristwatches are not the exception."[43] In the 1970s, anthropologist Casagrande found the Otavaleños "proud, clean, industrious, intelligent, and so on."[44] And his colleague Salomón said that they wore an eye-catching and beautiful outfit of white pants, blue ponchos, and large hats; produced crafts recognized for their quality; took advantage of modern technology; and performed multiple artisanal tasks that they combined with agricultural activities on their parcels of land.[45]

These oft-repeated positive remarks about the Otavalo Indians' character contrast with the negative ones that the same travelers and many others made about the deplorable social conditions and the cultural weaknesses of the indigenous peoples referred to in preceding chapters. Casagrande considered the singular traits of the Otavaleños surprising if compared to those of other indigenous peoples, who were seen as "lazy, drunken and dirty," among "other flaws of character."[46] A Jewish immigrant employed on a hacienda in the Province of Chimborazo, scandalized by the "wretched situation of the Indians," recalled the "Nazi barbarism" and "how absurd and cruel the concentration camps" where he had been were.[47]

Even though it is not possible to find sufficient explanations for the anomaly represented by the Otavalans in the indigenous world, it is worthwhile to put forward some tentative hypotheses.

It seems that the Incas allowed the Otavalans to maintain possession of their land even after their territories had been conquered. This fact surely made it possible for them to be more independent; and when the Spaniards arrived, it must have influenced the establishment of a more flexible social organization than that of other Andean provinces.[48] Until the end of the seventeenth century, in the area of Otavalo there was a sparse white and mestizo population, which reduced the possibilities that the Indians would be exploited by the Creoles, as had occurred in other areas. To these favorable elements were added the measures taken by Antonio Murga, one of the presidents of the Audiencia of Quito (1615–1636), to improve the organization of the obrajes, curtail the abuses against the Indians, and oblige the Spaniards and Creoles to return the land that they had usurped. He also prohibited their residence there and visits by merchants.[49] These situations and policies must have contributed to the fact that the domination and exploitation to which other highland Indians were exposed through the encomienda system, the obrajes, and the haciendas were mitigated in Otavalo.

Apparently, the Otavalans were already good weavers[50] before the conquest, since they made a cloth known by the name *cumbi*, whose texture and quality led Spaniards to compare it to European damask. In the case of Otavalo, the obrajes were the largest not only of the Audiencia of Quito but also of the Spanish colonies,[51] and they served to improve the Indians' crafts. The business operations of the obrajes must have entailed a complex production structure that called for great efficiency. In Otavalo there were five hundred workers, up to five times more than the number employed in other textile mills. It was necessary to supply them with raw material from different places: cotton from the warm valleys and wool from the plains. The manufacturing process had a certain degree of specialization, and the distribution of final products in distant consumption centers, some located outside the country, posed innumerable difficulties.

The fact that important obrajes in Otavalo belonged to the Spanish Crown and were overseen by Spaniards, better prepared and perhaps more compassionate than the cruel Creoles, probably made it possible to attribute greater importance to the organization of factory processes than to the merciless exploitation of labor. This explains why the Indians would have preferred to work in the obrajes rather than in agriculture. All of this must have contributed to reaffirming the Otavalans' tradition of independence and to developing habits of organization, discipline, management, hard work, and innovation. This manufacturing tradition must have also influenced the fact that at the end of the nineteenth century "the country's largest cotton factory" was installed in Otavalo.[52]

To these historical elements must be added the system of work that the Otavalans adopted in their business activities, as well as the influences that the indigenous community received from abroad because of their frequent trips.

The fact that they worked without a schedule in their workshops and in the commercialization of their products, even on weekends, made it possible for them to increase their output. Since the heads of household performed these tasks along with their wives, children, and other relatives, labor costs were reduced; and more importantly, everyone felt committed to the success of the economic activity in which they were involved because they considered themselves the owners. The strong sentiments of reciprocity that developed for this reason made families help each other, with money and with labor; do favors for each other when needed; and opportunely return those favors.

The sense that Otavalans have of the economical use of time means that rest for them is not stopping work but rather "switching from one task to another," because if they tire of being seated at a loom "all day long" they occupy themselves in a different task.[53] These characteristics of Otavalan enterprise made it possible to make production less expensive, increase savings, accumulate capital, improve competitiveness, and thus expand artisanal and commercial operations.

Aníbal Buitrón described the Otavalans' widespread practices of mutual support in the following terms: The *"parcialidad* is the core and the basis for indigenous organization" in which "all of the members have the obligation of mutually supporting each other whenever a contingent [larger than the family] is necessary" to perform some task such as erecting a house, holding a wedding, offering a reception, or performing stewardship. Those who did not collaborate with other members of the *parcialidad* in meeting their needs could not expect reciprocity when they found themselves in a similar situation.[54]

The tourism generated by the beautiful geography of the Province of Imbabura and the appealing open-air Indian market of Otavalo led to a substantial increase in the sales of handicrafts. The demand fostered diversification of production as well as expansion into apparel, accessories, and a variety of decorative or utilitarian articles. Those who traveled to Europe, North America, and other Latin American countries, where they sometimes lived for long periods, brought with them lessons, skills, and innovations that they applied to their businesses upon returning to their homeland. Thanks to them, the importance of knowing how to read, write, and do math; mastering the Spanish language; sending their children to school; and "avoiding conflicts and difficulties"[55] became apparent.

As seen previously, the Protestant influence[56*]—through the positive effects that evangelical preaching produced on the economic behavior of its followers—contributed to favoring savings due to the elimination of wasteful spending on celebrations and drinking. It also accentuated the Otavalans' interest in making profits and seeking their own destiny.

---

*The author noted that, for decades, missionaries and representatives of the evangelical, Baha'i, and Mormon faiths have gone to Otavalo and surrounding communities and have won over converts and built places of worship. According to the Indians, this is due, among other reasons, to the fact that it has allowed them to eliminate alcohol consumption and the traditional festivities (supposedly Catholic) that were "very expensive."

CONTRIBUTIONS FROM IMMIGRANTS

In the first half of the twentieth century, immigrants arrived from Europe and other Old World regions, especially Arabs, Italians, Germans, Spaniards, and Chinese. Jews joined these groups in mid-century. Regardless of their geographical origin, their contribution was very important for the modernization of Ecuador because their knowledge, experience, and enterprise filled the national void—and because of them the country could take advantage of the opportunities created by the economic growth of the 1950s, 1960s, and 1970s. At the end of the century, Colombian immigrants also arrived, in a number far larger than the sum of all those who had come before from other parts of the world. Even though this immigration was more heterogeneous, it was also positive for the country; for example, improving sales techniques and customer service, which were so far behind in Ecuador. However, because the Arab and Jewish immigrations are the oldest and had the most important economic and cultural effects, only they will be analyzed here.

The Arabs and the Jews that came to Ecuador had to face the same difficulties that hindered Ecuadorians' progress, and even greater difficulties since they were making their way in an environment that was strange to them. They did not know Spanish, they suffered marginalization, they were taken advantage of, they lacked capital, and they did not have access to the connections and friendships that counted for so much in the success of the natives. However, they managed to overcome the difficulties that they encountered, and in only a few years managed to get ahead. Their success was due to the fact that they had attributes that were scarce among Ecuadorians, such as constancy, savings, and willingness to do manual labor. To this was added the imperious need that they had of earning their daily bread, since some of them came to feel hunger. To survive or to realize their dreams, they undertook all sorts of initiatives that led them to organize personal businesses or establish companies, thanks to which, following years of sacrifices, they managed to leave poverty behind, to live comfortably, and in many cases to build important net worth that they left as a legacy for their descendants.

The Arabs made a significant contribution to the progress of Guayaquil in an era in which the port was the land of opportunity, while the Jews contributed to Quito's rising out of the backwardness in which it had been immersed for hundreds of years. Both groups promoted Ecuador's development, just as immigrants of other nationalities had. The initiatives they took, the businesses they started, and the companies they founded allowed the country to discover economic possibilities that had gone unnoticed, to enjoy services that had been lacking, and to acquire new knowledge and technologies. Their contribution has been so important that seven of the seventeen companies mentioned in chapter 4 as leaders in their respective sectors belong to descendants of immigrants, even though these groups do not account for even 5 percent of Ecuador's total population.

The economic success of European, Arab, Asian, and Colombian immigrants—in addition to contributing to the country's development—produced a beneficial demonstration effect that helped Ecuadorians to abandon habits that had been detrimental for individuals to carve out their own destiny, for companies to progress, and for Ecuador to construct its future. Because of immigrants, quite a few discovered that people's dignity should be respected no matter what their social condition; that an enterprising spirit opened doors to progress; that effort bore fruits; that hard work and merit mattered more than favors, recommendations, and godfathers; that without savings little could be done economically;* that time should not be wasted; that objectives were achieved with perseverance; that the use of technical resources was indispensable; that personal hygiene and cleanliness of the home were essential; that there was no better pastime than culture; and that women could work outside their homes as professionals or businesswomen, or even performing less prestigious activities.

The dissemination of these cultural lessons was aided by the evidence apparent to all Ecuadorians: many immigrants—despite being Europeans and, therefore, whites—undertook work and performed trades, sometimes with their own hands, that upper-class Ecuadorians had always refused to do because they considered them unbecoming and beneath them.

Successful Arabs

Few Lebanese, Syrian, and Palestinian immigrants arrived in Ecuador in the second half of the nineteenth century, but many did in the first half of the twentieth. They were known by the euphemism "Turks" due to the passports that they arrived with, since back then their countries formed part of the Ottoman Empire. They brought with them little knowledge; their education was only a few grades in school, and their skills were those befitting a people of merchants. All of them were Orthodox Christians or said they were. None of them professed the Muslim religion, and when they

---

*Alberto Di Capua, manager of the pharmaceutical company LIFE, went to work by bus for twelve years and then in the company car, until finally getting a car of his own after twenty-five years of service.

came to Ecuador they joined the Catholic Church.[57] Many were peasant farmers and, save a few exceptions, people of scarce resources and knowledge who pooled all of the money they could to finance the costly trip from the Middle East to South America. They traveled to Guayaquil, attracted by a certain renown that the port had acquired due to the wealth created by cacao exports, and with the hope of finding some fellow countryman who would accept them in his home and help them find a job or set up a business, as did in fact happen in many cases.

Once in Guayaquil they had to have at least some means of covering the cost of their subsistence for a few months until getting a job or undertaking a lucrative activity. Crawford said that "the ones that had already settled welcomed the newcomers, lent them money, provided them with a pack of merchandise on credit, gave them advice on how to sell, and had an experienced peddler accompany them around the most remote places in the country."[58] Even though some went around Ecuador as traveling salesmen for Guayaquil's commercial houses, most of them devoted themselves to selling fabrics, woolen cloth, and trinkets as street peddlers in cities and towns, or in shops that they set up on the port's main streets. Those who had a certain amount of capital had connections in Europe,[59]* and they founded import companies that proved to be very profitable because of the demand created on the coast due to the cacao wealth, and in the highlands due to the populations that were incorporated into the market following construction of the railroad.

For the Arab immigrants it proved relatively easy to compete with Ecuadorians, and over time to achieve a certain monopoly in commercial activities. They arrived when possibilities for progress were appearing in Ecuador thanks to the economic growth of the coast and the construction of roads. They operated in a country in which well-to-do Ecuadorians had no interest in commerce, which they viewed as a trade for people of lower social status. And insofar as the other social classes, few of their members were willing to do the grueling work that traveling poor and unknown roads entailed to, after so many difficulties, end up with small volumes of sales and uncertain profits. On the other hand, the newcomers, with packs of merchandise on their backs, crossed rivers, traveled rugged paths and long distances, visited remote towns, stayed in poor lodging, and went into the coastal haciendas as peddlers.[60]

They acted humbly, treated everyone with cajoling courtesy and, despite their scant knowledge of Spanish, did not let themselves be defeated

---

*The author cited the case of Gabriel Farah, whose siblings had a store in Paris.

by language difficulties when they were making a sale. So, they seldom let a customer get away without buying something. In performing these activities they had the invaluable help of their wives, who during their husbands' absences covered for them at the counter of urban shops or went door to door with merchandise under their arms to sell cloth in the houses of the cities where they lived. This activity became easier once they were prospering and could build a house, which was planned with a ground-floor shop and second-floor housing.[61] This work style allowed them to avoid paying employees' salaries and do without hiring managers, while committing family members and friends to the success of the business in which they were involved. In this way, they lowered the costs of their commercial operations, increased their profits, and put together their first capitals that later grew year by year.

In the decades following their arrival in Ecuador, the fortune that smiled on all of the Arab immigrants—on some more and others less—as a reward for their bold work, their habit of saving, and their enterprising abilities, allowed them to broaden their commercial activities in the area of importation and to start exporting and undertaking other activities such as agriculture, industry, banking, and services. Many came to amass fortunes catalogued among the largest in Ecuador, despite which they suffered from marginalization, more in Guayaquil than in Quito. The condescending whites disdainfully referred to them as "Turks" and even refused to accept their invitations to parties and weddings. The members of the elite "militantly refused to accept the Lebanese among their ranks" and blocked their entry into Guayaquil clubs until in 1975 they managed to be admitted to the exclusive Club de la Unión.[62] By that time, the "colony," as residents of Guayaquil called the Arab community, had managed to become related to Ecuadorian families by marriage, even to upper-class families. These ties extended so widely that it currently proves difficult to find a traditional family in Guayaquil that has not had some members of Lebanese, Syrian, or Palestinian origin. The social barriers imposed on the Arabs by the Ecuadorians were broken more easily in the cities of the highlands, which is curious if one recalls the aspirations of nobility of the residents of Quito and of highlanders in general.

The social margination suffered by the Arabs proved economically profitable in two ways. Since they could not have access to the networks of influence to receive favors and obtain benefits, they had to depend on themselves in all aspects and had to redouble their efforts to overcome the difficulties they had encountered and get ahead. This not only educated them in perseverance, reciprocal support, and solidarity, but also allowed them to accumulate savings, by virtue of the fact that they did not have to incur the heavy expenditures demanded by the social life of well-to-do families in Guayaquil.

The modest educational background of Arab immigrants and the types of commercial activities in which they built their fortunes initially did not help them contribute to technological progress, to the introduction of innovations, to industrial development, and to the modernization of Ecuador. Nor did they contribute to a change in the Ecuadorian cultural habits analyzed in preceding pages, except for pursuing profit through hard work and valuing economic success. Instead, the behaviors of the immigrants in other realms were quite in sync with those of old, common to Ecuadorians; for example, ignoring the law, evading taxes, and not honoring commitments. Their second- and third-generation descendants, on the other hand, because of their better education and the industrial, agricultural, fishing-industry, and service activities they undertook, have made important contributions to the country's progress in recent decades, especially in Guayaquil, whose economic advancement could not be explained without the presence of the powerful Arab "colony." People in the know mention the Isaías, Antón, Dassum, Kronfle, and Eljuri families, the last one residing in Cuenca, as those who distinguished themselves for the net worth they have accumulated, the variety of businesses they have undertaken, and the influence they have attained.*

Arab immigrants did not stand out in the field of culture,[63] but they did in public life, where they have been notable players despite continuing to be a community of small numbers with respect to the rest of the Ecuadorians. So great is their influence that two politicians of Arab descent were elected as President of the Republic (Abdalá Bucaram and Jamil Mahuad), one as Vice-President (Alberto Dahik), and many others as prefects, mayors, and Cabinet ministers.

Jewish Entrepreneurs

The Jews came to the unfamiliar country of Ecuador toward the middle of the twentieth century. They were given visas and welcomed when they were fleeing Nazi persecution, which they could only escape by leaving Europe. Most of them arrived between the years 1937 and 1939, and then after World War II. For a country that had not received massive

---

*The author specifically mentions the names of Olga Eljuri, Paco Villar, Antonio Kronfle, Astris Achi, and Henry Kronfle.

immigrations, their number was considerable because they totaled five thousand. Over time, many returned to Europe or settled in the newly established Israel because their businesses were not flourishing, the country's backwardness closed the doors to those who were the best educated, and they did not find an environment in which their religious beliefs fit in; but above all, because they wanted to seek a more secure future in the prosperous economy of the United States. Such emigration processes have produced a gradual reduction in the Jewish community, which currently has no more than five hundred members, almost all of whom reside in Quito, with only a few in Guayaquil and Cuenca.

As had occurred with the foreign travelers who arrived in previous times, the country's absolute backwardness, widespread poverty, subordination of the Indians, alongside the dirtiness of people, homes, lodgings and taverns, and the habit—still alive in the twenty-first century—of urinating just about anywhere, did not fail to amaze them and make them feel uncomfortable.[64] Yet, others were impressed in Guayaquil with the "white sand, blue sky, brilliant sun, and pleasant smell of fried fish."[65] Everyone lived through the same experience when the ship left them in the poverty-stricken town of La Libertad and they boarded the outdated autocarril that took them to Guayaquil. For a few days they stayed in that city, which some of them reached directly by the Guayas River, and then took the train to Quito and saw the capital and other highland cities. These discomforts were overlooked because they were grateful to the country that had allowed them to save their lives and that offered them the possibility of living in peace without fear of being spied on, detained, and sent to an extermination camp. Some knew hunger because they had no money. They arrived with only the clothes on their backs, but they were aided by fellow countrymen who had arrived earlier, or by the Jewish community association that was organized later.

Few opted to live in Guayaquil, a city they left due to the annoyances caused by "families that came from the great European cities," the humid tropical heat, the cockroaches, and the crickets "that in the rainy season covered the area like rugs, crunched under the feet of those that passed by and disturbed the evenings with their chirping."[66] Initially, they were scattered in the provinces of the highlands. However, over time they became concentrated in Quito, despite its backwardness, since they felt more at home with the climate. They settled in the center of the city and then later in the north, in the América and Mariscal neighborhoods that were beginning to take shape, and to whose beautification they later contributed with the elegant houses they built. The less well-to-do rented rooms and apartments or stayed at boarding-houses where they were welcome tenants because "they paid the rent on time" and "treated the rental property well."[67] Whereas the visas they received from the Ecuadorian government were issued for them to work in agricultural activities, few found employment there. And except for a few, those who did abandoned their jobs because of the backwardness of the countryside and its isolation, which did not allow them to educate their children and have the comforts they were accustomed to. Because of their physical appearance and because almost none of them spoke Spanish, many people called them "gringos" and, believing them to be such, tried to deceive them, sometimes successfully.*

Unlike immigrants of other nationalities, the Jews in general had technical training, professional experience, a business background, a high level of education and culture, and some had university degrees. In certain cases they had had important businesses in their countries of origin and had formed part of Europe's intellectual elite. However, above all, they were imbued with values that had accompanied the Hebrew people during their millenarian history: a hardworking spirit, an obsession with savings, a lack of prejudices, a sense of organization, willingness to do manual labor, initiative, perseverance, aptitude for innovation, commitment to fulfilling obligations, austerity in both personal and business matters, and a practical sense of life, that is, a mentality completely different from that which prevailed in the Ecuador of those days.[†]

These cultural values allowed them to be more innovative and competitive, as can be seen in just a few examples. They introduced sales with installment payments and home delivery; opened up large windows in the dark, enclosed shops of Quito; and used glass cases to display their wares. Such selling devices had been unknown in the city till then. The paper bags made at one of their factories replaced the sheets of newspapers used previously, and their pots and pans were used by housewives and servants to pack or transport the food they bought in grocery stores, markets, butcher-shops,

---

*According to one Jewish immigrant, a barber by profession, "Back then the parameters of honesty in Ecuador were minimal, and they tricked us 'gringos' awfully." Lehmann, *Breve libro sin editar sobre la comunidad judía en el Ecuador desde 1938*, 129. Vera de Kohn tells the story of how a piece of property with a view of the city where, with her husband, who was an architect, they had planted a forest and built their home, was confiscated for an unbelievably low price "under the pretext that the presidential palace was going to be built there." Vera Kohn, *Terapia Iniciática* (Quito: Centro de Desarrollo Integral, 2006), 38.

†A Jewish man (Lehmann, *Breve libro sin editar sobre la comunidad judía en el Ecuador desde 1938*, 130–31) told the story of how a cobbler offered to repair a pair of shoes for him in three days but took a month. Constanza Di Capua also confessed to me that her husband Alberto worked until very late in his office at LIFE, even on weekends, and that, to save the company money, she entertained suppliers from abroad or important customers with dinners at their home, using their own resources.

and bakeries.[68] They also offered dry-cleaning services and the possibility of having clothes picked up at their customers' homes.

The construction of a good number of the bridges erected in Ecuador around the middle of the century was owed to the technology of the firm Siderúrgica. The Jews also developed the exportation of "ultra-light balsa wood" for the construction of planes, ships, and buoys during World War II; and later, for the production of household goods, acoustic and thermal insulation, and other articles. Their ideas, training, experience, and procedures made it possible to "improve the quality" of national manufactured goods, introduce "new products that until then were unknown or imported," and open up markets abroad, for example for pyrethrum, a raw material for pesticides.[69] The first computers, which used to take up a spacious room, were brought in by the Italian Jews who founded the pharmaceutical company LIFE. They established dozens of companies, many of them industrial ones. According to Kreuter, in 1948 these totaled fifteen exporters and some 140 industries, including fifteen hotels and boarding-houses that employed some two thousand workers.[70]

Their work and business virtues and the need to feed and clothe themselves led them to work incessantly without being concerned about the lack of resources; the dearth of implements, tools, and materials; the poor public services; the informality of the Ecuadorians; and the backwardness of the country. Because of the asylum that they had received and that had saved their lives, the difficulties seemed trifles to the Jews; and Ecuador, a "paradise." Their wives contributed to the success of their initiatives and businesses. In addition to occupying themselves with household chores, without the help of servants, they supported their husbands in any way they could: by keeping books, handling bureaucratic procedures, preparing and collecting invoices, making homemade products, and selling them door to door to obtain additional income. They also tapped their knowledge, experience, and connections in their countries of origin to establish import-export businesses. Finally, the fact that they were living in a country where everything was still to be done made it easy for them to find business niches that the Ecuadorians, due to their indolence, had not yet discovered.

Their professional and economic background, sometimes very notable, did not matter. Initially, the Jews performed any activity that would allow them to cover their basic needs, no matter how humble the work. One adolescent who came from Germany—and surely many more—earned a living as a domestic servant.[71] Since in Jewish families "the wife knew how to cook and the husband how to wash," they began producing articles of consumption at home (butter, bread, chocolates, cookies, cakes, noodles, cheese, cream, sausages, and hams). These were previously unknown in the country or manufactured with "an unsatisfactory quality for European taste." Until they could open their own shops, they sold their wares from house to house or at bakeries, or they took orders. They also took advantage of their culinary skills to install the first comfortable hotels and restaurants in Quito (the Cordillera, Savoy, and Colón), whose first customers were the members of the numerous Jewish colonies.

Those who managed to buy machines to make knits changed highland fashion by substituting warm sweaters for the large scarves and shawls that women wore to protect themselves from the cold. "A considerable number" worked in commerce, in stores, or as peddlers of all conceivable types of products. Some set up accounting offices or technical and commercial advisory firms; others devoted themselves to selling currency, insurance, and transportation services.[72] Those who managed to bring money and jewelry with them, or who managed to build up resources with the profits from their initial businesses, ventured into metal-mechanics, pharmaceuticals, chemicals, ceramics, paper, liquors, textiles, hotels, foodstuffs, cleaning, sawmilling, leather tanning, handicrafts, construction and furniture-making, clothing, shoes, jewelry, painting, and other areas.

Many of these activities were successful and eventually gave rise to large and prosperous companies. The most notable were LIFE (medicines), Ideal-Alambrec (metal mechanics), Siderúrgica (construction), Acero Comercial (materials), Mi Comisariato (supermarkets), La Competencia (business), Omega (paper bags), ATU (metal furniture), OSO (tire retreading), Kywi (hardware), and Paco (paper and office supplies). Among the pioneering Jewish businessmen, the most innovative were: Nussbaum, Klein, Deller, Pienknagura, Scharninsky, Kohn, Kywi, Freund, and Dorfzaun; and more recently, Heller, Attia, and Gutt. Despite the fact that many left and their businesses closed, according to Lehmann in 2005 Jewish enterprises directly employed about fifty thousand workers.[73]

Among the Jewish immigrants, there were also professionals, intellectuals, artists, musicians, singers, teachers, geologists, and writers. These included Alberto Di Capua, Giorgo Ottolenghi, Aldo Muggia, Francisco Breth, Hans Heiman, Leopold Levy, Paul Engel, Marco Turkel, Enrique Fenster, Benno Weiser, Victor Rosen, Hans Jacob, Nora Hahn, Gerardo Gottehelf, Rudolf Mendel, Lilo Linke, Bruno Moritz, Otto Glass, Egon Fellig, and Karl Kohn. Olga Fisch valued, rescued, and disseminated Ecuadorian popular art; Constanza Di Capua conducted archeological, anthropological, and colonial art studies; and Vera Schiller de Kohn was a psychologist and professor. At mid-century these activities were not of interest to Ecuadorian women, who usually lived relegated to their homes, without intellectual concerns and only preoccupied with social life.

The Jewish community also contributed to education by founding the school Colegio Alberto Einstein (1973), and to the spread of reading through the bookstores they opened. Simon Golberg, who had had the Goethe Bookstore of old books in Berlin, some of which he brought to Ecuador, founded the Librería Internacional.[74] Charles Liebman founded Su Librería, which operated on the main square and came to be the most important bookstore in Quito.

The Jewish community also contributed to awakening a fondness for classical music. The costly and modern concert hall known as the Casa de la Música, donated to Quito by Gi Neustatter at the beginning of the twenty-first century, serves as a testimony to this. Its well-attended weekly performances contrast sharply with what was available in the late 1950s, when a scant public, mostly comprised by Jews, attended occasional concerts offered by the National Symphonic Orchestra in the small Teatro Sucre.*

The Jews were not interested in politics, except for Pablo Better, a second-generation Ecuadorian Jew who held the offices of Minister of Economics and Finance and president of the Central Bank.

The contributions of the Jews, and their positive conduct's demonstration effect on the Ecuadorians, had much to do with the country's progress and with modern Quito's industrial, commercial, hospitality, and cultural development by the end of the twentieth century.

---

*Luis Levy, the son of a Jewish immigrant, told me that in the 1940s the members of his community gathered at the Jewish association's center to listen to concerts of classical music that were not played by a live orchestra but rather by a slate record that spun around on an old gramophone set up on a platform in the main meeting room.

FINAL REFLECTIONS

The cultural habits, attitudes, and beliefs analyzed in the preceding chapters were shaped during the sixteenth century and maintained during the colonial period and the early years of the republic. They kept the inhabitants of the Audiencia of Quito, and later of Ecuador, from progressing individually, kept economic activities from growing, and kept the country from developing. For almost five centuries there were only slight changes. The economic and social structures, the conformist discourse of the Catholic Church, the country's cloistered situation, extensive paternalism, stratified society, national backwardness, limited immigration, weaknesses in education, the absence of the rule of law, and modest outside influence—all contributed to this situation.

During hundreds of years, the Quiteños and Ecuadorians in general did not value effort, and they were not hardworking or interested in commerce. They were distrustful and did not take initiatives or launch innovations. They were not punctual and did not fulfill their commitments. They did not respect property rights, abide by laws, or obey the orders of authorities. They did not administer national assets and resources in an honest way, did not assume their responsibilities, and did not defend public interests. They were not open to new ideas, did not save to be able to invest, and were not concerned about cleanliness.

The segregationist, stratified society and widespread paternalism meant that merit was not recognized, good performance was not rewarded, and equal opportunities were not offered to citizens. Mediocre education, geographical isolation, limited immigration, and obstacles for the circulation of ideas kept people from abandoning inconvenient cultural values and adopting attitudes consistent with individual and collective progress, successful private initiative, and the country's development.

179

In Guayaquil the citizens' negative values began to change in the second half of the nineteenth century, and in the rest of Ecuador around the middle of the twentieth century. However, this was only with regard to interest in productive work, economic progress, and national development. Rich, poor, whites, Indians, mestizos, mulattos, and blacks realized that the economic status inherited from their parents could be modified if they routinely worked hard, took business initiatives, ran risks, took an interest in commerce, established industries, and sought to build wealth. For its part, the state awakened from its lethargy and accepted the challenge of promoting development. To this end, it undertook the construction of infrastructure, expanded public services, implemented structural reforms, enacted laws, and promoted economic and social programs.

The economic growth fostered by exports, first of bananas and later of oil, contributed to this cultural renovation, as did the decline in the importance of agricultural activities; the breakdown of the social organization of the hacienda; the appearance of productive urban activities; the arrival of fresh ideas; the presence of foreign companies, investments, and immigrants; the new systems of communications; the urbanization of the cities; the reforms promoted by international organizations; the liberalization of the economy; Ecuador's international openness; and the revolution caused by globalization and the Internet.

Even though in the twenty-first century most Ecuadorians are motivated by work and economic success, equivalent changes have not occurred in behaviors related to individual well-being, entrepreneurial initiatives, productivity, honesty, and trust. Despite the fact that the tendency to idleness has been left behind, the prejudices regarding manual labor have decreased, and working on a daily basis has become habitual, work is not diligent and efficient, especially among those that perform tasks as employees under contract, and above all in the case of public servants. Regardless of their economic status and professional level, people are not hardworking, efficient, and persevering. Rather, they are indolent, inconsistent, routine-oriented, and given to unproductive spending and not to saving. For this reason, companies and the broader economy are not innovative and competitive, nor do they have enough resources to grow and achieve an international projection.

Arriving late for appointments is frequent, as is being late in fulfilling commitments, implementing a contract, performing a task, finishing a project, providing a service, and paying a debt. Since economical use is not made of time, tasks are not done quickly: what should be done immediately is left for later, and what could be done today is postponed for tomorrow. Also, there is widespread distrust regarding the good faith with which the parties will act in making a business deal, setting up a company, implementing a contract, or undertaking an economic activity. There is no assurance that people will act with transparency, fulfill their commitments, and respect agreements, even in the case of transactions backed by deeds, contracts, letters of credit, IOUs, checks, and guarantees.

Morally permissive attitudes and behaviors begin early when students copy homework, cheat on exams, and plagiarize papers and theses in schools and colleges. These attitudes and behaviors later find expression in all aspects of national life, in both the public sector and the private sector, regardless of the social background of the individuals and the activities they carry out. Such is the case of tax evasion, because citizens do not see paying taxes as their primary civic obligation. Few consider the state a political body that should protect general interests, ensure legitimate rights, demand obligations, attempt to achieve the common good, and guarantee the rule of law. In fact, many consider it an instrument whereby individuals, union organizations, economic groups, private-sector companies, public officials, political leaders, and individuals themselves can obtain favors, benefits, and privileges, and get rich.

Personal merits are not recognized and rewarded due to the power and influence that personal relations have in a stratified and paternalistic society in which many decisions are based on the exchange of loyalty and favors. The predomination of personal relations over institutional ones means that decision makers, above all in the public sector, think about the person or group who will be benefited from a decision, and not about its merits, needs and rights, nor about national conveniences. Friendship, kinship, and the relationship between godparents and their godchildren's parents, as well as political affinities, union affiliations, and the so-called *esprit de corps* are examples of ties that weigh more heavily.

The law does not usually establish guidelines for the conduct of people in everyday life, in private-sector economic relations, and in public activities, nor is it in a position to offer guarantees that rights will be respected, obligations will be met, and equal opportunities will be offered to all citizens. There are multiple causes for this, but the most important one is the fact that legal principles are not present in the mind of people when they are conducting their activities. Instead, what prevails is the proclivity to get around the law through loopholes and shortcuts. Noncompliance with the law by individuals, companies, social organizations, and authorities keeps legal security from existing in the country, that is, the certainty that the parties' behavior will be in keeping with the law; and in the case of disputes, that the decisions of judges, magistrates, and administrators will abide by the law. The absence of the rule of law generates an atmosphere of distrust that leads economic agents to postpone their business decisions, make projects more expensive to protect themselves from unforeseen risks, and prefer speculative activities that provide rapid profits over long-term investments.

Those who form part of a private enterprise or a public entity, at different levels, do not link their interests to those of the institution they serve nor to those of the country in which they carry out their activities. For this reason, they are not naturally inclined to fulfill their obligations, give up something, or make sacrifices for the general benefit, or to take on extra tasks when critical circumstances arise. Their low sense of social responsibility affects others: owners, bosses, authorities, and governments.

Paternalism and populism deprive the state of its subsidiary nature and make it the first option to which citizens resort with their problems, even personal ones. A demagogic discourse laden with offers to set things right and other promises, along with the gratuitous distribution of benefits and public resources to voters, keep people from becoming aware of their own blame and from assuming their own responsibilities. The populist policies of governments and congresses result in wasting public resources, creating privileges, tending to private matters, creating regressive subsidies, and carrying out projects that are not priorities. Over time, they lead to crises that cause economic slumps, hikes in inflation, and increased poverty, all of which conspire against national development.

Because they constitute a cultural phenomenon, the cultural habits, beliefs, and attitudes studied herein have been shared by all of the inhabitants of Ecuador, regardless of their ethnic background, economic condition, social status, educational level, and the responsibilities they have had in the public sector or the private sector.

However, geographical location—in other words, the place where individuals live—has been an element of cultural differentiation that has given rise to different economic behaviors in the country's two main regions. On the coast, especially in Guayaquil, the enterprising spirit is widespread, and shrimp-farming is a good example of this. However, the tendency to save is more widespread in the highlands, as demonstrated by the size of the bank deposits, which are almost twice as high as on the coast, despite the fact that the latter is a much wealthier region.

There are also ethical differences between the two regions, as seen in chapter 4. "Black losses" are much higher in the power companies of the coast (34 percent) than in those of the highlands (14 percent), the per capita amount of taxes that the inhabitants of the Province of Pichincha pay (after subtracting those paid by foreign and domestic companies) is almost three times as high as in Guayas, and overdue payments on bank loans are 70 percent higher in Guayas than in Pichincha. Opinion polls show that the residents of Guayaquil are more given to pay bribes and to justify them than those of Quito, and they also view public interests with less concern.

The first four chapters of this book contribute innumerable pieces of evidence of how the Ecuadorian way of life has posed all sorts of stumbling-blocks for the economic success of individuals, the sound performance of entrepreneurial activities, the efficient management of public activities, and general welfare and development in Ecuador. For these reasons, the economy has not been able to grow at high enough rates or to sustain high rates over the long run. In addition, people, companies, and the state have not tapped the opportunities to advance that have been provided to them at the national and worldwide levels. It has proven impossible to build institutions to regulate economic, social, and political relations and to achieve a society that offers its citizens equal opportunities. It has also been impossible to improve the population's standard of living and to eliminate poverty. Furthermore, the country has one of the lowest rankings in international indexes for competitiveness and one of the highest for corruption. It is evident that in Ecuador the society is not organized like, and does not function like, the societies that in the last quarter-century have managed to rise out of their backward state, overcome poverty, and develop: Korea, Singapore, Spain, and Ireland, among others.

The approach that underscores the role of cultural values in the progress of peoples and in the development of nations calls for not blaming external forces but rather situating within the borders of the country and among its inhabitants the responsibility for taking Ecuador out of its backwardness and making it a developing society. This entails locating the cause of national problems and the lack of solutions at the opposite extreme of the theories of imperialism and dependency. Despite the fact that such proposals have been abandoned—even by those who conceived them, in light of the ample evidence that the states that opened up to the world were those that prospered—many continue to attribute Ecuador's underdevelopment to the industrialized countries' actions and omissions, to policies promoted by international organizations, and to the presence of foreign companies and capital. This is still another example of the national inclination to shift responsibility onto others and of Ecuadorians' traditional resistance to opening up to the world and to new ideas.

This research effort contributes evidence that certain behaviors, beliefs, and attitudes have kept the country from developing in the way that would have been possible. Hopefully, it will also contribute to the citizens' awareness of their responsibilities and to cultural patterns compatible with the needs of individual and collective progress, as well as to the authorities' and institutions' decisions to take measures and promote policies that will encourage the adoption of cultural values that will make the Ecuadorian people assume their responsibility in constructing their own destiny.

In this regard, it is worthwhile to recall that people's cultural values are not immutable, nor inherent to a given race, religion, or social class. They can change through the action of institutions, laws, and leaders; through economic, social, and political reforms; educational processes; and external influences, as has occurred in other countries of the world. Spain, which many years ago was culturally very similar to Ecuador, constitutes the best example of this.

The cultural changes produced in Guayaquil, Otavalo, and Cuenca demonstrate that it is possible for individuals and groups of people to leave aside conduct that hinders individual and collective progress and, instead, to adopt values consistent with the needs of national development and personal well-being. The analysis of the economic success of both Arabs and Jews, despite the fact that they had to deal with more obstacles than the Ecuadorians, leaves no doubt that their success was due to their capabilities, sacrifices, efforts, and sound decisions, and not to reasons of a different nature.

Even though the notable progress made in Quito in recent years has been mentioned, a more in-depth analysis would contribute to identifying the reasons that the greater distance separating it from Guayaquil in the twentieth century has reappeared. Furthermore, this study does not address the progress made by two medium-sized cities, one on the coast and one in the highlands. Manta is experiencing an economic boom thanks to its successful fishing activities and the industrial processing of tuna. Ambato is experiencing a similar boost, based on small and medium-sized commercial and industrial enterprises. In Ambato a habit of punctuality has also been implemented in public and private ceremonies and in social engagements and business appointments. Among the twenty largest payers of income tax, the number of people in Ambato exceeds the number in Guayaquil.

There are also positive experiences in small groups of people, among which it is worthwhile to mention two. The Centro del Muchacho Trabajador (Working Boys' Center) in Quito, promoted by an American Jesuit, John Halligan, takes children off the street to educate and train them. The program's graduates have managed to double the national averages for saving, starting businesses, finding stability in their work, and improving their families' levels of well-being through their efforts. In a poor indigenous community of the rural parish of Salinas, located in the province of Bolívar, the illiteracy rate was 85 percent in 1970, and the infant mortality rate 45 percent. However, thanks to initial technical and financial assistance from the Swiss Cooperation Agency, a company was set up to produce cheese. The Indians' disciplined and persevering efforts have made it possible to build up a prosperous dairy products industry (Queseras Bolívar) that competes with the most well-known brands in terms of quality and price. Illiteracy in the community has dropped to 24 percent and infant mortality to 14 percent, and the Indians' income and standard of living have improved.

Along the lines of promoting changes in cultural values to make them compatible with national development needs, the assembly that issued the Political Constitution of 1998 introduced an article on the duties that Ecuadorians should fulfill to be good citizens. Until then, the constitutions had emphasized citizens' rights and said nothing about their obligations. To relate the mandates of Article 97 of that constitution to individuals' day-to-day activities, in 1999 I published a manual entitled *Deberes y responsabilidades para ser buenos ecuatorianos*. It has been used by social organizations, the civil society, and Catholic establishments for values education purposes. An initiative of CORDES that received economic support from USAID also made it possible for the Ministry of Education to reform the school curriculum so as to incorporate values education and train teachers in this area.

To climb out of its backwardness, develop, and improve the well-being of its inhabitants, Ecuador has to resolve many problems, in almost every field. However, just as has occurred in the past, whatever is done to achieve these objectives will be insufficient if the Ecuadorians' cultural habits do not change.

NOTES

CHAPTER 1: CULTURAL CHARACTERISTICS OF THE AUDIENCIA OF QUITO

1. John Leddy Phelan, *El reino de Quito en el siglo XVII* (Quito: Banco Central del Ecuador, 1995), 81.

2. Gironaldo Benzoni, *Historia del Mondo Nuevo* (Madrid: Alianza Editorial, 1989), 323.

3. Mario Cicala, *Descripción histórico-topográfica de la provincia de Quito de la Compañía de Jesús* (Quito: Biblioteca ecuatoriana Aurelio Espinosa Pólit-Instituto Geográfico Militar, 1994), 1:149.

4. William Bennet Stevenson, *Narración histórica y descriptiva de 20 años de residencia en Sudamérica* (Quito: Abya-Yala, 1994), 436, 392.

5. Michael T. Hamerly, *Historia Social y Económica de la Antigua Provincia de Guayaquil, 1763–1842* (Guayaquil: Archivo Histórico del Guayas, 1973), 67.

6. Charles La Condamine, *Viaje a la América Meridional* (Madrid: Espasa-Calpe S.A., 1921), 41.

7. Alexander Humboldt, *L' Amerique Espagnole en 1800* (Paris: Calmann-Lévy, 1965), 242–43.

8. Phelan, *El reino de Quito en el siglo XVII*, 102–03.

9. Lawrence Clayton, *Los Astilleros de Guayaquil Colonial* (Guayaquil: Casa de la Cultura Ecuatoriana Núcleo del Guayas, 1978), 114.

10. Jorge Juan and Antonio De Ulloa, *Noticias Secretas de América* (Madrid: Dastin, 2002), 218, 224.

11. Stevenson, *Narración histórica y descriptiva*, 397–98.

12. Francisco José Caldas, *Obras de Caldas* (Bogotá: Imprenta Nacional, 1912), 9:143.

13. José María Vargas, *La Economía Política del Ecuador durante La Colonia* (Quito: Editorial Universitaria, 1957), 93–95.

14. Nicholas Cushner, *Farm and Factory: The Jesuits and the Development of Agrarian Capitalism in Colonial Quito, 1600–1767* (Albany: State University of New York Press, 1982), 67.

15. Clayton, *Los Astilleros de Guayaquil Colonial*, 114–15.

16. Osvaldo Hurtado, *El Poder Político en el Ecuador* (Quito: Ediciones de la Universidad Católica, 1997 [1977]), 41.

17. Lois Crawford de Roberts, *Los Libaneses en el Ecuador* (Fundación Cultural Ecuatoriano-Libanesa, 1997), 12–13. The author cites a thesis: Eilif V. Miller, *Ecuadorean Soils and Some of Their Fertility Properties* (Ph.D. thesis, Cornell University, 1948), 3, 6.

18. Juan and De Ulloa, *Noticias Secretas de América*, 148.

19. Stevenson, *Narración histórica y descriptiva*, 464–65.

20. Cicala, *Descripción histórico-topográfica*, 1:149.

21. Quoted in María Luisa Laviana, *Guayaquil en el Siglo XVIII: Recursos Naturales y Desarrollo Económico* (Sevilla: Escuela de Estudios hispanoamericanos, 1987), 166.

22. Vargas, *La Economía Política del Ecuador*, 94.

23. Christian Büschges, *Familia, honor y poder* (Quito: FONSAL, 2007), 43–44.

24. Ibid., 115–34.

25. Juan and De Ulloa, *Noticias Secretas de América*, 395–99.

26. Florence Trystram, *El Proceso con las Estrellas* (Quito: Ediciones Libri Mundi, 1999), 67.

27. Büschges, *Familia, honor y poder*, 115–16, 268–69.

28. Alexander Humboldt, *Diarios de viaje en la Audiencia de Quito* (Quito: Occidental Exploration and Production Company, 2005), 139, 194.

29. Romualdo Navarro, "Idea del Reino de Quito," *La Economía Colonial.* (Quito: Corporación Editora Nacional, Quito, 1984), 155.

30. Jorge Juan and Antonio De Ulloa, *Relación Histórica del Viaje a la América Meridional* (Madrid: Fundación Universitaria Española, 1978), 1:365, 372–73.

31. Stevenson, *Narración histórica y descriptiva*, 414.

32. Federico González Suárez, *Historia general de la República del Ecuador* (Quito: Daniel Cadena, 1931), 449, 454.

33. Luis Robalino Dávila, *Orígenes del Ecuador de Hoy* (México: Cajica, 1967), 37.

34. Francisco Aguirre Abad, *Bosquejo Histórico de la República del Ecuador.* (Guayaquil: Corporación de Estudios y Publicaciones, Sección de Investigaciones Histórico-Jurídicas, 1972), 144.

35. Juan Domingo Coleti, "Relación inédita de la ciudad de Quito," in *Quito a través de los siglos,* ed. Eliécer Enríquez (Quito: Biblioteca Municipal, 1941), 2:62.

36. Cicala, *Descripción histórico-topográfica*, 2:30–45.

37. Benzoni, *Historia del Mundo Nuevo*, 321–22.

38. Juan and De Ulloa, *Noticias Secretas de América*, 288–90.

39. Stevenson, *Narración histórica y descriptiva*, 440.

40. Belisario Quevedo, *Historia Patria* (Quito: Banco Central del Ecuador 1982), 112–13.

41. González Suárez, op. cit., 1970, 954.

42. Martin Minchon, *El pueblo de Quito 1690–1810* (Quito: FONSAL, 2007), 169–74.

43. Cicala, *Descripción histórico-topográfica*, 2:32.

44. Juan and De Ulloa, *Noticias Secretas de América*, 148–49, 290.

45. Juan and De Ulloa, *Relación Histórica del Viaje*, 1:365–66.

46. Cicala, *Descripción histórico-topográfica*, 2:39.

47. Quoted in Pilar Ponce Leiva, *Certezas ante la incertidumbre: Elite y Cabildo de Quito en el siglo XVII* (Quito: Abya–Yala, 2000), 241.

48. Cicala, *Descripción histórico-topográfica*, 1:585–97.

49. Phelan, *El reino de Quito en el siglo XVII*, 351.

50. Robson Brynes Tyrer, *Historia Demográfica y Económica de la Audiencia de Quito* (Quito: Banco Central, 1988), 104.

51. Hugo Arias Palacios, *Evolución Socio Económica del Ecuador: Sociedades Primitivas y Período Colonial* (Guayaquil: Biblioteca Ecuatoriana 24, 1980), 172.

52. Tyrer, *Historia Demográfica y Económica de la Audiencia de Quito*, 93.

53. Stevenson, *Narración histórica y descriptiva*, 442.

54. Tyrer, *Historia Demográfica y Económica de la Audiencia de Quito*, 93.

55. Juan and De Ulloa, *Noticias Secretas de América*, 269–70.

56. Cicala, *Descripción histórico-topográfica*, 2:43.

57. Alfonso María Mora, *La Conquista Española juzgada jurídica y sociológicamente* (Buenos Aires: Editorial América Lee, 1944), 201. Cites a report.

58. Anonymous writer in English, translated into Italian, *Storia Degli Stabilimenti Europei in sei parti, Volume Primo* (Venecia: MDCCLXIII), 288–89.

59. Juan and De Ulloa, *Relación Histórica del Viaje*, 375–77.

60. Trystram, *El Proceso con las Estrellas*, 128.

61. Caldas, *Obras de Caldas*, 162.

62. Stevenson, *Narración histórica y descriptiva*, 414.

63. Quevedo, *Historia Patria*, 112.

64. Juan and De Ulloa, *Relación Histórica del Viaje*, 372–79.

65. Tyrer, *Historia Demográfica y Económica de la Audiencia de Quito*, 260.

66. Trystram, *El Proceso con las Estrellas*, 74.

67. Coleti, "Relación inédita de la ciudad de Quito," 52, 61–62.

68. Cicala, *Descripción histórico-topográfica*, 1:118, 220.

69. José Jouanen, *Historia de la Compañía de Jesús en la Antigua Provincia de Quito* (Quito: Editorial Ecuatoriana, 1941), 76.

70. Humboldt, *Diarios de viaje en la Audiencia de Quito*, 219.

71. Friedrich Hassaurek, *Cuatro años entre los ecuatorianos* (Quito: Abya-Yala, 1997), 128.

72. Caldas, *Obras de Caldas*, 230–31.

73. Manuel Villavicencio, *Geografía de la Política del Ecuador* (New York: Imprenta de Robert Craighead, 1858), 223.

74. Victorino Brandini, "De Quito, de su decadencia, voto por su regeneración," in *Quito a través de los siglos*, ed. Eliécer Enríquez (Quito: Biblioteca Municipal, 1941), 2:146.

75. Humboldt, *Diarios de viaje en la Audiencia de Quito*, 212.

76. Cicala, *Descripción histórico-topográfica*, 1:139.

77. Jouanen, *Historia de la Compañía de Jesús*, 644.

78. Cicala, *Descripción histórico-topográfica* 1:349–53.

79. Cushner, *Farm and Factory*, 15, 16, 86, 87, 89, 175–76.

80. Cicala, *Descripción histórico-topográfica*, 1:634.

81. Stevenson, *Narración histórica y descriptiva*, 372.

82. Clayton, *Los Astilleros de Guayaquil Colonial*, 150.

83. Ibid., 372–73.

84. Laviana, *Guayaquil en el siglo XVIII*, 45–46.

85. Stevenson, *Narración histórica y descriptiva*, 365.

86. María Luisa Laviana Cuetos, *Estudios sobre el Guayaquil Colonial* (Guayaquil: Archivo Histórico del Guayas, 1999), 25.

87. Ibid., 25.

88. Stevenson, *Narración histórica y descriptiva*, 379, 392.

89. Ibid., 375.

90. Clayton, *Los Astilleros de Guayaquil Colonial*, 153.

91. Stevenson, *Narración histórica y descriptiva*, 415.

92. Ponce Leiva, *Certezas ante la incertidumbre*, 213.

93. Ibid., 267.

94. Quevedo, *Historia Patria*, 110.

95. Robalino Dávila, *Orígenes del Ecuador de Hoy*, 63.

96. Humboldt, *L' Amerique Espagnole en 1800*, 237.

97. Richard Konetzke, *Historia Universal Siglo XXI, América Latina II: La Epoca Colonial, Siglo XXI* (Madrid: Siglo XXI, 1971), 70.

98. Phelan, *El reino de Quito en el siglo XVII*, 96.

99. Villavicencio, *Geografía de la Política del Ecuador*, 8.

100. Aguirre Abad, *Bosquejo Histórico de la República del Ecuador*, 144.

101. González Suárez, op. cit., 3:330.

102. Coleti, "Relación inédita de la ciudad de Quito," 57, 58, 61.

103. Caldas, *Obras de Caldas*, 235–36.

104. Humboldt, *Diarios de viaje en la Audiencia de Quito*, 115.

105. Juan and De Ulloa, *Relación Histórica del Viaje*, 371.

106. Stevenson, *Narración histórica y descriptiva*, 414.

107. Juan and De Ulloa, *Relación Histórica del Viaje*, 319–20.

108. Villavicencio, *Geografía de la Política del Ecuador*, 9.

109. Alberto Landázuri Soto, *El Régimen Laboral Indígena en la Audiencia de Quito* (Madrid: Imprenta de Aldecoa, 1959), 16–32.

110. Hurtado, *El Poder Político en el Ecuador*, 34.

111. Clayton, *Los Astilleros de Guayaquil Colonial*, 104.

112. Joaquín De Merizalde, *Relación histórica, política y moral de la ciudad de Cuenca* (Cuenca: Editorial Casa de la Cultura Ecuatoriana, 1957), 27.

113. Juan and De Ulloa, *Noticias Secretas de América*, 188.

114. Clayton, *Los Astilleros de Guayaquil Colonial*, 98.

115. Laviana, *Guayaquil en el siglo XVIII*, 44–45.

116. Hamerly, *Historia Social y Económica*, 57.

117. Laviana, *Guayaquil en el siglo XVIII*, 50–51.

CHAPTER 2: CULTURAL VALUES IN THE NINETEENTH CENTURY

1. Hamerly, *Historia Social y Económica*: 100.

2. Joaquín De Avendaño, *Imagen del Ecuador: Economía y sociedad vistas por un viajero del siglo XIX* (Quito: Corporación Editora Nacional, 1985), 299.

3. Hamerly, *Historia Social y Económica*, 52.

4. Pedro Fermín Cevallos, *Resumen de la historia del Ecuador* (Puebla-México: Biblioteca Ecuatoriana Mínima, 1959), 385.

5. Cicala, *Descripción histórico-topográfica*, 1:23.

6. James Orton, *The Andes and the Amazon* (New York: Harper & Brothers Publishers, 1870), 74.

7. Alexandre Holinski, *L'Ècuateur: Scènes de la vie Sud-amèricaine* (Paris: Amyot Editeurs, 1861), 132, 210.

8. Thomas MacFarlane, *Hacia los Andes: Botas de viaje a América del Sur -1876–* (Quito: Abya-Yala, 1994), 138–39; F. W. UP DE Graff, *Cazadores de Cabezas del Amazonas* (Madrid: Espasa-Calpe, 1961), 39–40.

9. Graff, *Cazadores de Cabezas del Amazonas*, 39–40.

10. Hamerly, *Historia Social y Económica*, 109.

11. For a broader analysis of the institution of the hacienda, see: Hurtado, *El Poder Político en el Ecuador*, 55–72.

12. Ibid., 61; Graff, *Cazadores de Cabezas del Amazonas*, 34.

13. Graff, *Cazadores de Cabezas del Amazonas*, 34.

14. Hassaurek, *Cuatro años entre los ecuatorianos*, 336.

15. Graff, *Cazadores de Cabezas del Amazonas*, 32, 34–37.

16. De Avendaño, *Imagen del Ecuador*, 133–34.

17. Holinski, *L'Ècuateur: Scènes de la vie Sud-amèricaine*, 170.

18. Mark Van Aken, *King of the Night: Juan José Flores and Ecuador 1824–1869* (Berkeley: University of California Press, 1989), 43; Manuel Chiriboga, *Jornaleros y Gran Propietarios en 135 Años de Exportación Cacaotera, 1970–1925* (Quito: Consejo Provincial de Pichincha, 1980), 50.

19. Hassaurek, *Cuatro años entre los ecuatorianos*, 215.

20. Hurtado, *El Poder Político en el Ecuador*, 66–70.

21. Holinski, *L'Ècuateur: Scènes de la vie Sud-amèricaine*, 186–88.

22. Hassaurek, *Cuatro años entre los ecuatorianos*, 158–59.

23. Ibid., 247–49.

24. De Avendaño, *Imagen del Ecuador*, 143, 145.

25. Orton, *The Andes and the Amazon*, 74.

26. Hassaurek, *Cuatro años entre los ecuatorianos*, 223, 247.

27. Orton, *The Andes and the Amazon*, 73–74; Hassaurek, *Cuatro años entre los ecuatorianos*, 223.

28. Edward Whymper, *Entre los Altos Andes del Ecuador* (Quito: Imprenta Nacional, 1921), 224.

29. Hassaurek, *Cuatro años entre los ecuatorianos*, 223.

30. Orton, *The Andes and the Amazon*, 72.

31. De Avendaño, *Imagen del Ecuador*, 126–27.

32. Teodoro Wolf, *Geografía y geología del Ecuador* (Quito: Casa de la Cultura Ecuatoriana, 1975), 579–80.

33. Hassaurek, *Cuatro años entre los ecuatorianos*, 162, 215, 224, 155.

34. Ibid., 231.

35. Orton, *The Andes and the Amazon*, 72–73.

36. Ibid., 49, 139, 222–23.

37. Whymper, *Entre los Altos Andes del Ecuador*, 136

38. Orton, *The Andes and the Amazon*, 73.

39. Adrian Terry, *Viajes por la región ecuatorial de América del Sur* (Quito: Ediciones Abya—Yala, 1994), 216.

40. Reginald Enock, *Ecuador: Geografía Humana* (Quito: Corporación Editora Nacional, 1980), 260.

41. Orton, *The Andes and the Amazon*, 68.

42. Hassaurek, *Cuatro años entre los ecuatorianos*, 155.

43. Terry, *Viajes por la región ecuatorial*, 78.

44. Gaetano Osculati, *Exploraciones de las Regiones Ecuatoriales* (Quito: Abya-Yala, 2000), 1:45–46.

45. Holinski, *L'Ècuateur: Scènes de la vie Sud-amèricaine*, 184.

46. Hassaurek, *Cuatro años entre los ecuatorianos*, 27–28.

47. Orton, *The Andes and the Amazon*, 30, 79.

48. Joseph Kolberg, *Hacia el Ecuador: Relatos de Viaje* (Quito: Abya-Yala, 1996), 225.

49. Hassaurek, *Cuatro años entre los ecuatorianos*, 152, 49, 223.

50. Graff, *Cazadores de Cabezas del Amazona*, 43.

51. Osculati, *Exploraciones de las Regiones Ecuatoriales*, 1:38.

52. Whymper, *Entre los Altos Andes del Ecuador*, 27, 180, 61, 87.

53. Enock, *Ecuador: Geografía Humana*, 262.

54. Holinski, *L'Ècuateur: Scènes de la vie Sud-amèricaine*, 128, 220; Gonzalo Ortiz Crespo, *La incorporación del Ecuador al mercado mundial* (Quito: Corporación Editora Nacional, 1988), 198.

55. José Peralta, *Tipos de mi tierra (cuadros al natural)* (Cuenca: Casa de la Cultura Ecuatoriana, 1974), 294; Graff, *Cazadores de Cabezas del Amazona*, 43.

56. Ortiz Crespo, *La incorporación del Ecuador*, 198.

57. Graff, *Cazadores de Cabezas del Amazona*, 43.

58. Terry, *Viajes por la región ecuatorial*, 216, 217.

59. Orton, *The Andes and the Amazon*, 72–73.

60. Hassaurek, *Cuatro años entre los ecuatorianos*, 138–39.

61. Orton, *The Andes and the Amazon*, 72.

62. Wolf, *Geografía y Geología del Ecuador*, 386.

63. Francis Hall, *Colombia: Its Present State and Inducements to Emigration* (Philadelphia, 1825); Hassaurek, *Cuatro años entre los ecuatorianos*, 148–49.

64. Quoted in Andrew McKenzie, *Las aventuras de Archer Harman*, trans. C. A. Salazar (1901), 5.

65. Hassaurek, *Cuatro años entre los ecuatorianos*, 153.

66. Orton, *The Andes and the Amazon*, 72.

67. Whymper, *Entre los Altos Andes del Ecuador*, 176.

68. Cevallos, *Resumen de la historia del Ecuador*, 464.

69. Hassaurek, *Cuatro años entre los ecuatorianos*, 62–63.

70. Orton, *The Andes and the Amazon*, 73.

71. Graff, *Cazadores de Cabezas del Amazona*, 43.

72. Orton, *The Andes and the Amazon*, 73.

73. Wolf, *Geografía y Geología del Ecuador*, 247.

74. MacFarlane, *Hacia los Andes*, 94, 95, 101, 152.

75. Wolf, *Geografía y Geología del Ecuador*, 255.

76. Hassaurek, *Cuatro años entre los ecuatorianos*, 28, 38.

77. Osculati, *Exploraciones de las Regiones Ecuatoriales*, 55, 37.

78. Kolberg, *Hacia el Ecuador*, 274–75.

79. Holinski, *L'Ècuateur: Scènes de la vie Sud-amèricaine*, 161, 186.

80. McKenzie, *Las aventuras de Archer Harman*, 31.

81. MacFarlane, *Hacia los Andes*, 153.

82. Hassaurek, *Cuatro años entre los ecuatorianos*, 222.

83. McKenzie, *Las aventuras de Archer Harman*, 27.

84. Kolberg, *Hacia el Ecuador*, 16, 17, 186.

85. Osculati, *Exploraciones de las Regiones Ecuatoriales*, 1:46.

86. MacFarlane, *Hacia los Andes*, 134.

87. Kim Clark, *La Obra Redentora* (Quito: Universidad Andina Simón Bolívar, Corporación Editora Nacional, 2004), 36, 107.

88. McKenzie, *Las aventuras de Archer Harman*, 30.

89. Hurtado, *El Poder Político en el Ecuador*, 76.

90. Holinski, *L'Ècuateur: Scènes de la vie Sud-amèricaine*, 186.

91. Ibid., 219.

92. Quoted in Carlos Arcos, "El Espíritu del Progreso: Los Hacendados en el Ecuador del 1900," in *Clase y Región en el Agro Ecuatoriano,* ed. Miguel Murmis (Quito: Corporación Editora Nacional, 1986), 277.

93. Enock, *Ecuador: Geografía Humana*, 389.

94. McKenzie, *Las aventuras de Archer Harman*, 48–49.

95. Hassaurek, *Cuatro años entre los ecuatorianos*, 111.

96. McKenzie, *Las aventuras de Archer Harman*, 25.

97. Enock, *Ecuador: Geografía Humana*, 405.

98. Julio Estrada Ycaza, *Los Bancos del Siglo IX* (Guayaquil: Archivo Histórico del Guayas, 1976), 12.

99. Quoted in Clark, *La Obra Redentora*, 60.

100. Hassaurek, *Cuatro años entre los ecuatorianos*, 135.

101. Ibid., 140.

102. Holinski, *L'Ècuateur: Scènes de la vie Sud-amèricaine*, 142, 160, 172.

103. Orton, *The Andes and the Amazon*, 60, 65, 78.

104. Enrico Festa, *En el Darien y el Ecuador: Diario de viaje de un naturalista* (Quito: Abya-Yala, 1993), 287.

105. Graff, *Cazadores de Cabezas del Amazona*, 42.

106. De Avendaño, *Imagen del Ecuador*, 145.

107. Hassaurek, *Cuatro años entre los ecuatorianos*, 188.

108. Graff, *Cazadores de Cabezas del Amazona*, 30, 31, 43.

109. Whymper, *Entre los Altos Andes del Ecuador*, 101.

110. Hamerly, *Historia Social y Económica*, 140

111. Osculati, *Exploraciones de las Regiones Ecuatoriales*, 23

112. Julio Estrada Ycaza, *El puerto de Guayaquil* (Guayaquil: Archivo Histórico del Guayas, 1973), 3:232–33.

113. Osculati, *Exploraciones de las Regiones Ecuatoriales*, 22–23.

114. Kolberg, *Hacia el Ecuador*, 210–11.

115. MacFarlane, *Hacia los Andes*, 152.

116. Kolberg, *Hacia el Ecuador*, 191.

117. Holinski, *L'Ècuateur. Scènes de la vie Sud-amèricaine*, 22, 19.

118. Whymper, *Entre los Altos Andes del Ecuador*, 381.

119. Terry, *Viajes por la región ecuatorial*, 215

120. Carlos Wiener, *"Viaje al Río de las Amazonas y a las Cordilleras"* in *El Ecuador Visto por los Extranjeros Viajeros de los Siglos XVIII y XIX*, ed. Humberto Toscano (México: Editorial Cajica, 1959), 13:455.

121. Kolberg, *Hacia el Ecuador*, 193.

122. Hamerly, *Historia Social y Económica*, 131.

123. Toscano, *El Ecuador Visto*, 75.

124. Hamerly, *Historia Social y Económica*, 49–62.

125. Festa, *En el Darien y el Ecuador*, 105.

126. McKenzie, *Las aventuras de Archer Harman*, 12.

127. De Avendaño, *Imagen del Ecuador*, 194.

128. Whymper, *Entre los Altos Andes del Ecuador*, 10.

129. Clark, *La Obra Redentora*, 37, 80.

130. Hamerly, *Historia Social y Económica*, 111.

131. Alfredo Espinosa Tamayo, *Psicología y sociología del pueblo ecuatoriano* (Guayaquil: Biblioteca Ecuatoriana, Imprenta Municipal, 1918), 137.

132. James D. Rudolph, "Historical Setting," in *Ecuador: A Country Study*, ed. Dennis M. Hanratty (Washington, DC: Library of Congress, 1993), 90.

133. Jacinto Jijón y Caamaño, *Política Conservadora Volumen II* (Quito, 1934), 541.

134. Junta de Planificación, *Reforma de la Estructura de Tenencia de la Tierra y Expansión de la Frontera Agrícola, Plan General de Desarrollo* (Quito, 1962), 71; Carlos Wiener, *Guayaquil a través de los siglos* (Quito: Talleres Gráfico Nacionales, 1964), 467; Crawford, *Los Libaneses en el Ecuador*, 1:79, 81.

135. *Los Libaneses en el Ecuador*, 79, 81.

136. Wiener, 467.

137. Pedro Fermín Cevallos, *Historia del Ecuador desde su origen hasta 1845*, vol. 1 (Quito-Guayaquil: Ariel, 1972), 103.

138. Hassaurek, *Cuatro años entre los ecuatorianos*, 186.

139. Wiener, *Guayaquil a través de los siglos*, 459.

140. Van Aken, *King of the Night*, 45.

141. Orton, *The Andes and the Amazon*, 89.

142. MacFarlane, *Hacia los Andes*, 147.

143. Hassaurek, *Cuatro años entre los ecuatorianos*, 234–35.

144. Osculati, *Exploraciones de las Regiones Ecuatoriales*, 1:44.

145. Hamerly, *Historia Social y Económica*, 140–41.

146. Hassaurek, *Cuatro años entre los ecuatorianos*, 186.

147. Wolf, *Geografía y geología del Ecuador*, 590.

148. Orton, *The Andes and the Amazon*, 79.

149. De Avendaño, *Imagen del Ecuador*, 127, 213.

150. González Suárez, *Memorias Íntimas* (Quito-Guayaquil: Clásicos Ariel, 1972), 86.

151. Holinski, *L'Ècuateur: Scènes de la vie Sud-amèricaine*, 189, 196.

152. Hassaurek, *Cuatro años entre los ecuatorianos*, 197, 234, 265.

153. Holinski, *L'Ècuateur: Scènes de la vie Sud-amèricaine*, 19–20.

154. Wiener, *Guayaquil a través de los siglos*, 454–55.

155. McKenzie, *Las aventuras de Archer Harman*, 11.

156. Hassaurek, *Cuatro años entre los ecuatorianos*, 66.

157. Kolberg, *Hacia el Ecuador*, 489.

158. Wolf, *Geografía y geología del Ecuador*, 591.

159. Hassaurek, *Cuatro años entre los ecuatorianos*, 341.

160. De Avendaño, *Imagen del Ecuador*, 116.

161. Holinski, *L'Ècuateur: Scènes de la vie Sud-amèricaine*, 28.

162. Osculati, *Exploraciones de las Regiones Ecuatoriales*, 43.

163. Hassaurek, *Cuatro años entre los ecuatorianos*, 198.

164. Orton, *The Andes and the Amazon*, 78-79.

165. Hassaurek, *Cuatro años entre los ecuatorianos*, 194.

166. Cevallos, *Historia del Ecuador desde su orígen hasta 1845*, 434–43.

167. Graff, *Cazadores de Cabezas del Amazonas*, 29.

168. Hassaurek, *Cuatro años entre los ecuatorianos*, 185, 164.

169. Ibid., 217.

170. Holinski, *L'Èciateur: Scènes de la vie Sud-amèricaine*, 30.

171. Clark, *La Obra Redentora*, 94–95.

172. Washington Padilla J., *La Iglesia y los Dioses Modernos: Historia del Protestantismo en el Ecuador* (Quito: Corporación Editora Nacional, 1989), 142, 225.

173. Ibid., 142.

174. Hassaurek, *Cuatro años entre los ecuatorianos*, 24.

175. Holinski, *L'Èciateur: Scènes de la vie Sud-amèricaine*, 21.

176. McKenzie, *Las aventuras de Archer Harman*, 2

177. Terry, *Viajes por la región ecuatorial*, 139.

178. Hassaurek, *Cuatro años entre los ecuatorianos*, 213, 222.

179. De Avendaño, *Imagen del Ecuador*, 95.

180. Whymper, *Entre los Altos Andes del Ecuador*, 87–90.

181. McKenzie, *Las aventuras de Archer Harman*, 30.

182. Orton, *The Andes and the Amazon*, 68.

183. Hassaurek, *Cuatro años entre los ecuatorianos*, 152, 247.

184. Terry, *Viajes por la región ecuatorial*, 221.

185. Hassaurek, *Cuatro años entre los ecuatorianos*, 357–358.

186. Terry, *Viajes por la región ecuatorial*, 219.

187. Van Aken, *King of the Night*, 72, 74.

188. Enrique Onffroy de Thoron, *América Ecuatorial*, Primera Parte (Quito: Corporación Editora Nacional, 1983), 157–58.

189. Holinski, *L'Èciateur: Scènes de la vie Sud-amèricaine*, 63.

190. Lois Crawford de Roberts, *El Ecuador en la Época Cacaotera* (Quito: Editorial Universitaria UCE, 1980), 101, 102.

191. Hassaurek, *Cuatro años entre los ecuatorianos*, 363.

CHAPTER 3: CULTURAL CHANGES IN THE FIRST HALF OF THE TWENTIETH CENTURY

1. McKenzie, *Las aventuras de Archer Harman*, B, 3–9.

2. Crawford de Roberts, *El Ecuador en la Época Cacaotera*, 50, 62.

3. United Nations, *Statistical Yearbook*, 1951. Provided by the Economic Commission for Latin America and the Caribbean (ECLAC), http://www.cepal.org.

4. Hurtado, *El Poder Político en el Ecuador*, 88–90.

5. Ludwig Bemelmans, *El Burro por Dentro* (Quito: Editora Moderna, 1941), 79.

6. Padilla J., *La Iglesia y los Dioses Modernos*, 356.

7. Crawford de Roberts, *El Ecuador en la Época Cacaotera*, 113.

8. Bemelmans, *El Burro por Dentro*, 23.

9. J. Fred Rippy, "German Investments in Latin America," in Crawford, *El Ecuador en la Época Cacaotera*, 51.

10. McKenzie, *Las aventuras de Archer Harman*, 4.

11. Albert Franklin, *Ecuador: Retrato de un Pueblo* (Quito: Corporación Editora Nacional, 1984), 319.

12. Hans Meyer, *En Los Altos Andes del Ecuador* (Quito: Abya-Yala, 1993), 72.

13. Blair Niles, *Correrías casuales en el Ecuador* (Quito: Abya-Yala, 1995), 37–47.

14. Empresa Periodística Prensa Ecuatoriana, *América Libre, Guayaquil en 1920* (Guayaquil, 1920), 126, 127, 186.

15. Niles, *Correrías casuales en el Ecuador*, 92, 123.

16. Ibid., 77, 78.

17. Belisario Quevedo, *Ensayos Sociológicos, Políticos y Morales* (Quito: Banco Central del Ecuador, Corporación Editora Nacional, 1981), 233.

18. Clark, *La Obra Redentora*, 66–67.

19. Ibid., 108, 109, 120, 149.

20. Franklin, *Ecuador: Retrato de un Pueblo*, 178.

21. Henri Michaux, *Ecuador, diario de viaje* (Barcelona: Tusquets Editores, 1983), 32.

22. Meyer, *En Los Altos Andes del Ecuador*, 73.

23. J. A. Delebecque, *Travers l'Amérique du Sud: Plon-Nourrit et. Cie. Impremeurs-Éditeurs* (Paris: Impremeurs-Éditeurs, 1907), 121.

24. Bemelmans, *El Burro por Dentro*, 131.

25. Arthur Weilbauer, *Mi largo camino: Relato de un refugiado de la Alemania Nazi* (Quito: unpublished manuscript, 1982), 34–35.

26. Quevedo, *Ensayos Sociológicos, Políticos y Morales*, 227, 231, 234, 191–93.

27. Espinosa Tamayo, *Psicología y sociología del pueblo ecuatoriano*, 21, 124, 125.

28. Clark, *La Obra Redentora*, 60.

29. Delebecque, *Travers l'Amérique du Sud*, 122.

30. Guillermo Reed, quoted in Padilla J., *La Iglesia y los Dioses Modernos*, 315.

31. Espinosa Tamayo, *Psicología y sociología del pueblo ecuatoriano*, 83–84.

32. Meyer, *En Los Altos Andes del Ecuador*, 25.

33. Michaux, *Ecuador, diario de viaje*, 135–37.

34. Franklin, *Ecuador: Retrato de un Pueblo*, 126, 228, 292.

35. María Luiza Kreuter, *¿Dónde Queda el Ecuador?* (Quito: Abya-Yala, 1997), 57.

36. Ray Bromley, "Market Center, and Market Place in Highland Ecuador," in Whitten, *Cultural Transformation and Ethnicity in Modern Ecuador*, 251–52.

37. Claudio Malo González, *Pensamiento Indigenista del Ecuador* (Quito: Corporación Editora Nacional, 1988), 17.

38. Bemelmans, *El Burro por Dentro*, 58, 185.

39. Espinosa Tamayo, *Psicología y sociología del pueblo ecuatoriano*, 81.

40. Meyer, *En Los Altos Andes del Ecuador*, 425.

41. Franklin, *Ecuador: Retrato de un Pueblo*, 150, 154, 111.

42. Kreuter, *¿Dónde Queda el Ecuador?*, 57.

43. Quevedo, *Ensayos Sociológicos, Políticos y Morales*, 279.

44. Delebecque, *Travers l'Amérique du Sud*, 68, 49, 106.

45. Bemelmans, *El Burro por Dentro*, 33, 35, 37.

46. Espinosa Tamayo, *Psicología y sociología del pueblo ecuatoriano*, 110, 11.

47. Meyer, *En Los Altos Andes del Ecuador*, 98.

48. Ibid., 97.

49. Franklin, *Ecuador: Retrato de un Pueblo*, 81, 263, 264, 299.

50. Quevedo, *Ensayos Sociológicos, Políticos y Morales*, 225, 226, 232, 234, 236.

51. Niles, *Correrías casuales en el Ecuador*, 102.

52. Michaux, *Ecuador, diario de viaje*, 136.

53. Espinosa Tamayo, *Psicología y sociología del pueblo ecuatoriano*, 29, 32, 78, 83, 84, 111, 121, 122, 126, 184.

54. Emilio Bonifaz, "Comportamiento," in Malo, *Pensamiento Indigenista del Ecuador*, 462.

55. Clark, *La Obra Redentora*, 56, 88.

56. Meyer, *En Los Altos Andes del Ecuador*, 37.

57. Weilbauer, *Mi largo camino*, 47.

58. Franklin, *Ecuador: Retrato de un Pueblo*, 185, 186, 193.

59. Kreuter, *¿Dónde Queda el Ecuador?*, 58.

60. Clark, *La Obra Redentora*, 185–90, 203.

61. Crawford de Roberts, *El Ecuador en la Época Cacaotera*, 144.

62. Quevedo, *Ensayos Sociológicos, Políticos y Morales*, 280.

63. Franklin, *Ecuador: Retrato de un Pueblo*, 79.

64. Weilbauer, *Mi largo camino*, 48.

65. Delebecque, *Travers l'Amérique du Sud*, 19–20.

66. Crawford de Roberts, *El Ecuador en la Época Cacaotera*, 101–03.

67. Quevedo, *Ensayos Sociológicos, Políticos y Morales*, 280.

68. Ibid., 280.

69. Espinosa Tamayo, *Psicología y sociología del pueblo ecuatoriano*, 91.

70. Michaux, *Ecuador, diario de viaje*, 41.

71. Espinosa Tamayo, *Psicología y sociología del pueblo ecuatoriano*, 32.

72. Franklin, *Ecuador: Retrato de un Pueblo*, 231, 273–76.

73. Padilla J., *La Iglesia y los Dioses Modernos*, 358.

74. Weilbauer, *Mi largo camino*, 71.

75. Niles, *Correrías casuales en el Ecuador*, 46.

76. Bemelmans, *El Burro por Dentro*, 169.

77. Clark, *La Obra Redentora*, 118.

78. Espinosa Tamayo, *Psicología y sociología del pueblo ecuatoriano*, 123.

79. Michaux, *Ecuador, diario de viaje*, 141–42.

80. Crawford de Roberts, *El Ecuador en la Época Cacaotera*, 107, 112.

81. Espinosa Tamayo, *Psicología y sociología del pueblo ecuatoriano*, 123–24.

82. Ibid., 71.

83. Quevedo, *Ensayos Sociológicos, Políticos y Morales*, 241–42.

84. Espinosa Tamayo, *Psicología y sociología del pueblo ecuatoriano*, 163.

85. Crawford de Roberts, *El Ecuador en la Época Cacaotera*, 106.

86. Espinosa Tamayo, *Psicología y sociología del pueblo ecuatoriano*, 82, 89.

87. Peralta, *Tipos de mi tierra*, 74.

88. Clark, *La Obra Redentora*, 67, 69–70.

89. Espinosa Tamayo, *Psicología y sociología del pueblo ecuatoriano*, 87, 99.

90. Alfredo Espinosa Tamayo, "El problema de la enseñanza en el Ecuador," *El Arielismo en el Ecuador* (Quito: Banco Central, Corporación Editora Nacional, 1986), 126, 180.

91. Quevedo, *Ensayos Sociológicos, Políticos y Morales*, 279.

92. Espinosa Tamayo, *Psicología y sociología del pueblo ecuatoriano*, 78–80, 90, 99.

93. Franklin, *Ecuador: Retrato de un Pueblo*, 185–87.

94. Meyer, *En Los Altos Andes del Ecuador*, 409.

95. Franklin, *Ecuador: Retrato de un Pueblo*, 237.

96. Quevedo, *Ensayos Sociológicos, Políticos y Morales*, 201.

97. Espinosa Tamayo, *Psicología y sociología del pueblo ecuatoriano*, 159–60.

98. Luis Monsalve Pozo, "El indio, cuestiones de su vida y su pasión," Malo González, *Pensamiento Indigenista del Ecuador*, 124.

99. Alfredo Pérez Guerrero, "La Télesis Social y la Raza India," in *Teoría de la Cultura Nacional*, ed. Fernando Tinajero (Quito: Banco Central del Ecuador, Corporación Editora Nacional, 1986), 95.

100. Quevedo, *Ensayos Sociológicos, Políticos y Morales*, 236.

101. Franklin, *Ecuador: Retrato de un Pueblo*, 167.

102. Ibid., 82.

103. Bemelmans, *El Burro por Dentro*, 184.

104. Espinosa Tamayo, *Psicología y sociología del pueblo ecuatoriano*, 90, 195.

105. Quevedo, *Ensayos Sociológicos, Políticos y Morales*, 231.

106. Franklin, *Ecuador: Retrato de un Pueblo*, 120.

107. Delebecque, *Travers l'Amérique du Sud*, 28, 31.

108. Meyer, *En Los Altos Andes del Ecuador*, 72.

109. Crawford de Roberts, *El Ecuador en la Época Cacaotera*, 104–07.

110. Clark, *La Obra Redentora*, 122, 123, 205, 132.

111. Espinosa Tamayo, "El problema de la enseñanza en el Ecuador," 187.

112. Clark, *La Obra Redentora*, 118, 124–32.

CHAPTER 4: CULTURAL CHANGES IN THE SECOND HALF OF THE TWENTIETH CENTURY

1. Germánico Salgado, *Del Desarrollo al Espejismo* (Quito: Corporación Editora Nacional, 1995), 157.

2. Mitchell A. Seligson, *Auditoría de la Democracia: Ecuador 2006* (Latin American Public Opinion Project [LAPOP], Vanderbilt University–Cedatos Gallup, 2006), 106.

3. Osvaldo Hurtado, *Deuda y Desarrollo en el Ecuador Contemporáneo* (Quito: Planeta, 2002), 89, 96.

4. Joseph Casagrande, "Strategies for Survival: The Indians of Highland Ecuador," in *Cultural Transformations and Ethnicity in Modern Ecuador*, ed. Norman E. Whitten (Urbana: University of Illinois Press, 1981), 261.

5. Hugo Burgos, *Relaciones Interétnicas en Riobamba* (Quito: Corporación Editora Nacional, 1997), 405.

6. Andrade, *Protestantismo indígena*, 83.

7. Blanca Muratorio, "Protestantism, Ethnicity, and Class in Chimborazo," in Whitten, *Cultural Transformations*, 514–29.

8. Andrade, *Protestantismo indígena*, 165.

9. The World Bank, *World Development Indicators* (Washington, DC: 2004).

10. Michael Handelsman, *Culture and Customs of Ecuador* (Westport, CT: Greenwood Press, 2000), 43.

11. Ernesto J. Lehmann, *Breve libro sin editar sobre la comunidad judía en el Ecuador desde 1938* (Quito: Editorial Delta, 2005), 341.

12. Ibid., 129.

13. Superintendencia de Bancos y Seguros, www.superban.gov.ec; Superintendencia de Compañías, www.supercias.gov.ec. *Anuario Estadístico del Mercado de Valores*.

14. See Osvaldo Hurtado, *Los Costos del Populismo* (Quito: CORDES, 2006), 30.

15. Virginia Fierro and Mónica Salvador, "Reorientación del gasto público: del servicio de la deuda externa al financiamiento del gasto social," in *Cuestiones Económicas No. 30* (Quito: Banco Central del Ecuador, 1997), 190.

16. *Diario El Universo*, December 11, 2005.

17. Seligson, *Auditoría de la Democracia*, 56–57.

18. Ibid., 57.

19. Handelsman, *Culture and Customs of Ecuador*, 38.

20. Ibid., 47.

21. Ibid., 39.

22. Daniel Kaufmann, Aart Kraay, and Máximo Mastruzzi, *Governance Matters V: Aggregate and Individual Governance Indicators for 1996–2005* (Washington, DC: The World Bank, 2006), Statistical Appendix.

23. Casagrande in Whitten, *Cultural Transformations*, 269.

24. De Avendaño, *Imagen del Ecuador*, 471.

CHAPTER 5: IN PURSUIT OF ECONOMIC SUCCESS

1. Delaporte, *Le Voyageur Francois ou La Connoissance et du Nouveau Monde* (Paris: Chez L. Cellot, Imprimeur-Libraire rue Dauphine, 1770), 255–56.

2. De Merizalde, *Relación Histórica*, 43.

3. Juan De Velasco, *Historia del Reino de Quito* (Venezuela: Biblioteca Ayacucho, 1981), 400.

4. Trystram, *El Proceso con las Estrellas*, 99.

5. Caldas, *Obras de Caldas*, 181, 196.

6. De Merizalde, *Relación Histórica*, 26.

7. Cicala, *Descripción histórico-topográfica*, 1:501, 506, 508.

8. Trystram, *El Proceso con las Estrellas*, 175–81.

9. Juan Cordero Iñiguez, *Historia de Cuenca y su región: Siglo XVI* (Cuenca: Municipalidad de Cuenca, 2007), 86.

10. Juan and De Ulloa, *Relación Histórica del Viaje*, 434.

11. Delaporte, *Le Voyageur Francois*, 255.

12. De Merizalde, *Relación Histórica*, 26, 28.

13. Cicala, *Descripción histórico-topográfica*, 1:509, 502.

14. De Velasco, *Historia del Reino de Quito*, 392.

15. Silvia Palomeque, *Cuenca en el siglo XIX: La Articulación de una Región* (Quito: FLACSO, Abya-Ayala, 1990), 18.

16. Juan Chacón, Pedro Soto, and Diego Mora, *Historia de la Gobernación de Cuenca (1777–1820)* (Cuenca: Instituto de Investigaciones Sociales, 1993), 16–17.

17. Tyrer, *Historia Demográfica*, 76.

18. Jorge Nuñez Sanchéz, "Cuenca: La Capital Colonial del Sur Quiteño," in *Memorias del Encuentro de Historia y Realidad económica y social de Ecuador y América Latina*, vol. 1 (Cuenca: Universidad de Cuenca, 1994), 90–92.

19. Fernando Jurado Noboa, "Formación de clases sociales en Cuenca en el siglo XVI," in *Memorias del Encuentro de Historia y Realidad económica y social de Ecuador y América Latina*, vol. 1 (Cuenca: Universidad de Cuenca, 1994), 114.

20. Cordero Iñiguez, *Historia de Cuenca*, 80, 81, 109, 111.

21. Palomeque, *Cuenca en el siglo XIX*, 18, 39, 45, 46, 48, 49, 52, 53, 118, 145.

22. McKenzie, *Las aventuras de Archer Harman*, 65.

23. Festa, *En el Darién y el Ecuador*, 274.

24. Franklin, *Ecuador: Retrato de un Pueblo*, 251–55.

25. Conversation with Constanza Di Capua.

26. Díaz, "La psicología del pueblo Azuayo."

27. De Avedaño, *Imagen del Ecuador*, 227.

28. Data prepared by INEC.

29. INEC, *Censo de Población y vivienda 2001* (Quinto, 2002).

30. Beatie Saltz, "El uso del tiempo: hábitos de trabajo y modalidades de trabajo," in *Indianistas, indianófilos, indigenistas* (Quito: Abya-Yala, 1992), 140.

31. Aníbal Buitrón, *Investigaciones sociales en Otavalo* (Otavalo: Instituto Otavaleño de Antropología, 1974), 46.

32. Gina Maldonado, *Comerciantes y viajeros* (Quito: FLACSO-Abya-Yala, 2004), 32–33.

33. Revista Diners, No. 284, Enero 2006.

34. INEC, *Censo de Población y vivienda 2001.*

35. Delaporte, *Le Voyageur Francois*, 251, 152.

36. Segundo Moreno, "Humboldt y su comprensión de los pueblos indígenas," in *El regreso de Humboldt* (Quito: Museo de la ciudad de Quito, 2001), 156.

37. Stevenson, *Narración histórica*, 441.

38. Holinski, *L'Ècuateur: Scènes de la vie Sud-amèricaine*, 179.

39. Kolberg, *Hacia el Ecuador*, 283.

40. De Avendaño, *Imagen del Ecuador*, 126, 209.

41. Bemelmans, *El Burro por Dentro*, 172.

42. Franklin, *Ecuador: Retrato de un Pueblo*, 293.

43. Lilo Linke, *País de contrastes*, 3rd ed. (Oxford, UK: Oxford University Press, 1960), 63.

44. Casagrande in Whitten, *Cultural Transformations*, 260.

45. Frank Salomón, "Weavers of Otavalo," in Whitten, *Cultural Transformations*, 420, 423.

46. Casagrande in Whitten, *Cultural Transformations*, 260.

47. Lehmann, *Breve libro sin editar sobre la comunidad judía en el Ecuador desde 1938*, 90, 93.

48. Unpublished paper by Cristiana Bochart de Moreno.

49. Phelan, *El Reino de Quito en el Siglo XVII*, 129–31.

50. Rocío Rueda Novoa, *El obraje de San Joseph de Peguche* (Quito: Abya-Yala, 1988), 54.

51. Tyrer, *Historia Demográfica*, 101.

52. McKenzie, *Las aventuras de Archer Harman*, 34.

53. Buitrón, *Investigaciones sociales en Otavalo*, 62.

54. Ibid., 72–75.

55. Ibid., 42-43.

56. Lynn Meisch, *Andean Entrepreneurs* (Austin: University of Texas Press, 2002), 37.

57. Crawford de Roberts, *Los libaneses en el Ecuador*, 85.

58. Ibid., 62.

59. Ibid., 60.

60. Ibid., 62–63.

61. Ibid., 63.

62. Ibid., 81, 144–45, 158.

63. Ibid., 151.

64. Lehmann, *Breve libro sin editar sobre la comunidad judía en el Ecuador desde 1938*, 130.

65. Kreuter, *¿Dónde Queda el Ecuador?*, 51.

66. Ibid., 84, 85.

67. Ibid., 59, 60.

68. Ibid., 63.

69. Ibid., 87, 304.

70. Ibid., 304.

71. Lehmann, *Breve libro sin editar sobre la comunidad judía en el Ecuador desde 1938*, 102.

72. Kreuter, *¿Dónde Queda el Ecuador?*, 61–69.

73. Lehmann, *Breve libro sin editar sobre la comunidad judía en el Ecuador desde 1938*, 40.

74. Kreuter, *¿Dónde Queda el Ecuador?*, 58.

GLOSSARY

aparcería: an agricultural contract whereby one person provided the land and another the work, with the commitment of sharing the harvest.

audiencia: a political institution of colonial administration that represented the authority of the Spanish monarchy in the territories that, following Independence, comprised Ecuador.

autocarril: a small train similar to a bus.

cabildo: a municipal government council in colonial times.

cacique: a local or regional caudillo.

canton: a territory corresponding to a municipality.

cascarilla: the tree bark from which quinine was extracted for use in the treatment of malaria.

caudillo: a national political leader whose power is based on arms and/or popular support and who usually exercises absolute authority above the law and parties.

cédula: generic name for a law issued by a Spanish monarch.

chacra: small plot of farmland.

cholo: pejorative term for a mestizo or for an acculturated Indian.

chulla: Quechua term for people who simulated a social condition that did not correspond to their family background and economic resources.

compadrazgo: extended relations tied to godparenthood.

concertaje: a form of farmworker recruitment whereby a hacienda owner paid out advances in money or in kind, to be repaid by the peon's work, under the threat of imprisonment if he failed to do so.

corregimiento: an institution of colonial administration corresponding to a part of the audiencia. Presided over by a corregidor.

Costa: tropical coastlands, originally a jungle region, located in the western area of the country.

ECLAC: Economic Commission for Latin America and the Caribbean; a United Nations regional organization.

encomienda: a colonial institution whereby a colonist was given a certain number of Indians from whom he collected tributes or whom he obliged to work for his benefit.

finquería: a form of labor recruitment in the coastal region.

FTA: the Free Trade Agreement that was being negotiated with the United States.

FUT (Frente Unitario de Trabajadores): a workers federation that groups the main labor unions.

hacienda: an institution that organized large-scale agricultural and live-stock production through the work of Indians in the highlands and montubios on the coast, who were subordinate to the hacendado or hacienda owner.

huasicama: an Indian who did temporary, seasonal work as a domestic servant in the home of a hacienda owner.

huasipungo: a small plot of land that a hacienda owner gave an Indian family to work for their own benefit. The Indians were called huasi-pungueros.

INCAE (Instituto Centroamericano de Administración de Empresas): Central American Institute of Business Administration.

intendente: intendant; a government official for a specific territory.

latifundio: a hacienda with a significant territorial expanse.

longo: a pejorative term for a mestizo or an acculturated Indian.

mestizaje: ideology of "the blending" or mixing of race, ethnicity, or culture.

mestizo: a person with a racial mix of white and Indian.

mita: a form of recruitment of Indian laborers.

montubio: a peasant farmer from the coastal region.

mulatto: a person with a racial mix of white and black.

obraje: an exploitative "factory" or mill that produced textiles during the colonial period, using forced labor from Indians.

oidor: a judge during the colonial period.

Oriente: the Amazon jungle region, located in the eastern part of the country.

palanca: a "connection" or influential person that can obtain benefits from a third party.

pendejo: a silly, stupid person.

Quechua: the language of the imperial Inca, spoken by the Indians of Ecuador.

parcialidad: a group of Indians located in a given territory.

patrón/patrono: a "boss"; the name used to refer to a hacienda owner.

reales: coins used from colonial times through the 1970s.

Reino de Quito: Kingdom of Quito; term used by historian John Leddy Phelan to refer to the Audiencia of Quito.

runa: an indigenous person in the Quechua language.

sembraduría: form of peasant farmworker recruitment in the coastal region.

servicia: an Indian peasant farmworker who works seasonally as a domestic servant in the home of a hacienda owner.

Sierra: the highlands of the Ecuadorian Andes.

sucre: Ecuador's currency until the country adopted the U.S. dollar in the year 2000.

zambo: a person with a racial mix of Indian and black.

BIBLIOGRAPHY

Aguirre Abad, Francisco. *Bosquejo Histórico de la República del Ecuador*. Guayaquil: 1972.

Almond, Gabriel A., and Sidney Verba. *The Civic Culture*. Newbury: Sage, 1980.

Andrade, Susana. *Protestantismo indígena: procesos de conversión religiosa en la provincia de Chimborazo*. Quito: Flacso, Abya-Yala, Ifea, 2004.

Anonymous English writer translated into Italian. *Storia Degli Stabilimenti Europei in sei parti, Volume Primo*. Venice: 1763.

Arcos, Carlos. "El Espíritu del Progreso: Los Hacendados en el Ecuador del 1900." In *Clase y Región en el Agro Ecuatoriano*, ed. Miguel Murmis. Quito: Corporación Editora Nacional, 1986.

Arias Palacios, Hugo. *Evolución Socio Económica del Ecuador: Sociedades Primitivas y Período Colonial*. Guayaquil: Biblioteca Ecuatoriana 24, 1980.

Banco Central del Ecuador. *Memoria del Gerente General*. Quito: 1959.

———. *Sesenta y cinco años de Información Estadística: 1927–2002*. Quito: 2002.

Banfield, Edward C. *The Moral Basis of a Backward Society*. New York: The Free Press, 1967.

Bemelmans, Ludwig. *El Burro por Dentro*. Quito: Editora Moderna, 1941. *The Donkey Inside*. New York: Viking Press, 1941.

Benzoni, Gironaldo. *Historia del Nuevo Mundo*. Madrid: Alianza Editorial, 1989.

Bonifaz, Emilio. "Comportamiento." In *Pensamiento Indigenista del Ecuador*, ed. Claudio Malo González. Quito: Corporación Editora Nacional, 1988.

Brandini, Victorino. "De Quito, de su decadencia, voto por su regeneración." In *Quito a través de los siglos*, vol. 2, ed. Eliécer Enríquez. Quito: Biblioteca Municipal, 1941.

Burgos, Hugo. *Relaciones Interétnicas en Riobamba*. Quito: Corporación Editora Nacional, 1997.

Büschges, Christian. *Familia, honor y poder*. Quito: Fonsal, 2007.

Caldas, Francisco José. *Obras de Caldas*, vol. 9. Bogotá: Imprenta Nacional, 1912.

Casagrande, Joseph. "Strategies for Survival: The Indians of Highland Ecuador." In *Cultural Transformation and Ethnicity in Modern Ecuador*, ed. Norman Whitten. Urbana: University of Illinois Press, 1981.

Cevallos, Pedro Fermín. *Historia del Ecuador desde su Origen hasta 1845*, vol.1. Quito–Guayaquil: Ariel, 1972.

Chacón, Juan, Pedro Soto, and Diego Mora. *Historia de la Gobernación de Cuenca (1777–1820)*. Cuenca: Instituto de Investigaciones Sociales, 1993.

Chiriboga, Manuel. *Jornaleros y Gran Propietarios en 135 Años de Exportación Cacaotera, 1970–1925*. Quito: Consejo Provincial de Pichincha, 1980.

Cicala, Mario. *Descripción histórico-topográfica de la provincia de Quito de la Compañía de Jesús*. Quito: Biblioteca Ecuatoriana Aurelio Espinosa Pólit-Instituto Geográfico Militar, 1994.

Clark, Kim. *La Obra Redentora*. Quito: Universidad Andina Simón Bolívar, Corporación Editora Nacional, 2004.

Clayton, Lawrence. *Los astilleros de Guayaquil Colonial*. Guayaquil: Casa de la Cultura Ecuatoriana Núcleo del Guayas, 1978.

Coleti, Juan Domingo. "Relación inédita de la ciudad de Quito." In *Quito a través de los siglos*, vol. 2, ed. Eliécer Enríquez. Quito: Biblioteca Municipal, 1941.

Comité Interamericano de Desarrollo Agrícola (Cida). *Ecuador: tenencia de la Tierra y Desarrollo Socioeconómico del Sector Agrícola*. Washington, DC: Unión Panamericana, 1965.

Cordero Iñiguez, Juan. *Historia de Cuenca y su región: Siglo XVI*. Cuenca: Municipalidad de Cuenca, 2007.

Corporación Latinobarómetro. *Latinobarómetro 2005*. Santiago: 2005.

———. *Latinobarómetro 2007*. Santiago: 2007.

Crawford de Roberts, Lois. *El Ecuador en la Época Cacaotera*. Quito: Editorial Universitaria UCE, 1980.

———. *Los libaneses en el Ecuador*. Quito: Fundación Cultural Ecuatoriano-Libanesa, 1977.

Cushner, Nicholas P. *Farm and Factory: The Jesuits and Development of Agrarian Capitalism in Colonial Quito: 1600–1767*. Albany: State University of New York Press, 1982.

Dávila, Luis Robalino. *Orígenes del Ecuador de Hoy*. México: Cajica, 1967.

De Avendaño, Joaquín. *Imagen del Ecuador, economía y sociedad vistas por un viajero del siglo XIX*. Quito: Corporación Editora Nacional, 1985.

Delaporte. *Le Voyageur Francois ou La Connoissance et du Nouveau Monde*. Paris: Chez L. Cellot, Imprimeur-Libraire rue Dauphine, 1770.

Delebecque, J. A. *Travers l'Amérique du Sud: Plon-Nourrit et. Cie*. Paris: Impremeurs-Éditeurs, 1907.

De Merizalde y Santiesteban, Joaquín. *Relación Histórica, política y moral de la ciudad de Cuenca*. Quito: Casa de la Cultura Ecuatoriana, 1957.

De Tocqueville, Alexis. *La Democracia en América*. Madrid: Guadarrama, 1969.

De Velasco, Juan. *Historia del Reino de Quito*. Venezuela: Biblioteca Ayacucho, 1981.

Díaz, Octavio. "La psicología del pueblo Azuayo." In *Monografía del Azuay*, ed. Luis F. Mora and Arquímedes Landázuri. Cuenca: 1926.

Empresa Periodística Prensa Ecuatoriana. *América Libre*. Guayaquil: 1920.

Enock, Reginald. *Ecuador: Geografía Humana*. Quito: Corporación Editora Nacional, 1980. *Ecuador*. New York: 1914.

Espinosa Tamayo, Alfredo. "El problema de la enseñanza en el Ecuador." In *El Arielismo en el Ecuador*, ed. Nancy Ochoa Antich. Quito: Banco Central—Corporación Editora Nacional, 1986.

———. *Psicología y sociología del pueblo ecuatoriano*. Guayaquil: Biblioteca Ecuatoriana, Imprenta Municipal, 1918.

Estrada Ycaza, Julio. *El puerto de Guayaquil*. Guayaquil: Archivo Histórico del Guayas, 1973.

———. *Los Bancos del Siglo XIX*. Guayaquil: Archivo Histórico del Guayas, 1976.

Festa, Enrico. *En el Darién y el Ecuador. Diario de viaje de un naturalista*. Quito: Abya-Yala, 1993.

Fierro, Virginia, and Mónica Salvador. "Reorientación del gasto público: del servicio de la deuda externa al financiamiento del gasto social." In *Cuestiones Económicas No. 30*. Quito: Banco Central del Ecuador, 1997.

Fitch, Samuel. *The Armed Forces and Democracy in Latin America*. Baltimore: The Johns Hopkins University Press, 1998.

Franklin, Albert. *Ecuador: Retrato de un Pueblo*. Quito: Corporación Editora Nacional, 1984. *Ecuador: Portrait of a People*. Garden City: Doubleday, Doran and Company Inc., 1943.

Fukuyama, Francis. *Confianza*. Buenos Aires: Ediciones Atlántida, 1996.

Goffin, Alvin M. *The Rise of Protestant Evangelism in Ecuador, 1895–1990*. Gainesville: University Press of Florida, 1994.

González Suárez, Federico. *Memorias Íntimas*. Quito-Guayaquil: Clásicos Ariel, 1972.

———. *Historia general de la República del Ecuador*, Quito: Daniel Cadena, 1931.

Graff, F. W. UP DE. *Cazadores de Cabezas del Amazonas*. Madrid: Espasa-Calpe, 1961.

Grondona, Mariano. *Las Condiciones Culturales del Desarrollo Económico*. Buenos Aires: Ariel, 2000.

Hall, Francis. *Colombia: Its Present State and Inducements to Emigration*. Philadelphia: 1825.

Hamerly, Michael T. *Historia Social y Económica de la Antigua Provincia de Guayaquil, 1763–1842*. Guayaquil: Archivo Histórico del Guayas, 1973.

Handelsman, Michael. *Culture and Customs of Ecuador*. Westport, CT: Greenwood Press, 2000.

Harrison, Lawrence E. *The Central Liberal Truth*. New York: Oxford University Press, 2006.

———. *El Subdesarrollo está en la Mente*. Buenos Aires: Rei, 1987.

Harrison, Lawrence, and Samuel P. Huntington, eds. *Culture Matters*. New York: Basics Books, 2000.

Hassaurek, Friedrich. *Cuatro años entre los ecuatorianos.* Quito: Abya-Yala, 1997. *Four Years among the Ecuadorians.* Abridged version of *Four Years among Spanish-Americans,* ed. C. Harvey Gardiner. Carbondale: Southern Illinois University Press, 1967 [1867].

Holinski, Alexandre. *L'Èquateur: Scènes de la vie Sud-amèricaine.* Paris: Amyot Editeurs, 1861.

Humboldt, Alexander. *Diarios de viaje en la Audiencia de Quito.* Quito: Occidental Exploration and Production Company, 2005.

——. *L'Amerique Espagnole en 1800.* Paris: Calmann-Lévy, 1965.

Huntington, Samuel P. *¿Quiénes Somos?* Madrid: Paidós, 2004.

Hurtado, Osvaldo. *Deuda y Desarrollo en el Ecuador Contemporáneo.* Quito: Planeta, 2002.

——. *El Poder Político en el Ecuador.* Quito: Ediciones de la Universidad Católica, 1997 [1977].

——. *Los Costos del Populismo.* Quito: CORDES, 2006.

INEC. *Censo de Población y vivienda 2001.* Quito: 2002.

Informe Confidencial. *Encuestas de Coyuntura.* Quito: 2007.

Jijón y Caamaño, Jacinto. *Política Conservadora.* Quito: 1934.

Jouanen, José. *Historia de la Compañía de Jesús en la Antigua Provincia de Quito.* Quito: Editorial Ecuatoriana, 1941.

Juan, Jorge, and Antonio De Ulloa. *Noticias Secretas de América.* Madrid: Dastin, 2002.

——. *Relación Histórica del Viaje a la América Meridional.* Madrid: Fundación Universitaria Española, 1978.

Junta de Planificación. *Reforma de la Estructura de Tenencia de la Tierra y Expansión de la Frontera Agrícola, Plan General de Desarrollo.* Quito: 1962.

Jurado Noboa, Fernando. "Formación de clases sociales en Cuenca en el siglo XVI." In *Memorias del Encuentro de Historia y Realidad económica y social de Ecuador y América Latina,* vol. 1. Cuenca: Universidad de Cuenca, 2002.

Kaufmann, Daniel, Aart Kraay, and Máximo Mastruzzio. *Governance Matters V: Aggregate and Individual Governance Indicators for 1996–2005.* Washington, DC: The World Bank, 2006.

Kohn, Vera. *Terapia Iniciática.* Quito: Centro de Desarrollo Integral, 2006.

Kolberg, Joseph. *Hacia el Ecuador: Relatos de Viaje.* Quito: Abya-Yala, 1996.

Konetzke, Richard. *Historia Universal Siglo XXI, América Latina II: La Época Colonial.* Madrid: Siglo XXI, 1971.

Kreuter, María Luiza. *¿Dónde Queda el Ecuador?* Quito: Abya-Yala, 1997.

La Condamine, Charles. *Viaje a la América Meridional.* Madrid: Espasa-Calpe S. A., 1921.

La economía colonial. Quito: Corporación Editora Nacional, 1984.

Landázuri Soto, Alberto. *El Régimen Laboral Indígena en la Audiencia de Quito.* Madrid: Imprenta de Aldecoa, 1959.

Landes, David. *The Wealth and Poverty of Nations.* New York: W.W. Norton, 1998.

Laviana Cuetos, María Luisa. *Estudios sobre el Guayaquil Colonial*. Guayaquil: Archivo Histórico del Guayas, 1999.

————. *Guayaquil en el siglo XVIII: Recursos Naturales y Desarrollo Económico*. Sevilla: Escuela de Estudios Hispanoamericanos, 1987.

Lehman M, Ernesto J. *Breve libro sin editar sobre la comunidad judía en el Ecuador desde 1938*. Quito: Editorial Delta, 2005.

Linke, Lilo. *País de contrastes*. 3rd ed. Oxford, UK: Oxford University Press, 1960.

MacFarlane, Thomas. *Hacia los Andes: Notas de viaje a América del Sur 1876*. Quito: Abya-Yala, 1994.

Maldonado, Gina. *Comerciantes y viajeros*. Quito: Flacso-Abya-Yala, 2004.

McKenzie, Andrew. *Las aventuras de Archer Harman*. Unpublished manuscript, 1901.

Meisch, Lynn. *Andean Entrepreneurs*. Austin: University of Texas Press, 2002.

Meyer, Hans. *En Los Altos Andes del Ecuador*. Quito: Abya-Yala, 1993.

Michaux, Henri. *Ecuador, diario de viaje*. Barcelona: Tusquets Editores, 1983.

Minchon, Martin. *El pueblo de Quito 1690–1810*. Quito: FONSAL, 2007.

Monsalve Pozo, Luis. "El indio, cuestiones de su vida y su pasión." In *Pensamiento Indigenista del Ecuador*, ed. Claudio Malo González. Corporación Editora Nacional, 1988.

Mora, Alfonso María. *La Conquista Española juzgada jurídica y sociológicamente*. Buenos Aires: Editorial América Lee, 1944.

Moreno, Segundo. "Humboldt y su comprensión de los pueblos indígenas." In *El regreso de Humboldt*. Quito: Museo de la ciudad de Quito, 2001.

Muñoz, Marta de Arosemena. *Marta Muñoz solamente*, ed. Rosa Guzmán. San Juan de Puerto Rico: 1996.

Muratorio, Blanca. "Protestantism, Ethnicity, and Class in Chimborazo." In *Cultural Transformation and Ethnicity in Modern Ecuador*, ed. Norman Whitten. Urbana: University of Illinois Press, 1981.

Navarro, Romualdo. "Idea del Reino de Quito." In *La Economía Colonial*. Quito: Corporación Editora Nacional, Quito, 1984.

Niles, Blair. *Correrías casuales en el Ecuador*. Quito: Abya-Yala, 1995. *Casual Wanderings in Ecuador*. 1923.

Núñez Sánchez, Jorge. "Cuenca: La Capital Colonial del Sur Quiteño." In *Memorias del Encuentro de Historia y Realidad económica y social de Ecuador y América Latina. Tomo I*. Cuenca: Universidad de Cuenca.

Onffroy de Thoron, Enrique. *América Ecuatorial, Primera Parte*. Quito: Corporación Editora Nacional, 1983.

Ortiz Crespo, Gonzalo. *La incorporación del Ecuador al mercado mundial*. Quito: Corporación Editora Nacional, 1988.

Orton, James. *The Andes and the Amazon*. New York: Harper & Brothers Publishers, 1870.

Osculati, Gaetano. *Exploraciones de las Regiones Ecuatoriales*. Quito: Abya-Yala, 2000.

Padilla J., Washington. *La Iglesia y los Dioses Modernos: Historia del Protestantismo en el Ecuador.* Quito: Corporación Editora Nacional, 1989.

Palomeque, Silvia. *Cuenca en el siglo XIX: La Articulación de una Región.* Quito: Flacso Ecuador/Abya-Yala.

Paz, Octavio. *El ogro filantrópico.* México: Joaquín Mortiz, 1979.

Peralta, José. *Tipos de mi tierra (cuadros al natural).* Cuenca: Casa de la Cultura Ecuatoriana, 1974.

Pérez Guerrero, Alfredo. "La Télesis Social y la Raza India." In *Teoría de la Cultura Nacional,* ed. Fernando Tinajero. Quito: Banco Central del Ecuador, Corporación Editora Nacional, 1986.

Peyrefitte, Alain. *La sociedad de la confianza.* Santiago de Chile: Editorial Andrés Bello, 1996.

Phelan, John Leddy. *El Reino de Quito en el Siglo XVII.* Quito: Banco Central del Ecuador, 1995. *The Kingdom of Quito in the Seventeenth Century.* Madison: The University of Wisconsin Press, 1967.

Ponce Leiva, Pilar. *Certezas ante la incertidumbre: Elite y Cabildo de Quito en el siglo XVII.* Quito: Abya-Yala, 2000.

Prófitas. *Estudio de estimación del contrabando.* Quito: 2005.

Putnam, Robert D. *Making Democracy Work.* Princeton, NJ: Princeton University Press, 1993.

Quevedo, Belisario. *Ensayos Sociológicos, Políticos y Morales.* Quito: Banco Central del Ecuador-Corporación Editora Nacional, 1981.

———. *Historia Patria.* Quito, 1982.

Rangel, Carlos. *Del buen salvaje al buen revolucionario.* Caracas: Monte Ávila Editores, 1976.

Riding, Alan. *Vecinos Distantes.* México: Joaquín Mortiz/Planeta, 1985.

Robalino Dávila, Luis. *Orígenes del Ecuador de Hoy.* México: Cajica, 1967.

Rudolph, James D. "Historical Setting." In *Ecuador: A Country Study,* ed. Dennis M. Hanratty. Washington, DC: Library of Congress.

Rueda Novoa, Rocío. *El obraje de San Joseph de Peguchi.* Quito: Abya-Yala, 1988.

Salgado, Germánico. *Del Desarrollo al Espejismo.* Quito: Corporación Editora Nacional, 1995.

Salomón, Frank. *Weavers of Otavalo.* In *Cultural Transformation and Ethnicity in Modern Ecuador,* ed. Norman Whitten. Urbana: University of Illinois Press, 1981.

Salomón, Jorge. *Las familias palestinas en el Ecuador.* Guayaquil: Mimeo, 2003.

Saltz, Beatie. "El uso del tiempo: hábitos de trabajo y modalidades de trabajo." In *Indianistas, indianófilos, indigenistas.* Quito: Abya-Yala, 1992.

Seligson, Mitchell A. *Auditoría de la Democracia: Ecuador 2006.* Latin American Public Opinion Project (LAPOP). Vanderbilt University–Cedatos Gallup, 2006.

Stevenson, William Bennet. *Narración histórica y descriptiva de 20 años de residencia en Sudamérica.* Quito: Abya-Yala, 1994. *Historical and Descriptive Narrative of 20 Years' Residence in South America,* vol. 2. London: 1829.

Superintendencia de Bancos e Instituciones Financieras. *Índices de provisiones de Riesgo de Crédito de Colocaciones.* Santiago: 2006.

Superintendencia de Bancos y Seguros. *Reporte Gerencial.* Quito: 2006.

Superintendencia de Compañías. *Anuario Estadístico del Mercado de Valores.* Quito: 2006.

Terry, Adrian. *Viajes por la región ecuatorial de América del Sur.* Quito: Ediciones Abya-Yala, 1994.

The World Bank. *World Development Indicators.* Washington, DC: 2004.

Toscano, Humberto. *El Ecuador Visto por los Extranjeros: Viajeros de los Siglos XVIII y XIX*, vol. 13. México: Editorial Cajica, 1959.

Trystram, Florence. *El Proceso con las Estrellas.* Quito: Ediciones Libri Mundi, 1999.

Tyrer, Robson Brynes. *Historia Demográfica y Económica de la Audiencia de Quito.* Quito: Banco Central, 1988.

United Nations. *Statistical Yearbook.* 1951.

Van Aken, Mark. *King of the Night: Juan José Flores and Ecuador 1824–1869.* Berkeley: University of California Press, 1989.

Vargas, José María. *La Economía Política del Ecuador durante La Colonia.* Quito: Editorial Universitaria, 1957.

Villavicencio, Manuel. *Geografía de la Política del Ecuador.* New York: Robert Craighead Press, 1858.

Weber, Max. *La Ética Protestante y el Espíritu del Capitalismo.* Mexico City: Fondo de Cultura Económica, 2003.

Weilbauer, Arthur. *Mi largo camino: Relato de un refugiado de la Alemania Nazi.* Quito: Unpublished manuscript, 1982.

Whymper, Edward. *Entre los Altos Andes del Ecuador.* Quito: Imprenta Nacional, 1921. *Travels Amongst the Great Andes of the Equator.* London: John Murray, 1892.

Wiener, Carlos. *Guayaquil a través de los siglos*, vol. 1, ed. Eliécer Enríquez. Quito: Talleres Gráficos Nacionales, 1964.

Wolf, Teodoro. *Geografía y Geología del Ecuador.* Quito: Casa de la Cultura Ecuatoriana, 1975.

ABOUT THE AUTHOR

Osvaldo Hurtado is president of the *Corporación de Estudios para el Desarrollo* (Corporation for Development Studies, CORDES) in Quito, the focus of which is conducting studies on topics of interest to development efforts. He also gives lectures, writes articles, provides advisory services, and participates in several nongovernmental organizations.

Among his previous books, it is worthwhile to mention *El poder político en el Ecuador (Political Power in Ecuador)*, which has been published in sixteen editions and translated into English and Portuguese. His papers on Latin America have been included in collections published in Argentina, Austria, Brazil, Chile, Colombia, France, Germany, Mexico, Peru, Spain, Switzerland, and the United States.

In 1977, he chaired the commission that prepared the referendum on elections and political parties, which laid out the guidelines for re-establishing democracy in the country. In 1979 he was elected Vice-President of the Republic and then, following the death of Jaime Roldós, served as President from 1981 to 1984. He also chaired the constituent assembly that approved the Constitution of 1998.

Breinigsville, PA USA
05 December 2009
228635BV00002B/2/P